6, 17, 1926 Melfort Fair. ... ... of 4 horses & 10 cattle. We secured $143⁰⁰ in prizes & two silver cups. The cups were for the best beef bull, and the best fat steer respectively.

I have received a letter from Rayner of the Extension Dept, University, Saskatoon asking me to judge cattle, sheep, & swine at Canora, Kamsack, Togo, Verigin, Wapella, Broadview, Whitewood, & Grenfell. I left Melfort for Canora to-day.

Canora Summer Fair. This marks my debute as an official judge of live stock. Met Brother Bales. He smokes a wicked pipe when away from home. We had 60 head of cattle, 25 hogs, & 9 sheep in the competitions. One half of Canora are Galatoirs & ½ of the other half are Jews. Jas. Brooks who once worked for Vanstone & Rodgers is judging. He is in his 75ᵗʰ year.

Kamsack fair. (100 head of cattle, 35 pigs, & 15 sheep) I had to judge a sweepstake bull class in which a Holstein, Ayrshire, Red Poll, Hereford, Angus, & Shorthorn came out. The purple ribbon went to the Ayrshire owned by Hamlin. I also had to judge bees, honey, & wool (Duncan of Verigin showed Holsteins, Jas. King of Runnymede, Mac Laughlin of Kamsack showed Shorthorns, & Duncan had some real nice yorkshire.

Togo Fair (75 cattle, 35 sheep, 25 pigs) The big event of the afternoon was a bull fight following the judging of the Hereford bulls. The 1st & 2nd prize winners broke loose & fought it out, practically destroying a buggy ...

Everyone's
Grandfather

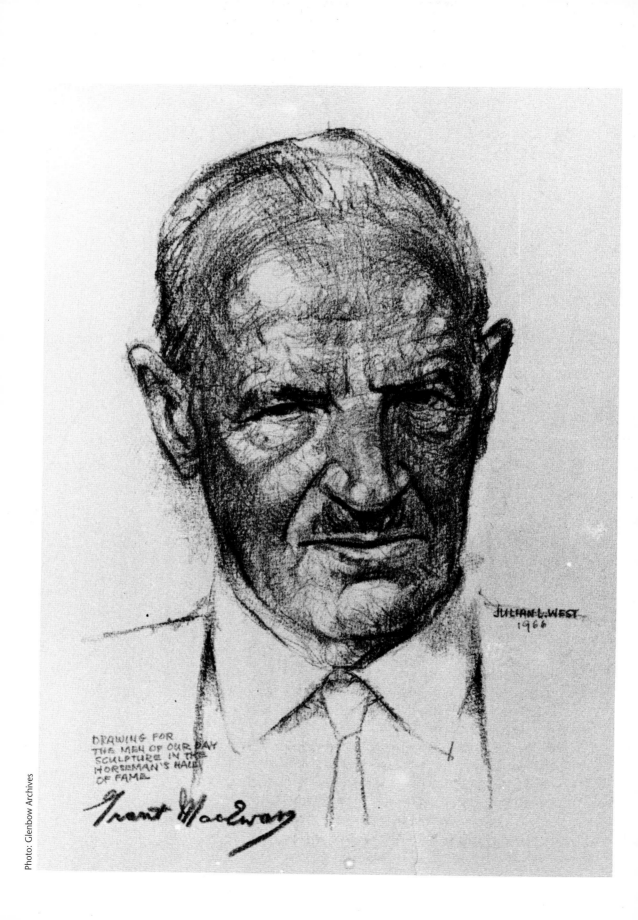

JULIAN L. WEST
1966

DRAWING FOR
THE MEN OF OUR DAY
SCULPTURE IN THE
HORSEMAN'S HALL
OF FAME

Grant MacEwan

Everyone's Grandfather

The Life & Times of Grant MacEwan

Donna von Hauff

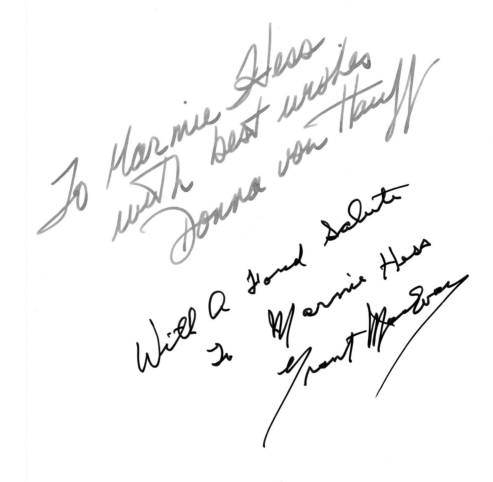

To Marnie Hess
with best wishes
Donna von Hauff

With a fond salute
To Marnie Hess
Grant MacEwan

Published by Grant MacEwan Community College Foundation/ Quon Editions

Design by Studio 3 Graphics

Printed by D.W. Friesen

Printed in Canada

von Hauff, Donna, 1952-
    Everyone's grandfather : the life and times of Grant MacEwan
    Includes bibliographical references and index.
    1. MacEwan, Grant, 1902- . 2. Lieutenant governors – Alberta –Biography. 3. Historians – Prairie Provinces – Biography. 4. Agriculturists – Prairie Provinces – Biography. 5. Politicians – Prairie Provinces – Biography. I. Grant MacEwan Community College Foundation. II. Title.
FC3675.1.M234V66 1993   971.2'0099   C93-090259-9
F1060.92.M33V66 1993

ISBN 0-9697125-0-2

MacEwan Creed

I believe instinctively in a God for whom I am prepared to search.

I believe it is an offence against the God of Nature for me to accept any hand-me-down, man defined religion or creed without the test of reason. I believe no man dead or alive knows more or knew more about God than I can know by searching.

I believe that the God of Nature must be without prejudice, with exactly the same concern for all His children, and that the human invokes no more, no less, of fatherly love than the beaver or sparrow.

I believe I am an integral part of the environment and, as a good subject, I must establish an enduring relationship with my surroundings. My dependence upon the land is fundamental.

I believe destructive waste and greedy exploitation are sins.

I believe the biggest challenge is in being a helper rather than a destroyer of the treasures in Nature's storehouse, a conserver, a husbandman and partner in caring for the Vineyard.

I accept, with apologies to Albert Schweitzer, "a Reverence For Life" and all that is of the Great Spirit's creation.

I believe morality is not complete until the individual holds all of the Great Spirit's creatures in brotherhood and has compassion for all. A fundamental concept of Good consists of working to preserve all creatures with feeling and the will to live.

I am prepared to stand before my Maker, the Ruler of the entire Universe, with no other pleas than that I have tried to leave things in His Vineyard better than I found them.

J.W. Grant MacEwan, 1969

MacEWAN *of Muckly*
("I grow green")

to grow green again
to grow strong again
to be rejuvenated
to revive
to flourish

Throughout this century, Western Canada has been served by the keen consciousness of John Walter Grant MacEwan. His quick wit and sharp eye continue to embrace the prairie landscape with a passionate concern for education, farming, agricultural sciences and the environment as a whole. Although he has been a historical author, politician and statesman — it is his personal qualities of integrity, determination and humor that have made him legendary.

RIDEAU HALL

Of Scottish lineage, Grant MacEwan was born on August 12, 1902 and grew up in a farming community in Manitoba and, later, in Saskatchewan. He was raised to exemplify the ideals his ancestry embraced: industry, respect for the environment and a sense of obligation to give back something in return for what is received.

As a child and, later, as a young man, Grant showed himself to be of exceptional character, dedication and compassion. A true pioneer's son, his life revolved around hard work and responsibility. During elementary school, he delivered newspapers, sold surplus vegetables from his family's garden, worked in a grocery store, yet so excelled that he skipped a grade in school.

MacEwan's physical prowess is the subject of hundreds of tales. As Lieutenant-Governor of Alberta, he asked his chauffeur to let him out of the car so that he might walk part of the way. He then had the bemused driver keep pace with him along the endless, dusty country road so that they could chat.

Canadians and Albertans alike have benefitted from the thought, words and deeds of Grant MacEwan. During this century of rapid change and uncertainty, he has been a traditional father figure, reaching out to people, walking the land and showing respect for the environment. Grant MacEwan is everyone's grandfather.

His Excellency the Right Honourable
Ramon John Hnatyshyn

FOREWORD

AUTHOR'S NOTES

"Dr. MacEwan," I asked innocently. "What do you think about during your spare time?" It was 1991, and I was in Grant MacEwan's Calgary home waiting for the British photographer Rosemary Calvert to set up her equipment. The noted Canadian writer, conservationist and statesman had written the foreword to my first book, *Alberta's Parks - Our Legacy.* I had wanted to capture an image of the man which matched the power of his message. The click of the shutter and his baritone answer were simultaneous. "Girls," he boomed.

John Walter Grant MacEwan is to thousands of Canadians the grandfather everyone wishes was theirs. He was born on August 12, 1902 on a Manitoba prairie farm to Bertha Grant and Alex MacEwan, both of Scottish lineage and Presbyterian affirmation. MacEwan was profoundly affected by the dynamics of the family he was born into. His people pioneered twice and went bankrupt once. It was these early hardships, experienced within the genuine isolation of the family's homestead, which caused him to believe that the most important qualities a person could develop were self-reliance and resourcefulness. His mother's Calvinistic beliefs instilled in him a strict code of ethics, and his father's admiration for Albert Schweitzer led him to accept a "Reverence For Life" as the true and effective basis for a civilized world.

These collective principles have guided his rise from being the son of a dirt farmer to the ninth Lieutenant-Governor of Alberta, but they also set him apart from, and in conflict with, contemporary thinking during much of his career. MacEwan's belief that human greed will result in the downfall of humanity has driven his moralistic and back to basics crusade in recent years. Public opinion has swung to his side, leaving politicians and media pundits scurrying to keep up. He has worked to "set thine house in order" and, perhaps, in doing so, has become the hero Canadians are searching for.

Grant MacEwan is respected for his environmental and humanistic beliefs, awed for his public commitment, and loved for his folksy accounts of Canada's vanguard. He has lived his life as a federalist and he believes that history will unfold as it should through institutionalized change. His literary contributions have helped to establish the Canadian identity. During the span of his life, he has come to know some of the early architects of this country. If ever there was a cheerleader for Western Canada, it is Grant MacEwan.

MacEwan has been described as, "driven — a man who does not acknowledge nor is conscious of the loneliness surrounding his life." By today's standards, it is difficult to comprehend how he juggled his professional and private life to accommodate his multiple roles. His career as an academic, politician and statesman competed with livestock judging, writing books, speaking tours, community service, a bank directorship, and management of a growing financial portfolio. And much of his career occurred before jet-travel and superhighways. His family, like those of many great men, paid for his fame in the usual way — time away and missed milestones. To them, Canadians owe a debt of gratitude.

As with all biographies, I owe thanks to many individuals from all walks of life and some explanations about editorial decisions. I have adopted the consistent use of MacEwan throughout the book rather than McEwan. While Grant changed the "Mc" to "Mac" during his early twenties, his parents' spelling of their surname remained unchanged. I have also included many well-known stories about everyone's grandfather, Grant MacEwan, and I have added new ones. If space, however, may have cost the exclusion of a personal favorite, please accept my apologies.

The research for this book was drawn from many sources. During early 1993, I travelled to Calgary once and twice a week to interview Dr. MacEwan. The use of a video-camera during these sessions allowed him to speak freely and there was no waiting for me to scratch down notes. The device also helped to abate the problem of his limited hearing. Our exchanges ranged from almost exact replays of Rusty Macdonald's earlier biography (just as if MacEwan was reading it to me), to tears shed about the death of brother George and wife Phyllis, to anger about the fiscal and environmental state of Canada. It is my intent to see this material turned into a documentary which will complement and parallel this book.

I am very grateful to Dr. MacEwan for the use of his diaries and for access to his personal papers. This research reaped a wealth of information about his life, and it also traced the development of Canada. To Heather MacEwan-Foran and her husband, Max, a special thanks for sharing the good, and the bad. Every great person has shadows, but they help serve to make the person human. Ultimately, it is the bottom line that counts, and the sum of Grant MacEwan's contributions to Canada outweigh any fault he may be seen to have.

Extraordinary efforts to source out information about Dr. MacEwan's life were made by the librarians and archivists at the Alberta Provincial Archives, the Glenbow Archives and Library, the University of Calgary Special Collections, the University of Saskatchewan, the University of Manitoba, the University of Guelph, Grant MacEwan Community College and the Royal Bank of Canada. The Edmonton Journal generously provided their collection of photographs to help illustrate the book. I am also very grateful to every journalist who has worked to capture, in quotes, the character of this western legend.

A special thanks goes to President Gerry Kelly, Barry Snowden, Tom Graham and Dianne Allen of Grant MacEwan Community College and its foundation. These individuals are deeply committed to both Dr. MacEwan and the college which bears his name. Their dedication to seeing Grant MacEwan's philosophies conveyed to other Canadians through the publishing of this book should be applauded. Foundation staffers Jennifer Stevenson, Miriam Moisan, and Karen Davis have also afforded tremendous assistance.

A number of individuals and organizations have provided valuable assistance to this project and deserve special thanks: Governor General Ray Hnatyshyn, the Honourable David Kilgour, Dr. Chuck Day, Link Byfield, Rusty Macdonald, Patricia Halligan-Baker, David Ward, Bill Weisenburger, Jim Mackie, Graham Underwood, Maureen Rennenberg, Treasury Branches of Alberta, Greyhound Lines of Canada, the Calgary Burns Club, the Historical Society of

Alberta, the Calgary Firefighters, the Calgary Foundation and the Calgary Golden Agers Club.

All authors need an editor. This book has benefitted from the expertise of two such experts, and one very dedicated proof-reader. Dr. Glenn Martin, who as senior editorial consultant, cheerfully imparted advice and experience. Dr. Ibrahim Alladin gave the content its global perspective. Ms. Dorothy Gray not only proof-read, she vetted the accuracy of the material contained herein. Her acquaintance with Dr. MacEwan dates back to 1954. Dorothy was also my companion during treks to Calgary, and her father, Charles, provided his home and hospitality to both of us.

To my husband, Peter, thank you for putting up with the other man in my life. Your desire to see Grant MacEwan's life written within the context of history remains, in my opinion, the most valuable recommendation made in shaping this biography. To my resourceful and self-reliant children — I hope you and your peers will strive to model your lives after everyone's grandfather, Grant MacEwan.

Donna von Hauff, 1994

Preface   7

Foreword   8

Section I - From the Highlands to the Prairies   14

Section II - New Beginnings   43

Section III - The University Years   62

Section IV - Professor Grant MacEwan   83

Section V - The Politician and Statesman   124

Section VI - The Circle Closes   164

Books by Grant MacEwan   188

Bibliography   189

Index   191

Section I

John Walter Grant MacEwan (circa 1930) — MacEwan-Foran Collection

From the Highlands to Saskatchewan

The heat was stifling. Beads of sweat welled along the man's dark hairline while dust devils whipped around his pant legs. His blue eyes surveyed the prairie landscape. Tumble weeds bounced freely, caught occasionally by the remains of a fence; Russian thistle flourished in the fields where crops once grew. In the distance, a small herd of gaunt cattle wandered around a modest shanty. Laundry fluttered between the house and a distant pole. Behind him sat the bus. The driver and some of the passengers stared into the open hood.

The Greyhound had coughed and sputtered from the time it left Rosetown, Saskatchewan. Each time the engine misfired, the dozing passengers startled from their slumber, and those still awake squirmed and sat upright in their seats. The caravan of the down-and-out, salesmen, drifters and a young couple were warned of an impending stop by a weathered sign that spelled Kindersley. One person got off.

The tiny settlement was long behind them when the engine choked, and ceased. An eerie stillness engulfed the passengers; the screech of the emergency brake punctured the silence. Their attention shifted to the sweat-stained back of the bus driver. Hitting the lever to open the door, and sliding out of his seat in a single motion, he announced: "Folks, I'll see what's wrong. You may want to get out and stretch your legs a bit."

The young couple — their union only hours old — looked calmly at each other. Unfolding his long frame out of the seat, the man left his wife, walked down the aisle, and stepped out into the scorching sun. Approaching the driver, whose head was partly emerged in the engine cavity, he cleared his throat and spoke. "MacEwan's the name." It was July 27, 1935.

Fifty-eight years later, Greyhound Lines of Canada dedicated coach 956 to John Walter Grant MacEwan ". . . in recognition of his longstanding service and contribution to his country." The prophet of the prairies described to the crowd how he and his bride, Phyllis, had left their wedding reception in Saskatoon, and travelled by train to Rosetown where they spent the night. The following morning, they boarded a bus for the West Coast. "I've always travelled by the means that takes the least charge of our environment," lectured MacEwan.

He recalled how it appeared that the travellers were going to be stranded for some time and noon hour was approaching. His wife unpacked their "ever-present" egg sandwiches and offered them around. "Well thunderation!" boomed the ninety-plus MacEwan. "The driver distinguished himself by adding his and it wasn't too long before all the passengers joined in and we had ourselves a potluck lunch in the middle of the Prairies."

Only months before the presentation, Grant MacEwan's lifetime accomplishments were consecrated in concrete at the opening of the Edmonton community college which bears his name. He had delighted the masses who came to hear him; he disappointed no one. "When I'm gone," he asserted, "the MacEwan name will live on in this institution. We had a daughter," he stated. "She had two daughters," he added. "I never had a son," he declared. "But I'm not dead yet."

During the applause, a young man turned to his friend and said, "Don't you wish he was your grandfather?"

John Walter Grant MacEwan (circa 1990) — Peter von Hauff

Just as the history of Canada reveals the enormous struggle of people to build a nation — so unravels the story of Grant MacEwan. It is also the intriguing saga of the Grant and the MacEwan clans — both of pure Scottish lineage and Presbyterian affirmation — whose patriarchs cast aside the mist of the moors and the familiar wail of the bagpipes for a new life in a new land.

It was a union of no small consequence when Alexander Hedley MacEwan and Bertha Gray Grant wed on January 18, 1900. Their ancestors, who arrived at vastly different times in the development of the new nation, knew full well the toil and tears that came with taming the land. John Walter Grant MacEwan was their first son.

Was it destiny or decision that caused Grant MacEwan to become Canada's modern day hero? He was, after all, just a typical prairie farmboy who, like his ancestors, experienced firsthand the harsh privation that comes from working the land. Was it those early beginnings that instilled in him the sentiments that would sustain his ascent into the powerful circles of academia and politics? Was it chance, or did MacEwan control his career, deliberately changing paths when the time was right?

When Canada bought Rupert's Land and the Territories from the Hudson's Bay Company following

Confederation, bright-eyed and enthusiastic young men focused their gaze on the "Last, Best West" — the Canadian frontier — with its clear blue skies, fertile soil and promise of free land. With the main expansion of the new Dominion advancing westward, and British Columbia joining Confederation as a full partner in 1871, the young country stretched for the first time — a mari usque ad mare — from sea to sea.

While the transfer of the North West to Canada had been one of the prime aims of the Confederation movement, Sir John A. Macdonald and the other founding fathers recognized that more than sentiment was needed to hold the young nation together. Without railways there would be and could be no Canada. The Canadian Pacific Railway — which would span the land and provide a link between the emerging agricultural expanses and primary industrial development to global markets — was soon to become a reality.

For those with fortitude and acceptance of the toil and hardship associated with conquering the land, the Homestead Act of 1872 made farms readily available. The prairies had been surveyed in numbered square sections of 640 acres each. In the even-numbered sections, farms could be obtained free if the homesteader satisfied certain conditions attached to developing his quarter-section of 160 acres. The odd-numbered sections were sold by the Dominion at moderate prices to raise a revenue. These sections also included the lands awarded to the Canadian Pacific Railway for construction of its line and other grants intended to capitalize the company's operations.

The Province of Manitoba was formed in 1870, and the remainder of the Northwest Territories was organized into administrative districts under a territorial Council by 1882. The threat of attack by western Indian tribes was all but eliminated by newly-signed treaties, and the North West Mounted Police, formed in 1873, maintained law and order.

The tough prairie sod was now being broken by improved agricultural machinery. Large tracts of land were being broken and disked in a fraction of the time that it had once taken the earlier souls who ventured onto the land. Newcomers, however, faced a myriad problems — building barns and houses, sod-busting, surviving cold winters and blazing summers — before they had a crop to sell. The bonanza farms were free but they exacted a high human cost in blood, sweat and tears.

"My people were pioneers. My father came west in 1889 and homesteaded the hard way. I was born on the farm which is a good place to be born."

The West had shipped its first sample of wheat eastward in 1876. The virgin prairie land with its few trees and stones was somewhat easier to prepare for seeding and the combination of new early-maturing, disease-resistant grains, and crop mechanization had increased the pace of progress and production. Moreover, the new milling techniques produced a higher yield of fine white flour which was heavy in gluten and praised by bakers. A premium price was paid for the wheat.

Government publicity material, railway promoters, real estate agents, and word-of-mouth told of the Prairie promise. The possibility of owning land symbolized wealth, honor, prestige, and security. When the first homestead was taken out on July 1, 1872, young and old alike appeared until it became a hotly-contested race for land in the last known frontier. By the time the railway reached Winnipeg and beyond, everything seemed to guarantee the settlement of Western Canada. However, its development was slowed by the Great World Trade Depression which began in 1873 and lasted until 1896 with only brief periods of recovery.

Foreign immigration was front and foremost to the settlement of the Prairies, although a vast majority of the early settlers were young men from the East and mainly of British origin. For young men from Ontario and the Maritimes, their only remaining hope for a free homestead lay in the West. It was this promise of free land and a bright future that attracted the first member of the Grant family in 1879.

Only a century before, the family had been wrested from the old Jacobite country of Glen Urquhart following the razing it suffered after Culloden. James Grant, together with his four children, Alexander, Margaret, Mary and Jane, were among the almost two hundred pilgrims who boarded the Dutch ship Hector at Loch Broom in the Western Highlands of Scotland and set sail for a new life in new land. When these immigrants sailed into Pictou Harbor on the northeastern shore of Nova Scotia on September 15, 1773, it was a feat of no small consequence.

The voyage was onerous. A fierce gale off Newfoundland had blown the ship so far off course that it took two weeks to regain its former position. Accommodations and provisions were inadequate in quality and quantity. And an outbreak of smallpox and dysentery resulted in the death of eighteen children. Water had to be rationed during the later

On September 15, 1773, the Dutch ship Hector *sailed into Pictou Harbor, Nova Scotia. On board were thirty-three families, twenty-five single men, their agent and a piper who had left Scotland for a new life in Canada. The piper is James Grant.*
— MacEwan-Foran Collection

John Walter Grant's house in Springville, Nova Scotia. — MacEwan-Foran Collection

stage of the voyage. Moldy scraps of food, discarded days earlier, were eaten during the last two days of the journey. These intrepid souls, thirty-three families, twenty-five single men, their agent and a piper, were the beginning of a wave of emigration from the Old World to the New which would continue into the mid-nineteenth century, and profoundly influence the growth and development of North America.

James Grant established a grist mill at Pictou Harbor and became widely known throughout the region for his philanthropic work and generous assistance to the scores of hungry settlers. His son Alexander, also a man of social conscience, carried on the family business. In 1816, "the year of the mice", he purchased one thousand dollars worth of flour and had it shipped by water from Halifax to New Glasgow where it was distributed to the starving settlers. The latter begat Jas, who was to become known as "the dyer", and he begat John Walter Grant, the maternal grandfather of Grant MacEwan.

John Walter Grant was the fourth generation of Grants to call Canada home. The family milling operations in Springville, on the East River, had made the family prosperous. However, the Great World Trade Depression brought John Walter Grant and his family of nine to the brink of economic collapse. It was then that his nineteen-year-old son, John Gray Grant, left the struggling family and ventured into the world to create his own destiny. Little did his siblings, eight-year-old Bertha and twelve-year-old James, know that they would follow in his path.

John Grant bought passage on the newly opened rail route to Western Canada, and when the track ended, he worked for the CPR. The money he earned would help him buy his homesteading equipment. By the time the rail construction crew reached the new province of Manitoba, he was anxious to get on with his life. At the capital, he bid farewell to his fellow teamsters, strapped what he could on his back, and walked 150 miles north into the uplands of the Assiniboine River.

There he filed claim to a parcel of 160 acres of fertile land, eight miles north of where the future railway was due to be built. With quiet determination, John Gray Grant joined the elite ranks of the prairie sod-busters. He broke the tough covering of prairie grass, seeded and harvested his first crop, built a house and outbuildings, and shortly thereafter, married Martha Cumming.

When Martha was pregnant with their third child, John beckoned his Nova Scotian sister to his Manitoba homestead for a visit. Bertha arrived in 1894, a tall, dark-haired twenty-three-year-old with a love for life, and for her God, and the same humor and laugh that the entire Grant clan were known for.

There were now three Grants living in Manitoba. James Alexander Grant had arrived three years earlier and his half-section farm was four miles east of John's. After a spell of separation, some fifteen years in length, three of the Grant siblings were finally reunited.

John Walter Grant and Chrissie Gray Grant, Springville, Nova Scotia, 1897. — MacEwan-Foran Collection

Bertha Grant remained in Manitoba. She was a warm and caring person who gave selflessly of her time and talents to her relatives and community, and it was these qualities that secured her a place in the nursing program of the newly constructed Brandon General Hospital. One of the first graduates of the program, Bertha joined the staff of the hospital in 1897.

It had been a little over one hundred years since the Hector and its pilgrim Scots had landed in Nova Scotia. They were a brave lot, faithful to their God, trustful that their future would be better than their past.

Graduation photo, Brandon General Hospital's first nursing class, 1898. Bertha Gray Grant is back row, center. — MacEwan-Foran Collection

George MacEwan and Agnes Cowan, 1910. — MacEwan-Foran Collection

The factories in Britain and western Europe had quickened their pace during the century. The requirement for food from their crowded industrial towns rose steadily. The western United States was now settled, and any remaining land was of poor agricultural value. Canada's 'Last, Best West' was the last great expanse of fertile soil in North America. Land which could grow crops to feed Europe's factory population.

Minister of the Interior, Clifford Sifton's marketing cry, "come to the Last Best West!" rang throughout the civilized world during the 1890s in a bid to populate the Prairies. "You may keep your language and religion, just come and till our prairie soil" read the posters circulated throughout North America. The posters destined for Europe promised prosperity for newcomers. Since 1763 the politicians and populace had maintained, given Quebec's central place in the creation of Canada, that this nation would protect the cultures of its founding nations. It would be this promise of prosperity, and later its multicultural makeup which would attract millions of immigrants to Canada's shores.

Sifton's belief that a peasant in a sheepskin coat, born on the soil, whose forefathers had been farmers for generations, with a stout wife and a half-dozen children was good quality, drove the selection process. Orientals, Italians, Jews or Blacks were banned because he concluded "they don't farm well" (in northern climates).

The first Grants were already established farmers in Brandon, Manitoba when eighteen-year-old Alexander Hedley MacEwan set off from Guelph, Ontario, in search of his dreams. The MacEwans had originated from Buchlyvie, Stirlingshire, Scotland, home of the famous Clydesdale. His father George MacEwan had come to Canada in 1857 when he was twelve-years old. He became a blacksmith, working on the York Road running out of Guelph until he became an engineer in the Raymond Sewing Machine Factory where he worked for forty years. In the year following Confederation, George MacEwan married Agnes Cowan, whose family shared lineage with Sir Walter Scott, and some two years later, in 1870, Grant MacEwan's father, Alexander Hedley MacEwan was born.

Grant MacEwan's father, Alex, albeit interested in machines, was determined to head West. He was going to be a cowboy and ride the ranges of Idaho or Nevada like the characters in the stories he read, an activity and a goal that his strict Presbyterian parents abhorred.

George MacEwan, Guelph, Ontario, circa 1900 — MacEwan-Foran Collection

By the time he was eighteen-years-old, Alex was energetic, strong and imbued with remarkable endurance yet tempered with a quiet nature. He had worked on neighboring farms after leaving school, contributing a portion of the money to his parents for his keep, and setting the rest aside for the day he could realize his dreams. By 1889 he was ready. The western United States was his goal.

Alex set off with his small savings and a letter of reference from the last farmer he worked for. He travelled on the Canadian Pacific Railway which by now traversed the new dominion. The CPR, he reasoned, would carry him across the country without having to transfer from one rail to another. The line would also drop him just north of his intended destination, Idaho.

The time for the opening of the West appeared to have arrived with the eighties. The greatest migration in Canadian history occurred in 1881. The traffic through the United States from St. Paul and down the Red River Valley tripled in volume. There were rumors that thousands of Ontario farmers were ready to colonize Manitoba. Winnipeg became the front door of a vast empire that revealed its resources with the years. It had churches and schools, and a university supported by all religious denominations, would soon be established. Law enforcement deterred gangs of vultures or land-sharks from forming, although like activities in the American West were enshrined in print. While the mid- to late-eighties would see the immediate crisis of the Riel Rebellion become central to Manitoba's history, young men such as Alex MacEwan, arriving toward the end of the decade, were far more interested in establishing a land claim than taking sides in a French fray.

Alex was broke by the time his train pulled into Manitoba, and he had no other choice but to work for a grubstake. He disembarked in Brandon to begin what would become a lifetime search for fortune. Failure would counter his successes, and at least one flier would leave his future family, including young Grant MacEwan, without a roof over their heads or food to fill their bellies.

Alex MacEwan was hired by farmer Moses Abbey, a bachelor with a single man's penchant for the simple life. His homestead was eight miles out of town. It was here that Alex MacEwan learned about the seeding and harvesting of crops,

Alex Cowan of Altrieve Farm, Galt, Ont. and Dr. William Cowan seated.
— MacEwan-Foran Collection

Altrieve Farm   *March 20th/89*
Galt, Ontario

Having had the services of the bearer, Mr. Alex MacEwan, for the past two years, it affords us pleasure to be able to certify, not only to his good moral character but to his thorough reliableness whether in the field or attending to the stock, and can recommend him as being trustworthy in every respect.

(signed) Alex M. Cowan and James S. Cowan

"My mother was a Grant and my father a MacEwan. One was a Scottish beer and the other a Scotch whisky. I'm a teetotaller."

and the care and feeding of livestock. He earned twenty dollars a month of which part he saved; the rest he sent home to help his family.

The young man was satisfied with his work, particularly looking after the cattle and horses. The meals, however, were a different matter. He was appalled by the fare the older man concocted. Sowbelly beans and salt pork, while full of protein held hazards for the diner. The pork, stored in a barrel in the shed, tended to develop a life of its own. The chickens, who roosted on this barrel during the night, had a significant influence on the chemistry of its contents. Alex was also no more impressed by the alternate menu item, bannock. Moses would fry globs of gray unleavened bread dough in lard which had been recycled for as long as he had lived on the homestead, and slap them onto the rough board table for Alex to choose the least repugnant portion!

Alex MacEwan worked for Moses Abbey for four years with the exception of one summer. He reasoned that he could make a lot more money by selling trees for an eastern firm who promised an attractive commission than working the land or shovelling piles of manure. He discovered, however, that farmers had no interest in spending their time or hard-earned money on decorative shrubs for their vegetable gardens.

Alex's dream of riding the range soon faded, and his wish to own a farm might have met the same fate if a homestead, south of the town of Chater, had not come up for sale. In 1893, he put up his grubstake and made financial arrangements for the remaining amount.

The quarter section of land was untouched by a plow, and it presented Alex MacEwan an immediate challenge. He joined the ranks of prairie sodbusters, breaking the entire 160 acres that summer with a ten-inch plow pulled by a team of horses. His first crop was harvested late in the summer of the following year, in part with an ancient cradle and flail. Two years later, the young farmer, with the evidence of his prosperity jingling in his pockets, returned to Guelph to show his friends and relatives that his hard work had been rewarded with success.

Both progressive in thought and blessed with ample courage to carry out his convictions, Alex MacEwan was one of the pioneer elite who with mind and spirit revolutionized the practice of agriculture in Western Canada. Profit, not mere existence, was the name of the game. He was willing to try whatever means, be it for land or beast, to reduce the work and increase the yield. Grant MacEwan recorded in his journal, many years later, that when his father expanded his arable land, he used a twelve-inch gang plow to break the prairie sod. He wrote, "One of his neighbors remarked it was neither practical nor respectable to farm in such a hurry."

In 1898, Alex MacEwan read an advertisement in an American publication which convinced him that he could speed up the process of harvesting, perhaps even cheat the climate from ruining a crop, and maybe make a bit of money. It was simple. All he had to do was buy a steam thresher complete with a self-feeder and blower and thresh the entire district. Fifty years later, Grant MacEwan penned in his book, *Sodbusters*, a humorous account of the challenge his father encountered when he was faced with controlling a mechanical monster with an agenda of its own.

The Canadian spirit took flight, inspired by the conviction and courage of men like Alex MacEwan. Like the oats and wheat he sowed into the fertile prairie soil, the seeds of nationalism began to germinate, encouraged in part by the success of an industry wherein the efforts of one could now feed fifty. It was the beginning of a proud legacy wherein the Canadian prairies became known as the "breadbasket of the world."

Alexander MacEwan's farm was but a stone's throw, just two-and-a-half-miles down the road, from the James Grant farm. James had come to know Alexander MacEwan as a clever and hard-working man, perhaps a touch stubborn, but nonetheless a dedicated farmer whose Clydesdale horses were groomed impeccably whether for work or the road. This man, thought James, was a potential suitor worthy of his sister, Bertha. James, however, having tangled with Bertha once before about her choice of suitors, was not about to tamper again.

Bertha had been nursing at the Brandon General when James had caught wind of her attending a dance with a chap he felt not deserving of her attention. The following day he went to the hospital with the intent of taking her home, and thereby putting an end to the unsatisfactory liaison. Bertha met his demand with puzzlement followed by gales of laughter replete with tears. James retreated to his farm, alone, and soon after married Bella Smith. As fate would have it, Bertha Grant and Alex MacEwan did meet, albeit the coincidence was

---

Sodbusters

Our Sodbuster made some money and then came the machine age and he put all his savings into a threshing outfit of the newest and biggest design. Manufacturers were competing to see who could build the mightiest steam engine and the biggest separator. The newest gadgets on threshing machines that year were self-feeders and wind stackers. His outfit consisted of a Minneapolis engine and a separator with a 40-inch cylinder. It was the first west of Portage la Prairie having both self-feeder and blower.

Homesteaders came for miles to see the monster in action, to see a separator building its own stack and eating up sheaves which didn't have to be forced into its throat. The only trouble was that the new feeder didn't work and had to be discarded. So instead of having four men pitching sheaves into the automatic feeder, they had to be satisfied with eight men at the feeder end, four pitching from the loads to the tables, two cutting bands and two forcing sheaves into the cylinder.

When noon time came and the threshing crew descended upon the farmer's kitchen, 23 ravenous men sat down to test the food resources and the patience of the good wife. But when things were going well, that big outfit threshed a lot of wheat. It threshed 1,000 bushels in three hours one time, to say nothing of the bushels that went into the straw pile. That record stood a while and when the big outfit had to move from one farm to the next, it broke another record, a record for slow motion. And it usually broke a few bridges, because bridge builders hadn't reckoned with any such mechanical monstrosity . . . Strangely enough the big outfit didn't ruin Alex and it didn't drive him crazy. Some who bought threshers weren't so lucky.

from the book Sodbusters
by Grant MacEwan

"Father was a rugged individualist, a good farmer. He had a good sense of conservation. He kept his thoughts to himself. He was a typical Highland Scot that didn't have much to say. He was a good man."

orchestrated by James. Alexander Hedley MacEwan and Bertha Gray Grant were married in her brother John's home on January 18, 1900.

Alex MacEwan brought his bride home to a farm that was well established with a two-storey frame house, barn and outbuildings. He had planted young spruce trees on the north, west, and east side of the farm to break the prairie winds. James Grant's homestead was within eyesight and both farms were walking distance from Chater. The growing town was four miles away. It had a railway delivery point, general store, post office, hotel, lumberyard, blacksmith shop, and grain elevators.

Alex had built a fine, but basic house with four rooms, two up and two down. The wood-burning black and chrome Great Majestic cook stove sat prominently in the kitchen, a tribute to the homesteader's efficiency and expediency for it could both cook and heat at the same time. A sleek wood-and-coal-burning heater stood in the corner of the parlor. Stove pipes from both, which threaded through holes in the ceiling, radiated heat as they ran through the upstairs bedrooms, the temperature controlled entirely by the fury of the fire and the fervor of the stoker. The kitchen was not only the largest room, it was the centre of activity. The parlor was reserved for special occasions. Bertha soon transformed the house into a home, and set about to fill the silence of its rooms with the voices of children.

The West advanced rapidly thanks to the inrush of settlement. Railway lines and roads traversed the land and towns sprang up where once only sod lay. Brandon, Regina and Saskatoon, Calgary and Edmonton, once trading posts and board shanties, were now growing cities. Frame dwellings replaced the primitive sod huts of settlers. Railways carried the lumber. Land surrounding the towns had long ago been claimed and turned into farms which produced bumper crops and supported good livestock. The population of Canada in 1901 was 5,371,315.

Red-brown grain elevators began to speckle the land and for as far as the naked eye could see, golden grain dipped and dived like Texas line-dancers under the hot, blue summer sky. Almost overnight, the plains had evolved from a wilderness existence of trapping and hunting to an expanding industry intent on raising wheat for world markets. Science and machinery replaced the cradle and flail, the once stalwart harvest tools which were wielded by the same hands that had painstaking planted each seed, one by one.

While rail lines had transported enthusiastic wannabe farmers by the carload, they had also created dependency by becoming the major carrier of food, fuel, and equipment to burgeoning cities and remote sidings. The wheat kingdom had been created by the iron horse, and only it had the capacity to move the millions of bushels of wheat to market. Red River carts became a relic of the past.

By 1900 Western Canada was producing 5,000,000 bushels of wheat, much of it coming from southwestern Manitoba. Boosters said there was no limit to the amount of money to be made in the West. Bankers pumped the callused hands of farmers for more than just friendship. Making money was an honorable quest, and those closest to the land were part of the pivotal industry which promised prosperity.

Roughly 400,000 homestead entries were made during the first decade of the new century. While some of the newcomers brought their own capital and equipment, thousands came with the shirt on their back and nothing else. Their needs created marketing opportunities and niche industries in centres such as Brandon. Tools, implements, seed, wagons, good horses and oxen were all in demand.

In 1902, permanent radio communication across the Atlantic to Britain was established by Guglielmo Marconi. In 1903, Canada had a total of 178 cars registered. Sir Wilfrid Laurier and his Liberals swept the country for the third time in the general election of 1904, retaining their term in office that began in 1896. Wealth and prosperity had come to be expected. Only the lazy or crazy were poor.

There was great joy in the MacEwan homestead when Bertha gave birth to their first child, Agnes, in 1901. However, the sounds of the infant were silenced within its first year. Bertha, despite her nursing skill and knowledge, could not save her young daughter from the clutch of death when diphtheria swept the Prairies.

The following summer, Bertha gave birth to her second child. John Walter Grant MacEwan was born on August 12, 1902. He was named after his maternal grandfather in Nova Scotia, John Walter Grant, whose name was spoken in one word sounding like "Jnwaltergrant" — to distinguish him from other Grants living in the area.

Young Grant MacEwan met his namesake when he was two-years old and his grandfather seventy-six years young.

Grant MacEwan, 1903.
— MacEwan-Foran Collection

Bertha Grant MacEwan holding two-year old Grant. Seated are Grant MacEwan's grandmother and great-grandmother Grant. Photo was taken in 1904 in Springville, Nova Scotia — MacEwan-Foran Collection

Bertha's parents had remained in Pictou, Nova Scotia although most of her siblings had long since left the family home to make their own way. The old man's efforts at mentoring his grandson were returned with an everlasting admiration. Their feelings for each other would eventually grow to close the generation gap. In his journal, Grant MacEwan wrote of his maternal grandfather: "He never knew what it was to possess much of this world's goods, but he raised a family of eight and enjoyed life . . . His crop land was small. He seeded but a few bags of grain annually. One horse provided all the power apart from hand power on the farm. A small band of sheep, about 12 to 15 cows, an orchard and a generous garden completed the sources of food and provisions."

Years later, when Grant MacEwan began to search for his place in the world, it was this old man's thoughts which guided his decision. "John," he said. The old man always used the boy's first name. "I would rather see you an independent farmer, than the richest doctor in Pictou County." What grandfather Grant could not have known was that farming would be just one of his grandson's many careers.

The birthplace of Grant MacEwan was not unlike a Utopia. Alex MacEwan had built his farm eight miles northeast of Brandon in the Assiniboine River uplands. Because of the elevation, it was possible to see Brandon's church spires, the chimney stack and water tower of the mental hospital. Fertile fields with millions of shafts of wheat surrounded the farmhouse. The house was comfortable but not lavish. A vegetable garden and livestock provided foodstuff from which Bertha prepared the family's mouth-watering meals. The aroma of her fresh baking would bring Grant MacEwan to the kitchen, on the run, to taste whatever fare his mother had turned out of her Great Majestic.

From a very early age, Bertha MacEwan impressed on Grant her faith and values. Presbyterianism challenged and met the spiritual and moral needs of the New World farmers, and though the fervor of the puritanical faith had waned during its westerly drift to Manitoba and beyond, it had steadfastly maintained its "one on one" style of worship with daily prayers.

Bertha expected Grant to develop habits of worship similar to her own, and in return, God would favor his life. When the mother and son prayed together — and it was on their knees — Bertha creatively fused reverence and thriftiness together by turning down the flame of the oil lamps during prayer. Many years later, MacEwan described his mother as being an early conservationist whose conscience was guided by her faith. "She thought thrift was a virtue," he explained, "and that waste was a sin."

Alex on the other hand, was a bit of a free spirit. His place of worship was in the tabernacle of the great outdoors and the service occurred without rite or ritual. The other parishioners came and went as they pleased. Eventually, Grant MacEwan would also move his own altar amongst the trees and sky, and expand his faith to give equal due to all living creatures.

Grant MacEwan's piercing blue eyes which were overshadowed by his high brow seemed to absorb the wonders of the fast-changing world. He had inherited from his mother a mop of jet-black hair, a fun-loving nature and a sense of humor that was oft punctuated with a good belly laugh. From his father, the lad acquired a quiet and reserved manner.

His education began in the farmyard and surrounding fields. For part of the day he would watch his father and the farmhand tend to the animals or machinery. The other half of day was devoted to his mother. The birds and animals were his earliest friends. Work was a way of life, and neither its virtues nor vices were lost upon young Grant. Moreover, if life on a farm did not instill the value of good work ethics, his mother's Presbyterian faith would!

Humesville Church Choir (North Brandon). Bertha MacEwan is seated first in second row from bottom.
— MacEwan-Foran Collection

"My mother was a very devoted church person. She took us boys to church, by foot or by horse and buggy. It was four miles each way. Her effort wasn't lost. I'm not a church-goer now, but I still talk to my God. And I listen when I think He's talking to me."

Grant was a curious child. While most of his days were spent outside observing the wonders of nature, on occasion he was able to negotiate a trip to town. These opportunities allowed him to study the developing urban sprawl with its churches, smokestacks, busy streets, horse-drawn buggies and wagons, and everywhere he looked, people. The CPR station thrilled the little boy. Not only was it the hub for travel, its role in mail and parcel delivery made it an exciting place for a child to visit.

Prairie communities were governed by a strict code of behavior, and offenses were dealt with by community elders, their duty assigned, as a rule, in the stable behind the church. One sinner in the community in which MacEwan grew up was spotted working in his fields on a Sabbath. The sinner discovered, however, there was an up side to being devoted.

Grant's uncle John Grant and another gentleman were asked to call upon the wrongdoer and to admonish him about his ways. The callers first ascertained that the farmer knew what day of the week it was, and if he was a believer. The farmer explained he was behind in his work and merely trying to get caught up. On hearing this, John Grant told him to stop his work immediately and promised to return the next day to help him complete his chores.

Just as life was a part of the community, so was death. Grant MacEwan in his book, *Hoofprints and Hitchingposts*, recalled a humorous prairie funeral during his childhood. A community member had passed on and was to be buried on a day when the regular livery team, which normally drew the wagon carrying the coffin, was already doing funeral duty elsewhere. The driver dispatched for the event was left with no choice but to hitch together a Standard Bred, with some racing in his background, and a young bronco.

By the time the service had ended and the coffin was loaded, the team was restless. The normally solemn procession set off, but before long the livery team and the minister's pacer were in a thundering race for the graveyard. The contest, wrote MacEwan, was won by the minister. One of the mourners, who also knew his horses, suggested a horse trade to the minister after the interment. However, the man of the cloth countered: "No thanks, not even if you throw in the Pearly Gates."

The Canadian West grew at a faster pace than the East during the first decade of the century. The nation, however, was receding from a predominantly rural and primary producing economy to one focussed on manufacturing and service for its growing urban population. Even though the prairies were being steadily populated with Canadian, British and European settlers, and wheat dominated the economy, the growth of cities began to steadily outstrip rural Canada.

The rustic lifestyle associated with living off the land, albeit harsh at times, gave ample opportunity for quality interaction between family and extended family, and community. Not a lot was needed for an excuse to have a house party, barn dance, ball game, or picnic. The advent of the automobile was still in the future. A trip was ten miles. Twenty miles was considered a day's journey. It was a time when families were intimate members of communities, and communities were but an extension of its families. Dominion Day and Christmas Day were the most important holidays.

The Grant and MacEwan families mingled and supported each other in whatever manner was needed. Aunts and uncles extended their parenting beyond their own children to their nieces and nephews. Love and doing things together wove the John Grant, James Grant and Alex MacEwan families into an even closer clan. And although Alex MacEwan had little to say during these get-togethers, his taciturnity was not viewed as lack of interest. Rather, when he did speak, people listened. Bertha, on the other hand, enjoyed these great family gatherings and the accompanying bedlam and din. Her tranquil and orderly home with two males, both of whom possessed quiet dispositions, was a stark contrast to her childhood and the large and noisy family she grew up in.

The death of Bella Grant in 1905 was therefore an especially devastating blow to the Grant and MacEwan families. Bella and James and their three girls were an integral part of these great gatherings. For Grant MacEwan, this was also the first family member to die during his young life. Soon after, Marion Grant, the spinster sister of James, John and Bertha came to help out. One look at the three motherless girls, however, was enough to keep her in the James Grant home for the remainder of her life.

On April 16, 1906, Bertha gave birth to her third child, George Alexander Grant. Once more the wails of an infant filled the quiet house on the prairies, and the Grant and MacEwan families had cause to rejoice. By this time Grant was showing signs of behavior and insight beyond his years.

"Mother was a conservationist. Some people would say she was tight or mean, but she wasn't. But she had some very strong beliefs about economy. She believed waste was a sin and thrift was a virtue like kindness, or honesty, or mercy. Maybe it's wishful thinking, but I like to believe I got more from my mother's philosophy about life."

George MacEwan (standing) and Grant MacEwan in 1912.
— MacEwan-Foran Collection

Perhaps the quiet mien he had inherited from his father allowed him more time to observe the world around him, and to contemplate its meaning. The hired-hand, even speculated that four-year-old Grant would become prime minister one day. The lad had learned to respond to the expectations of the people around him at a very early age.

The wheat boom supported industrial activity and the extent of both was truly astounding. Railway lines knotted where towns and cities sprang up. Real estate prices soared, and speculation on land or livestock became a respectable hobby for some. Prosperity was the central fact of the first decade of the century. Sir Wilfrid Laurier's boast of the twentieth century belonging to Canada seemed more an appraisal than a prophecy. The spiral of the boom would not crest until 1913.

On September 1, 1905 the province of Saskatchewan became part of Confederation. From 1901 to 1910, the population of the province quintupled, and between 1901 and 1905, the number of homesteads increased from 13,000 to 50,000. When Saskatoon was incorporated as a town in 1903, finding the necessary nine councillors who had lived in the city for a year was a problem. But by 1905 it had received its charter, and by the end of the decade the city was building a university and had a population of almost twelve thousand.

The Carrot River Valley line — owned by the Canadian Northern Railway — opened that year. Trains carrying specu-lators were a way for the lines to sell new districts. So when the Carrot River Valley line took a group of investors out to the district, 400 miles northwest of Brandon, Alex MacEwan was amongst them. He bought on a section of fertile land at Melfort.

A risk-taker with an eye to improving the existing, Alex floated the idea of a horse breeders' syndicate amongst his fellow farmers. He wanted to improve the horsepower available to farmers by selective breeding. The farmers pooled their means and purchased Flash Baron, sired by the world-renowned Baron's Pride. It was not long before the horse began winning championships. The quality of the horsepower in the district became noticeably improved.

For nineteen years, Alex had been a member of Canada's elite agricultural community. He had come a long way from when he broke the prairie sod and planted his first crop. He had a wife and two boys now, and he had developed a thriving farming operation which was the envy of many in the district. By beginning work at four o'clock in the morning, he had established a prosperous operation and accumulated a bank roll which could easily support his retirement. But at thirty-seven years of age, Alex MacEwan still had mountains to climb and rivers to ford. He needed a new challenge, a change of pace.

The MacEwan homestead was put on the auction block on March 26, 1908. The proceeds from the sale helped launch Alex into his next career of manufacturing fire extinguishers, and real estate investments. He had reasoned that with the number of wood frame houses being built in Brandon and the surrounding area, and at the rate they were being built, he could easily become a millionaire within short order. With the constant threat of fire as his ally, the sky would be the limit in this industry and he was going to get in on the ground floor. He was also concerned that the boys, six-year-old Grant and two-year-old George, would need a better education than the one-room school house in Chater could provide.

As with most auctions of the time, the neighbors gathered from far and near to see what they could secure for their farming operation. Friends were the stouthearted workers who polished and greased the machinery, and groomed the livestock. The food for the day (nary an occasion in rural life would be complete without food) was prepared by Bertha with the help of neighboring wives.

Perhaps the most peculiar happening of the day was the sale of Alex's prized Clydesdales. Grant MacEwan writes in his book *Between the Red and the Rockies*: "Bob Walker and the McCallum boys brought brass-fitted harness, top collars, and rings in abundance, to dress the horses for the sale. When Auctioneer T.C. Norris (later Premier Norris of Manitoba) arrived and saw the stylish display he enquired if there was a ring factory in the district. Bob Walker, instead of talking down the team he himself wanted to buy, braided tails, plaited manes and so adorned the animals that he was obliged to pay the high price of $525 for the pair."

A few days later, Bertha and the two boys boarded the train for Nova Scotia, and Alex followed some weeks later after tidying up the last details relating to the disposal of the homestead. With the farm gone, the MacEwans were free from the enslavement its way of life imposed upon its owners. In not so many years, they would also come to regret the loss of its security.

"Dad didn't go to church but he did have some convictions. He believed that horses and cattle and other animals had as much right to live as humans had. He was particularly thoughtful toward his horses. Horses had a rough time during the pioneer years. They were essential. They were our slaves. I think horses deserve credit for pioneer achievement just as much as the pioneers themselves."

It had been four years since Grant had met his namesake. He pushed his nose against the glass of the window during the long train trip and absorbed the sights of the alternating countryside, towns and sprawling cities. Cars were now a common sight, yet the horse and buggy still ruled the dirt road. The lush green landscape of the Maritimes, with its creeks and rivers, and salty ocean breeze was a stark contrast to the prairie landscape that was his home. *Anne of Green Gables* was published that year. Romanticism and prosperity gripped the land.

Grant MacEwan wrote in his journal: "Mother and two sons journeyed to Nova Scotia for the summer months, and were later joined by the head of the household. The beauties of Pictou County registered vividly, even upon the son of six tender years. It was there on the East River that I, in company with my highly respected Grandsire, caught my first fish. As I recall the fish, it probably did not exceed six inches in length, but it did seem to possess great proportions at that time. John Walter Grant Sr. (my grandfather) and John Walter Grant Jr. (myself) were devoted to each other and on the latter's departure from the old farm at Springville, the former offered him anything on the farm that caught his fancy. The selection was quickly made - it was a modest gimlet that had previously proven effective in making tiny holes in pieces of board."

The family stopped in Guelph on the way home where Grant met his paternal grandparents. This visit, together with the time Grant spent with his namesake, made a lasting impression. Where the Grant clan celebrated life and the pleasures it held, the MacEwan clan were an austere lot that held frugality next to godliness. On the way home he learned from his mother the ditty, "Wilful waste brings woeful want, and some day you may say, oh how I wish I had the crust, that once I threw away."

Manitoba had grown exponentially in the short time the MacEwans were in Nova Scotia. Communities sprang up. The demand for services and supplies grew by leaps and bounds. The boom was driven by bumper crops which commanded top prices on world markets. The population of Brandon was 11,000. Wood frame houses were being built on every city block. Alex MacEwan was convinced more than ever that he had made the right decision. Manufacturing and selling fire extinguishers would put him on easy street.

The family moved into 1316 McTavish Avenue, a two-storey clapboard house, on August 31, 1908. The following day, Grant MacEwan commenced his education at Alexander School. In addition to looking after George and Grant, Bertha became a member of the congregation of Knox Presbyterian Church. Alex, who could never be described as lazy, reverted back to beginning his work day at four o'clock in the morning.

The Brandon home was described by MacEwan as modest with an average number of comforts and conveniences, and always an abundance of simple wholesome foods. One day was about like another, except that Christmas Day was truly different, a real and undisputed holiday. Sundays were devoted to worship. Grant's attendance at Knox Sunday school was near perfect. He was a member of the Mission Band and a Boy Scout, and in 1912, he served as a member of the guard of honor for Canada's governor general, the Duke of Connaught. Summer holidays and travelling further than Forrest or Chater were practically unthought of. Both Grant and George were city boys in guise if not in spirit. Alex was busy with his fire extinguisher factory, and Bertha with her family and church.

Grant MacEwan transferred from Grade two in Alexander School to the corresponding grade at Park School on November 1, 1909, perhaps because the first school was overcrowded. He wrote in his journal that "public school days slipped around at the rate of one grade a year until the Fall of 1914 when I was promoted from Grade six to Grade eight. Miss Bertha Pilling, a very able girl, was my teacher in Grade six; and in my final year in the Brandon school, my teacher was Mr. J. Johanason, a good teacher of Icelandic origin. Had the family remained in Brandon I would have tried my entrance examinations in my twelfth year (Spring of 1915)."

Music attracted MacEwan's attention for a time. The Alexander School had an orchestra which the aspiring young musician wanted to join. At first, he was interested in the cornet or the trombone. But when he discovered the price of the instruments, his interest cooled. Instead, he sent away for a five dollar B-flat flute. After two years of practice and no measurable results the would-be musician withdrew from the band.

During his last three years in school, MacEwan expanded the base of his knowledge to include carpentry and basic mechanics by attending a manual training course at Central and, subsequently, Normal School in Brandon. He

"Erosion is a pretty serious business and it's not all in soil. Erosion of ideals, morals, and spiritual value. It makes me sad. One of our losses from the pioneer years is that spiritual sense.

Every rural family had church connection. It might be two or three miles away. I'm thinking of one when I was a small boy, the church was in Humesville, north of Brandon.. You'd think by the farm population around that they wouldn't be able to fill a pew. There were a few men that didn't go, they hung around the horses, maybe did some trading. But ninety percent of the church was filled. It filled a vacuum in peoples' lives.

It wasn't a one day a week affair. There was always a prayer meeting on Tuesday or Wednesday evening where people turned out the same as they did on Sunday. It was an hour given to sacred music and sacred prayer. But it was important enough that people hitched their horses to their buggies and drove to church. It was a force — a force with energy in it."

"I think I've preserved some of the essential things in a religious life, and I hope that young people will not overlook that there's something bigger, more mysterious, with a greater potential than a computer or radio. Maybe there are still some miracles. But in any case, it's something that's worth looking for, and it's the search that counts."

showed a hidden flair for both, and one might wonder whether his later well-known carvings of his friend, the beaver, found their genesis here. He also secured his first experience in cutting hair. Writes MacEwan in his journal: "Uncle Jim was going to a wedding the next day and he had to have a haircut. I confessed that I had never performed such a task but would do my best. . . when I was about half finished, my victim peered in a mirror and said to me, 'Great Caesar, Grant! I think you had better stop. I'll finish it myself.'"

Even with the building boom in Brandon, there was still a vacant lot or two that attracted a summer baseball game, or a frozen slough that served for a game of ice hockey during the long Manitoba winters. Like other lads of his age, Grant had an overabundance of energy and a need to run off steam. Perhaps the time he spent playing sports may have seemed frivolous to the MacEwan side of the family, but it was an activity which allowed the prepubescent boy a brief release from his heavy family responsibilities.

By the same token, MacEwan was the source of a normal amount of childhood mischief. He was playing with a match one day and he decided to put it behind a lace curtain to observe the flame. When the material ignited, the lad ripped the flaming drape down, forgetting entirely about the fire extinguisher which stood nearby. His mother's discipline was sure and swift.

Another time, the young scavenger brought home a whole roll of wire which he found still attached but just outside a new fence at the exhibition grounds. The bubble of his success was burst by his mother's consternation and lecture about the morality of stealing. The rebuke was followed by the ominous appearance of a police officer riding his bicycle down the back alley. That night, a remorseful Grant rented his chum's wagon a second time, and dragged the wire back to where he found it. No doubt the family reading from the Bible that night had concentrated on the happenings of the day. The experience had cost him ten cents, five to get the wire home and five to clear his conscience.

A journal entry about George suggests that Grant's younger brother contributed to some of the pranks about the home. "Geordie, with the face of a philosopher and the true mind of a scientist cut the rubber gas pipe to the stove to see if his new Christmas knife was really sharp. The results were well nigh fatal."

It was during Grant's early years in the Brandon school system that the seeds for documenting the flesh-and-blood characters of Canada's past were sown. The abysmal lack of Canadian content in school history texts was not only troublesome, it irked the pride of the young federalist. He fretted over the fact that he had to memorize names of monarchs and their years of rule while books about the colorful pioneers who helped to build and shape the character of his country were nonexistent.

As a wee lad he had sat on his maternal grandfather's knee and learned about the courage and conviction of the Hector pilgrims and the settlement of Nova Scotia by his Highland ancestors. Even his father had described the settlement of the wild west as the two did chores around the Brandon farm. It was not long before the thoroughly disgruntled schoolboy hated the very subject he would later turn into a lucrative avocation.

The little boy's life must have seemed complete when his Grandfather and Grandmother Grant decided, in 1910, to make their home with his Uncle James. His uncle had gone to Pictou County and accompanied a carload of livestock and farm effects to Brandon, including what MacEwan described as "a memorable one-horse dump cart." One of the cows,

Grade six class photo. Grant MacEwan stands fourth from left in back row. — MacEwan-Foran Collection

"I'm an admirer of Arnold Toynbee, the late English historian and philosopher. He studied the rise and fall of empires. He could name twenty or more great empires that came up fast but didn't manage to stay up, didn't manage to establish a plateau and remain. They came up and went down, and then disappeared.

Toynbee concluded that this was a normal part of civilization. That they could expect the next generation to produce the same ups and downs. He said the next ones to suffer would be the United States and Canada."

given to the MacEwan family so that their young sons could have fresh milk, would trigger Grant MacEwan's entry into the business world.

"It was my ambition, much more than that of other boys, to make money," wrote MacEwan in his daily journal. "A dollar earned meant a dollar saved." He prided himself on the fact that he never spent as much as five cents at one time during his early school years. Once in a while he spent a cent on sweets.

The young entrepreneur was introduced to the magic of money at school. On Monday mornings the teacher would call each student up to her desk so that they could deposit into their own account whatever money had been saved from the previous week. The teacher marked it down and showed the students their growing balances. Every week on the designated banking day the procedure was repeated. It was not long before the children grasped the mystery of addition, interest, and forecasting, and grew a tidy little savings account.

The graph which tracked MacEwan's savings showed a steady incline, with one exception. At one point in his short life, Grant felt that baby George got far more attention than was deserved. And he decided to run away. He withdrew ten dollars from his savings bank, went to Fitton's store and bought three cent's worth of candy, and set off with the change jingling in his pocket. But by the time the lad had walked a mile or two, the bank withdrawal weighed heavy on his conscience. The forlorn little mogul returned home, disheartened that the experience had made a dip in his graph.

One could speculate as to whether young Grant's cultural predisposition made him one of the best savers in the school, or if indeed, it was a natural inclination. Nevertheless, he recorded the following in his journal, perhaps after being chastised for his conservative spending habits. "The more generous and polite called the eldest MacEwan boy thrifty and businesslike while others said he was mean, stingy and full of the traits of 'the circumcised.'"

Certainly the money-handling habits he formed in these tender years were fed by his creative entrepreneurial enterprises. Old Polly, the milk cow, always managed to produce more than was required. So the young businessman sold the extra — between three and eight quarts a day — to the neighbors. Soon he combined fresh extra vegetables from the family garden, and, a bit later, the Brandon Sun. The importance of yield and marketable commodities was impressed on the young tycoon at an early age.

The summertime offered even more hours for Grant to make money. The Brandon Fair employees presented an opportunity to expand his customer base for milk, vegetables and newspapers. And after a rain one day, he discovered to his delight, that the fair's manure pile had become a mound of erupting mushrooms. With the utmost of caution, lest he give away his source of supply, he plucked the fresh fungi which commanded a high price, and added them to his inventory.

The fair became the Dominion Exhibition in 1913. MacEwan sold cigars and confectioneries on a twenty percent commission, and kept his overhead to nil by jumping the fence to avoid paying admission. That summer he was given two pairs of boots from the pilot, Alfred Blakely, who was the star attraction at the exposition. Although the size thirteen brown and black patent leather button-up boots were still too big for the eleven-year old, he could not have foreseen how thankful he would be for the gift, in the not so distant future.

That same summer James Cowan, a cousin of Alex MacEwan, gave Grant his first automobile ride. "It was a big day when Jim took me for a ride in the country, perhaps to test a car or maybe to get away for an hour. . . I accompanied him out First Street to the asylum, and a trail leading toward 18th Street was selected for the trial. The speed was a marvel to me. It was weeks before I forgot the thrill of travelling thirty miles per hour in a car."

Grant MacEwan was always on the prowl looking for ways to make money. When most twelve-year-old boys were spending their summer holiday playing baseball or riding their bikes, he worked in George Fitton's grocery store from eight in the morning until six at night. On Saturdays he worked until ten. It was 1914 and World War I had just been declared. His trustworthy nature earned the respect of Mr. Fitton and it was not long before Grant was making the bank deposits. And for a couple of weeks, he ran the store. On his way to the bank, he would stop at the Brandon Sun, read the war bulletins and bring back to Mr. Fitton a summary of the overseas news.

With the first stage of his schooling soon to end, and the coveted Grade Eight Certificate within sight, MacEwan was giving a lot of thought to his future. For a time, he flirted with the idea of becoming a doctor. His father didn't much care "as

"Someone asked him:

'Dr. Toynbee, what can we do to prevent a decline? We're up now. What can we do to stay there?'

He said: 'Revive some of the old-fashioned values, resourcefulness and self-reliance and thrift.'

We've got to restore that sense of spirituality. Toynbee wasn't a church man but he believed that the future of our nation depended on spirituality."

long as the boys become neither preachers, lawyers or bartenders." The lad was also aware of his mother's secret wish for him to become a minister. But it would be the poignant words of his mentor and namesake, "I would rather see you an independent farmer," that would influence the adolescent's life. From the age of twelve on, Grant was resolved to become a farmer and to raise good livestock.

An entry in his journal reads: "I attended the public auction sales at the city market, and with the few cents entrusted to my care, I on one occasion bought a serviceable pick for thirty cents and on another occasion, a hand scythe for forty cents." Not only would these implements form the nucleus of the family's future farm equipment, but the expression, "entrusted to my care" would become the title of MacEwan's landmark work which described his philosophy of conservation.

Initially, the winds of war were dismissed by most Canadians. The population had enjoyed more than a decade of harmony and order accompanied by prosperity. The wheat boom had driven the economy, and cities flourished thanks to the ever increasing demand for products and services. The population was growing at unparalleled rate, bolstered by a reasonably hospitable immigration policy. In 1913, over 400,000 people, the largest number ever, settled in Canada. The country had no more reason to guess than most, and perhaps less, that mankind had come to a fork in its history, a modern day watershed for humanity.

News reports began to filter into the country from far off places like St. Petersburg and Belgrade, Bosnia and Bulgaria, Salonika, Constantinople and Fez. The antics of the Balkan kingdom, the problems in North Africa and the rumblings from Russia, could hardly be considered a danger to a nation as securely situated as Canada. It was also incomprehensible to think that Germany would challenge Great Britain on the open seas. Many of these news reports were dismissed by Canadians as cultural craziness that could not and would not affect them. Thus, the news from Sarajevo in 1914 shocked the somewhat smug, albeit naive nation, to its senses.

Never a man to sit on his haunches if there was a buck to be made, Alex had entered the booming real estate market in 1913 with the intent of flipping properties for a quick and easy profit. He had taken the surplus from his business, after first providing for his family, and speculated rather liberally on

For most of his life, Grant MacEwan recorded the happenings in his life in a ledger-style journal. A 1914 entry with the words "entrusted to my care" became in later years the title of one of his books. — Wei Yew

city lots. The farmer who left his land with a substantial bank roll was now cash poor.

The situation went from bad to worse after war was declared. Within a short time, foreign capital, which had helped to propel the Prairie promise, evaporated. Workers became scarce, and wages and freight rates increased. All of this pushed the cost of manufacturing through the roof. Moreover, the opening of the Panama Canal reduced the quantity of rail freight being shipped to the Pacific, and this rendered a severe blow to Brandon, a town dependent on the CPR. Real estate prices plummeted, and the need for fire extinguishers ceased with the cessation of construction.

In a last desperate attempt to increase the factory's sales, and thereby bolster his cash flow, Alex invited people to the factory to observe firsthand how effective his extinguishers were in the event of a fire. With a crowd watching, he set a small fire alight inside the wood frame factory, and allowed it to grow before turning on his extinguisher. The device failed and the factory burned to the ground, the building and contents uninsured. The Manitoba Boom was over; Alex MacEwan was bankrupt and his family was destitute. The effects of the war imposed dual standards on the Canadian economy. While cities like Brandon wallowed in the effects of the prewar recession, the rural countryside entered yet another boom. The export of wheat, flour, meat and cattle soared. The price of wheat went from $1.32 per bushel to $1.60 between March and April of 1914. The British were looking for 40,000 horses. The volume of livestock handled by stock markets increased by upwards of six hundred percent. Almost as much prairie land was brought into production during the war years as had been farmed during 1913. With the conflict cutting off or destroying much of Europe's farming production, Canada's farmers played an immensely important role in feeding the western allies. The federal minister of agriculture, the Hon. Martin Burrell, pleaded with the farmers of Canada to stay home and grow food. Alex was in the wrong place at the wrong time.

Grant MacEwan notes in a spring 1915 entry to his journal: "My father's business enterprises less profitable than anticipated. Hard times for the family. Decided to go back to the land." His father traded some of his numerous and unprofitable parcels of city real estate on five quarters of land

"Religion isn't an exact science — it's an important search. The search for truth, the search for God, the search for the secrets of God's house, the house of Nature. And when kids find these — they will have found the secrets to many of the environmental and conservation problems of the world today."

"We pioneered twice and went bankrupt once. We had things pretty rough at times and we were pretty sorry for ourselves. But as it turned out, these reverses were a blessing in disguise and I'm very grateful for the opportunities I had to sample the bad with the good, or the good with the bad."

at Margo, Saskatchewan, sight unseen. Alex felt that if he could get back onto the land he could rectify his financial position. However, his lawyer, when told of the swap, sniped, "What, you're going to township forty-four? Should be the best place in the world to grow icicles, but what else can you grow?"

The MacEwans thought they were going to a farm with a house, sound fencing and nine horses which had harnesses and were ready to work. They believed the vendor when he told them that the fields were already cultivated and ready to seed. They could visualize the surrounding countryside which the man had described for them. It had numerous lakes with fresh fish, or so he said.

With little money to his name, Alex assembled a carload of settlers' effects. Old Polly, a crate of hens, a lawnmower, a pail and all of their furniture, dishes, bedding and utensils were readied for shipment. Grant would accompany his father to the farm, and Bertha and George would remain in Brandon until Alex got the furniture into the house. The family's only farm tools were the scythe and pickax which Grant had bought at the auction for seventy cents. It must have been a humiliating experience for Alex to have only enough cash to buy two "old plugs." He paid fifty dollars for each horse and loaded them under the cover of darkness.

Alex had free passage with his load because he was a settler. But to avoid the expense of a fare for Grant, his parents decided that the boy would hide himself amongst the family belongings. Abetting this deed must have created no end of tribulation and woe for Bertha MacEwan who had, in years gone by, rebuked this same son for innocently bringing home a roll of wire from the Brandon Fair.

Clearly, Bertha must have agonized over the family's plight. She and Alex were considerably younger during their first go-around at homesteading. Both were now forty-four years of age and penniless. The deception of their departure placated her Scottish pride and hid the truth from her parents and brothers, but it was a woebegone woman who chose to postpone reckoning with her Lord about the stolen fare until after her family's financial position improved.

Grant and his father set out on Saturday, April 17, 1915, aboard a freight train, their cargo billed for Margo, Saskatchewan. The young lad, having decided to look upon their future as an adventure, embraced the impending move

with an attitude of enthusiasm. With his grandfather's advice
to become an independent farmer ringing in his ears, a copy of
the book, *Souls in Action*, presented to him from the Knox
Church Mission Band, he withdrew from his grade eight class,
and took some fifty dollars from his bank account. The task at
hand was simple: get on the land, seed and harvest a crop, and
sell it in the buoyant market to redeem the family from its
present state of affairs.

"The trip was very interesting," wrote MacEwan. "I was
a stowaway and must keep under cover. On one occasion I was
in my hiding place and while dad was out in the town to get
some bread, one of the train crew came in, stole one of our
best hens and I was obliged to view the event in silence." As a
successful academic in later years, the same stowaway wrote to
the president of the rail company, apologized for his deed and
enclosed the outstanding fare. Conceivably the lecture his
mother imparted on him many years before about the morality
of stealing had found a receptive conscience.

The ragtag twosome arrived in Margo on April 20 and
spent the remainder of the day unloading and making contacts.
Their arrival in the small hamlet created quite a stir and
before long its children gathered to watch the affair. Blessed
with an easygoing nature, Grant had soon acquired some new
friends, found out about the local school, and offered to play
catcher for the community's baseball team.

In the meantime, Alex, with the help of Mr. De Galliers
and the elderly Mr. Chapman, arranged for the loan of a wagon
to transport his effects to the farm. The following day and
despite the rain, the two hitched the horses to the borrowed
wagon, tied Polly to the rear and set out to find the eight
hundred acre farm which neither the father nor son had ever
laid eyes on.

The journey took them over land where ragged poplar
bluffs silhouetted the somewhat stumpy hills. The depressions
were occupied by sloughs, not lakes. At midday they found the
first survey stake, and some minutes later, at the end of a
weed-infested and grown-up trail, the so-called homestead
appeared. "The land was not as described, the cultivated
acreage was not ready for crop, the buildings were quite
unsatisfactory," recorded MacEwan. There were no horses, no
fences, a dilapidated house, rundown outbuildings, and the
fields were far from ready to receive seed..

When Alex MacEwan traded his Brandon lots for the Margo farm, he thought that only the fickleness of Mother Nature could defeat his plan to be self-reliant. The possibility of deception never crossed his mind. He had gambled and lost, and no doubt the needs of his family weighed heavily on his shoulders at that moment.

Both the father and son were lost in their thoughts as they stared at the vestiges of the farm that was to have given them another chance. Alex sought a solution, Grant an explanation. Surely, if there was ever a time when a boy should come to judge the actions of his father, the time was now and Grant MacEwan had good reason. Wet and chilled to the bone by the rain, Alex MacEwan conceded to his son, "Well Grant, this is a failure."

New Beginnings

To Alex MacEwan, failures were merely inconveniences or obstacles to be overcome. He believed that good came from bad, and that there was an opportunity to be had in most of life's occurrences — one just had to look for it until one found it. Never a person to wallow in self-pity, it was this plucky pioneer spirit and ample dose of Highland self-reliance and resourcefulness which stood him firm in the face of this disaster.

As for young Grant MacEwan, he knew full well not to pester his father when he was deep in thought. Besides, the dilapidated image of the land his father had traded the Brandon lots for preoccupied his thoughts. If Grant was not aware of the seriousness of the situation before seeing the Margo farm, he now knew that little separated his family from the elements or starvation. It was a disconcerting thought for a boy who had never known need or experienced poverty. He was cold and wet and hungry.

By the time the two had covered the distance between the homestead and Margo, Alex had a plan. Some years before, he had speculated on a section of land in Melfort. He had bought it as an investment, never dreaming he would need it. Grant MacEwan recorded in his journal, "Our hopes were now directed toward a piece of land, one section, 23-44-12-2 in the Melfort district. This parcel of unimproved land was bought in 1906 for purely speculative purposes, but a kind providence prevented the resale." There was no house, no outbuildings and the land was still shrouded in tough prairie sod. It was, nevertheless, rich black soil that could produce bumper crops, barring, that is, the fury of Nature which frequently caused grief to many an over-optimistic farmer.

Grant and Alex MacEwan reloaded their effects onto the train and bade farewell to the townspeople who had so generously helped them. The only truly downcast faces belonged to Margo's beleaguered baseball team whose newfound catcher was departing on the next train.

Twenty-two years had passed since Alex MacEwan had joined the elite ranks of theses "sodbusters." He had established the north Brandon farm as a bachelor, with few needs and no dependents. It would be different this time, however, for he had a wife and two young boys. Somehow, Alex

SECTION II

"I think the real progress in my generation has come from the imaginative things in our lives."

*"Mine was a farming genera-
tion. The farming people weren't
highly educated, some weren't
educated at all, but that didn't
stifle their imaginations."*

would have to break sod and prepare the land for next year's
crop, and build or find a shelter for his family within four, and
at best, five months. The task at hand was enormous. Moreover,
there would be no cash crop for another year.

Melfort was larger than Margo. Situated in the Carrot
River Valley, it was surveyed in 1902, the same year Grant
MacEwan was born. The town had prospered with the building
of the railway, and it became a major supply point for
northwestern Saskatchewan. Like Manitoba, settlers had
flocked to the younger province, and there was little land left
to claim in the "Last Best West" by 1920.

For thirteen-year-old Grant MacEwan, the prospect of
working hand in hand with his father would prove, in future
years, to be truly a golden opportunity. It was also a period of
time and purpose which would have a profound effect upon the
adolescent. Over the next decade, Grant would come to fully
appreciate the pioneer spirit which founded the Canadian
Prairies. It was here that he developed a lasting respect for
their self-reliance and resourcefulness, no doubt triggered by
his father's response to his own failures and inadequacies.

Grant and Alex MacEwan arrived in Melfort,
Saskatchewan on Saturday April 24, 1915 after one week of
living in a boxcar on bread, cheese, Polly's milk, and
"twenty-five cents' worth of fancy biscuits." During that week,
when Grant discovered he could not sell Polly's extra milk, he
traded it for fresh baking. And only sheer wit and his own
efforts helped him to put out a fire that started in their boxcar
when two boys tossed a lighted match through the open door,
shortly after they arrived in Melfort.

Early the next morning, Grant and his father started
out to find their farm which was four miles south and west of
Melfort. Wrote MacEwan: "Dad and I went out (Dad on foot
and I on a bicycle) to see the farm. It didn't look very
promising to me. There was no fence, no house, no cultivation,
but an abundance of trees." For the next two nights, the two
camped at the Sparrow's barn at the east end of the town
where they had arranged to store some of their effects. On
April 27, Alex and Grant drove out to the farmstead with a load
of furniture and Polly, the old cow. Ironically, they used a bluff
just off the trail to make a temporary camp, the same location
they later chose as the site to erect the farm buildings.

While Grant and his father were in Saskatchewan, supposedly getting the Margo house and farm in order, Bertha and nine-year-old George were forced to role play that nothing was wrong, and all was well. It is interesting to note that throughout the entire ordeal of Alex's business failure and the family's displacement from Brandon, Bertha held the secret, never disclosing to her family the gravity of the family's predicament.

Alex, who adored his beautiful Bertha, truly wanted to spare her from as much privation as possible. He wired her from Margo and instructed her to stay put in Brandon for an additional few weeks. However, fearing the truth about their economic situation and the Margo fiasco would be exposed if she remained past her planned date of departure, she ignored her husband's instructions. Bertha and nine-year-old George arrived in Melfort on April 28. That night, the MacEwan family, who by and large held face as an important part of their ethic, slept in Isaac Poole's granary. There was no further need for pretence. Their life in Brandon was over, and all of their efforts were needed to make the Melfort homestead a success.

The requirement for shelter was an issue of urgency. MacEwan wrote: "Jas Durnin, a farmer to the south of us, agreed to let us use his old bedbug infested, log building which was in use as a granary. We used it for sleeping quarters, and by day lived in an enclosure made by crated furniture in the bluff." There was also no source of fresh water on the property.

The simplest of domestic chores became not only feats of accomplishment but each one, in itself, a small miracle. Perhaps, all that stood between Bertha's ability to function and a gradual slide toward madness was her belief in God. Grant was forever appreciative of his mother's stellar efforts, and in later years wrote kindly about those first days in Melfort. "I will never forget how acceptable was the first mess of boiled potatoes we cooked over an open camp fire beside the bluff."

Alex MacEwan had some fifty dollars on him when he arrived in Melfort, most of which went to the purchase a secondhand wagon. The shortage of cash posed a real problem. Alex, a pay-as-you-go person, placed a mortgage on the land for three thousand dollars. Those funds became the much needed start-up money.

Two weeks after their arrival in Melfort, Alex MacEwan purchased a one-room shack in town. It took all of one day and

"Pioneer humor didn't come from magazines or from radio programs. It wasn't hand-me-down humor. It came to these people when they were milking the cows or doing the plowing."

The 16-foot by 18-foot one-room shack which became the MacEwan's first Melfort home.
— MacEwan-Foran Collection

part of another for Alex and Grant to move the 16-foot by 18-foot wooden structure using two sets of wagon gear, one borrowed. For a family whose roof had been the stars and poplar trees the walls, the secondhand hut was the next thing to a castle. Within a short time, Bertha transformed the crude edifice into a home with the addition of curtains, doilies, tablecloths and the like, all vivid reminders of happier Brandon days.

The building of a stable followed, and less than a month from the day Alex strode and Grant biked onto the property, they found groundwater. MacEwan recorded in his journal, "A memorable evening. We struck a small vein of water with our seven-inch hand-boring auger. Depth thirty feet. Great encouragement. Gas bubbled in all evening and we were greatly excited." In later years, it was the notoriously poor quality of Saskatchewan water that convinced MacEwan to seek a life in Alberta.

The MacEwan homestead became a beehive of activity. With the exception of Sunday, Alex began every day at four-thirty in the morning, and Bertha, George and Grant, two hours later. Alex broke and seeded seven acres with oats, and saw that bags of potatoes were planted to ensure the family would have food during the upcoming winter and spring. Ever mindful of their precarious situation, every member of the MacEwan family worked hard to establish the new operation.

Rudolf Fillickener was hired to speed up the fencing operation. Grant MacEwan observed: "Rudolf was a character, possessed a temper that was not to be tampered with. For marathon swearing feats he has seldom been equalled." And while the neighboring Poole family themselves were helpful, one of their cows was not. According to Grant, ". . . Poole's long-legged fence-breaking red cow threaten[ed] to consume what little crop we have and also to disturb the harmony of the two families."

Alex MacEwan was very much aware that the speed with which the virgin land was broken was of the utmost importance to the well-being of his family. Therefore, he bargained with Jack Curtis of Mount Forest to break some fifty acres in the southeast quarter for three dollars per acre. Using the horses and hand plow would have cost him valuable time. MacEwan wrote in his journal: "Laughie MacPhaden (son-in-law of Curtis) came with the outfit, an old 25-horse, one-cylinder International Harvester tractor and a five-bottom breaking plow . . . The breaking was very rough and poorly done . . ."

The job of disking this area fell to Grant. That summer, a true appreciation for the role of the pioneer's horse was instilled in his impressionable mind. "I would like to suggest that if somebody wants to erect a memorial, there would be none more suitable than to that noble creature who has played such a great part in the development of the country. Would suggest that the 'Pioneer Horse' be depicted in a half-starved state, gaunt, ribs projecting, head low and back end partly submerged in bog." Fifty or so years later, he committed his admiration for these four-legged heroes to print in his book *Hoofprints and Hitchingposts*.

The year 1915 was a memorable one for Canadians, both in war and harvest. In April, Canadian troops experienced the horror of chlorine gas in Ypres. The Dominion casualties totalled 6,037 within a four-day period. Suicidal frontal attacks, the Allied strategy for the next three years, targetted Festubert and Givenchy.

The harvest of 1915 produced a record yield for most farmers in Western Canada. The MacEwan family, however, realized but a measly seven acres of oats to show for their herculean efforts. On September 20, 1915 MacEwan wrote: "Stacked 10 loads of oat hay from the seven-acre plot. . . We worked until after dark to complete the stack. I was a tired helper that night, but very proud of our first lowly harvest." Their disappointment, like most of those who till the land, was quickly replaced by optimism for a bumper crop — next year.

Alex and Grant forged a relationship of close interdependency during that first summer in Melfort. MacEwan's journal reveals a pride of accomplishment and a growing respect for his elder's way of getting things done. It would also seem that Alex MacEwan needed the physical help of his oldest son, to eke out a new livelihood from the Saskatchewan frontier, almost as much as he needed the boy's forgiveness for bringing this hardship upon the family.

One might speculate, though, whether all was smooth sailing between the two personalities. In 1994, when I prompted Grant MacEwan to elaborate about the relationship he had with his father, he offered the following comment: "I greatly admired my father for getting things done, and always

"In all the days I visited the old livery stable, and listened to the stories related by the people that created them while they were milking cows or plowing, I never heard a sexy story."

"Pioneer humor had a distinctiveness. It was based on farm operations."

doing a good job. But sometimes he took risks that were foolish and he brought terrible trouble to the family. That I didn't respect him for."

Bertha continued, as in Brandon, to ensure her boys were guided by the same religious principles which directed her. The three would walk over four miles to Melfort every Sunday to worship at St. James Presbyterian Church, and return home, thoroughly famished, in the mid-afternoon after Sunday school. Only in the worst of weather did the trio take a horse and buggy, for even beasts of burden were given the Sabbath off from work. Some years later during a radio interview, MacEwan commented: "It meant something to have a mother whose faith was as firm as Gibraltar and who thought sufficient of her God and church that she, with her two boys, would walk eight and one-half miles in addition to her regular housework."

Within three weeks of their arrival in Saskatchewan, George and Grant entered Spry school, the local one-room frame schoolhouse. Miss Olive Durnin, who presided over some thirty-five pupils in eight grades, dealt a disappointing blow to the elder MacEwan boy when she dropped him back to Grade 7, a grade he had skipped in Manitoba.

The walk to and from school allowed both boys to observe the native vegetation and wildlife. They carried their lunch, usually egg sandwiches, and occasionally jam made from the fresh berries which grew around the homestead. During the winter, Alex permitted them to use a small horse-drawn cutter to get to school. Concerned for their safety, he strapped a small log behind the cutter so as to spread out the snow, thus preventing the formation of ruts which would cause the sleigh to tip over.

Grant MacEwan, who by then was showing the physical signs of the large man he would become, wore to Spry school the size thirteen patent leather button-up boots he received from the pilot Alfred Blakely. Although the boots had belonged to a famous person, they weren't exactly the type of footwear most farmboys wore. He wrote in his journals: "I hardly knew whether to be proud or ashamed of them." It was, no doubt, a difficult time for the teen. There are but spotty entries in his journal which indicate how the family's financial reversal affected him. It is difficult to imagine that any adolescent, who experienced the deprivation which MacEwan did during his formative years, would not be permanently affected and perhaps, warped when it came to money matters.

Grant developed a strong sense of self and responsibility toward family during this time period. He debated issues of concern and offered alternative solutions. When his teacher asked each pupil to bring fifty cents to school to purchase materials for raffia work, he submitted ". . . that was a large sum for us boys. We talked it over at home and the next day when the matter was again under discussion in school, I took the bit in my teeth, arose in my seat and explained to teacher and all that the money would only be secured with difficulty in our home and perhaps others, and it would be more satisfactory for us if the time were devoted to something less costly. I suggested physical training or something equally novel."

If the harvest of 1915 was a bitter experience for the MacEwans, the winter promised to be an equally harsh ordeal. Their flimsy shelter afforded little protection from the frigid temperatures and biting winds which swept the barren prairie expanse. Fearing for their safety, Alex sent Bertha and the boys to the James Grant homestead in Brandon for the winter. He toughed it out in the primitive shelter, tending to the animals, planning for the future.

Grant, who had begun Grade 8 for a second time in the fall, kept abreast of his studies at the Turriff school in addition to helping out around his uncle's farm. On December 31, the lad's Melfort teacher, Miss Durnin, rewarded his sense of honesty and ambition by sending the Christmas exams to him. She was well aware of her star pupil's desire to possess his Grade Eight Certificate.

The year 1916 would be a memorable one for both the prairie women and Grant MacEwan. On January 27, Manitoba became the first jurisdiction in Canada to give women the right to vote in provincial elections, and also to hold office. Their Saskatchewan sisters followed in March, and Alberta in April. Perhaps it was this early exposure to the fight of women for equal rights which sensitized and made Grant MacEwan aware of their plight, or maybe it was simply his observation of his mother's important role in establishing the Melfort homestead. Nevertheless, he later became the first representative of the Monarchy to break with its rather sexist leanings. As Lieutenant-Governor of Alberta, he opened up the male bastion of the New Year's Levy to include the gentler sex.

"The farmers were dealing with cows and horses and pigs and sheep and things, and that meant that manure was manure, and constipation was constipation. It wasn't lurid or shameful. It was perfectly legitimate. A lot of the stories were tinged with manure. But that's better than what we have today.

The humor that was recited in the livery stable was heard by all the farm people. The farm women were there waiting to go home, the farm kids were there on Saturday."

Grant was introduced to the wonders of the internal combustion engine when he attended a course in Brandon in early March. He embraced the technology of mechanization just as ducks take to water, and today's children use computers. "I was sold to engines in general and to IHC engines in particular. I was amazed to discover that engines were not complete mysteries after all and that I could really grasp the fundamental principles without much trouble." The young, unabashedly devoted convert to the engine, however, found his Clydesdale-loving father somewhat slower to trade his confidence in horse- to engine-power. One could even speculate if Alex suffered from the same phobia which affects fifty-year-olds when they discover their favorite secretary is being replaced with a computer.

Recruitment officers pressed the mature-looking fourteen-year-old Grant MacEwan to enlist. The young pacifist, who refused to conform, appeared out of step with the wave of patriotism which swept the country. Throughout his life, MacEwan would continue to be true to his belief that all living creatures deserve respect, a value which often set him at odds with, and ultimately ahead of contemporary thought. Moreover, Grant's solitary and at times reclusive personality rejected regimentation. He had experienced cadet camp in Brandon, and commented in his journal, ". . . once was enough!"

Just as April returned, so did the MacEwan boys to Spry School. Grant, in addition to doing his farm chores, studied three and four hours a night to catch up the difference between the Manitoba and Saskatchewan curriculums. He wrote his exams in June and began the long wait for the results which came from Regina. It was a bitter blow when classmate Teet Arnold rode into the MacEwan yard and announced both Grant and he had failed. "The tears flowed freely," wrote MacEwan.

Teacher Durnin, who arrived just as the news was delivered, was so perplexed by her star pupil's so-called failure that she wheeled her horse and buggy around, and sped to town to check the marks for herself. With a quick look at the results, the teacher headed back out to the MacEwan homestead, burst into the shack where the family was gathered around the dinner table, commiserating about the failure, and shouted: "Mrs. MacEwan, where's Grant? He passed his departmentals with HONORS! The only one in the whole northern school division to get honors!" It had never occurred to Teet Arnold, a not so diligent student, to check the honors list.

"Dad and Miss Durnin were perhaps the most excited of the group, and I was the happiest," wrote MacEwan. But when a proud Alex said, "Grant, if you say so, we'll buy that purebred Clydesdale mare in town!" the young graduate declined. Although young in years, Grant MacEwan knew full well this purchase was beyond the present means of his family.

The rest of the summer was spent clearing land, cutting trees, digging roots and watching over the fifty acres which had been seeded with wheat. Anticipating a bumper crop, Alex bought an old binder for twenty-five dollars and set about to repair it. In September, Rod Reid arrived with his Case steam outfit to thresh the MacEwan's first crop. The anticipated bumper harvest, however, did not materialize. Rather, the area farmers reaped straw, the kernels having rusted away. Nature had cruelly intervened in the family's quest to escape destitution. With no money to pay for Grant's board while he attended high school in Melfort — the family's only funds would come from the sale of surplus eggs and milk — this was the end of his formal schooling. Furthermore, Alex needed him on the farm.

The winter, whose temperatures would dip below minus fifty degrees Fahrenheit, began on November 8, 1916 with a solid freeze. Food was scarce for humans and beasts, the cattle and horses existed on frozen oatsheaves and a little chop. Once again, Bertha and the boys retreated to the comforts and warmth of brother James's farmhouse in Brandon. Letters were their only link for the next four months.

While the warm spring rays of the sun signalled rebirth throughout the Canadian countryside, the war continued to rage in Europe, and the demand for food and natural resources continued, fuelling an almost crippling inflation. The young Dominion found out rather abruptly that it could no longer depend upon Britain for financial help, for the Queen of the Seas was pressed to the limit by war expenditures. In 1917, Canadians paid their first income tax which was said by the government of the day to be a temporary measure to raise money for the war effort. The forerunner of the Canada Wheat Board was also established. Its purpose was to handle and collectively market, on a global scale, the country's wheat crop. Canada was coming of age.

"Four letter words crowd out a lot of imagination."

Between Red and the Rockies

In the season all social intercourse ceased. Cows went dry because nobody had time to milk them. School attendance dropped to the point where the teacher was almost alone. Threshing season brought out the best and the worst in people, some loved it and some went insane.

Getting and holding a crew was not always an easy matter, especially late in the season when cold weather and snow added to the hardships. Frequently the teamsters were neighbors or homesteaders who left their land to make some extra money. Often they were the hard-hitting , hard-drinking men who worked in the lumber camps in the winter and came to the farming districts at harvest time. They received a dollar-and-a-half a day and all they could eat.

The acknowledged hero of the harvest season was the steam engineer. He had special qualifications, he held a certificate, and he commanded the biggest wages and the greatest respect. If he had a good outfit, he wasn't very busy. As he stood with folded arms on the great drive wheel of the tractor, and surveyed operations, he knew that he was the envy of everybody. When he placed his hand upon the throttle and the mighty wheels responded, young hero-worshippers resolved on the spot to become steam engineers. It took a good man to resist the virus of conceit.

For a normally susceptible engineer, probably the biggest thrill of all came when he pulled the cord of the steam whistle. The single long blast that meant quitting time was always welcome. There was one mule team that positively refused to move a load or tighten the traces after that quitting signal. Two long blasts brought a special message to the tank man, who was pumping at some distant slough or creek, that water was low. Three blasts reminded teamsters on the grain wagons to hasten along so there would be no delay for want of a place to deposit the grain, and a series of short toots warned the workers on the stook wagons to speed up or the machine would be left to idle. . . Another distinctive character was the old-time separator man. His dusty and dirty job was not glamorous. But he command-ed the second highest wage and upon his skill depended the success of the season. He was expected to have untold knowledge about bearings and concaves and pulleys,

A farmer's optimism for a bounteous crop is eternal, and the MacEwans were no exception. In 1917, with their crop all planted by May, Alex and Grant MacEwan began to break more land. The hard work was made more difficult by the emaciated condition of their horses. The poor beasts had wasted away to skin and bones due to the poor quality of their feed. "The crop in, we prepared to do more breaking. We had five horses in that season and my father and I worked together all summer. Feed was scarce so we made only seven or eight miles per half day with the teams (two drivers, one plow) and utilized all spare moments (while the horses were resting) cutting and grubbing along our lands." It was this experience which pointed Grant MacEwan to study, during his university years, the direct link between an animal's well-being and its ability to work.

The crop was ready for cutting by mid-August. Wrote MacEwan: "Dad drove the binder. We doubled up with Jack Robertson and cut our crop first. I did most of the stooking." Once again, Rod Reid threshed, but this time the land yielded some twenty bushels per acre. Grant hauled load after load to the Pleasant Valley elevator. He described this memory of the family's first bountiful harvest in his book, *Between the Red and the Rockies.*

Grant MacEwan spike pitching at Melfort farm.
— MacEwan-Foran Collection

The MacEwan farm produced 2,751 bushels of wheat, graded Number Two Northern, which Alex sold at an average price of two dollars per bushel. All in all, his cost to harvest — a mere $318.16 — was worth every penny when one considered the payback for the family's labors. With money jingling in his pocket for the first time in several years, Alex MacEwan vaccinated his eight head of cattle against blackleg, spent fifteen dollars trading an older horse for a younger one, and bought a new John Deere plow for one-hundred-and-thirty dollars.

The silence with which Bertha met these expenditures was deafening. In her mind, the living conditions of her family should have taken precedence over this spree of spending. While she was always welcome at her brother James's farm, wintering there was not an occurrence she wanted to make a habit. Furthermore, maintaining face was an important stance of the MacEwan and Grant ethic, and a husband who could not provide adequate housing for his family was seen, at least by Bertha, to be wanting as a provider. "My mother," said Grant MacEwan during an interview, "had a very effective way of getting her point across. Her silence could drown out any conversation."

Alex and Grant began excavation for the basement of their house on October 1, 1917. "The decision was made rather suddenly and the work commenced so soon after that little planning was done," wrote MacEwan. Since the season was late, the house was built on blocks. The concrete foundation would follow next year. Charlie Van Camp and his carpenters arrived on October 12, and by October 25, the structure, a two-story frame house, 30 by 30 feet, with a 12 by 16 foot kitchen addition and dormer windows, was sufficiently advanced for the family to move in. "It was foundationless, plasterless, and lacked the finished flooring, but it looked like a million dollars to us," wrote MacEwan.

On November 14, Bertha's mother died in Brandon and ten days later, the first freeze signalled the beginning of yet another prairie winter. Each member of the family became a willing participant in the finishing of the house during that winter. Little by little, the inside of the structure began to look more like a home.

In Brandon, Grant had delivered the local newspaper and sold surplus milk and vegetables in addition to other

and at lacing belts he was a master. Such knowledge came not from books but from years of experience. For fully half of his time he was squirting oil into holes which nobody but himself would have any hope of finding. . .

All in all, those big threshing crews represented a perfectly co-ordinated effort, and each of the fifteen or twenty-five members had his part to play on the team. More than that, it was a strictly co-operative undertaking in the community. The wagons, racks, and horse teams were assembled from farms about, chiefly from those which would be served by the outfit. And some of the dishes and pans used in the kitchen were requisitioned from willing neighbors. Thus the job of keeping the accounts was often difficult and complicated. If a man had a big crop and depended upon much outside assistance, all one side of the barn door might be needed to carry the figures and balance the account. It was an argument in support of bigger doors on barns.

One might marvel at the fortitude and stamina of the farm women who fed those big gangs of ravenous threshers. When threshers were coming, the kitchen table was extended by strange and ingenious means until it would seat fifteen to twenty-five men as the occasion demanded. There one learned to eat with elbows "in his pockets," and there one learned, by necessity which comes from competition, to eat in a hurry.

It wasn't much wonder that the thought of a breakdown or delay occasioned by wet weather terrified the farm women. Meals were provided as usual whether the weather was fit for threshing or not and it was common for the woman of the home to serve a total of 400- or 500-man meals before the fields were finally cleared of stocks.

— From Between Red and the Rockies by Grant MacEwan

"We had to make our own fun. People laughed. The funny thing is that even though there was hardship and no professional entertainment, people laughed more than they do today."

MacEwan farmhouse in Melfort — MacEwan-Foran Collection

undertakings to make money. Melfort, however, was an entirely different market. Also, the rural countryside had a different set of rules for reimbursement. Helping neighbors, for example, constituted a return favor, not a cash payment. He was forced to realign his money-making ventures away from the service sector and to primary production.

A year after they moved to Melfort, Grant proposed to his father that they should share the cost of buying a Holstein cow. The family would get the milk and Grant would get the calves. While the cow turned out to be a good milk producer, upwards of 150 pounds a day, her breeding capability, unfortunately for Grant, was dismal. Her first and only calf was stillborn. Fortunately, the boy recovered some of his investment when the animal was sold for slaughter.

For the first, and perchance the only time in his life, some investments cost rather than earned Grant money. When he bought a cow with calf at foot for $100, the calf turned out to be so wild and unruly that it could not be shown. Moreover, the next time the cow was ready to calf, she needed a veterinarian. By the time all was said and done, the calf died, the vet charged ten dollars for his services, and the cow dried up!

Grant was fond of his younger brother George and periodically included him in his money-making schemes. Business enterprises were encouraged by their father who saw it as way to teach self-reliance. On one occasion, the boys pooled their resources and bought a red cow in calf to Alex MacEwan's own Aberdeen Angus bull and owned by Ted Frank. When it came time to ready her splendid bull calf for the show ring, Grant sent his younger brother into Melfort to purchase three gallons of Cane Mola, a popular molasses additive for show animals, from the A.E. Code store.

George dutifully asked for three gallons of Coca-Cola by mistake and was sent along, amidst gales of laughter, to Graham's Confectionery. At the confectionery he got the instructions right, asked for three gallons of Cane Mola and was sent back to Code's feed store. Once again he muddled the instructions and ordered Coca-Cola. The ten-year-old, thoroughly discouraged and probably a bit disgusted with his older sibling for sending him on the wild goose chase, returned home without the Cane Mola.

The fighting of the First World War continued into 1918, as did the need for food production. Manpower remained the chief home and front dilemma. Finding enough men in Canada, a nation with a population of eight million people, to carry on the strenuous work of producing foodstuffs and arms was a major problem, particularly considering its heavy losses at the front.

The federal Department of Agriculture, and its minister, Hon. T.A. Crerar, responded to the need by urging farmers and their sons to stay on the land. They were counselled to do everything necessary to double and quadruple production. "We required more power to operate our holdings adequately," wrote Grant. "My father and I were somewhat interested in the advisability of purchasing a tractor . . ."

George and foal in Melfort barnyard.
— MacEwan-Foran Collection

Alex MacEwan and his team of horses, 1925. — MacEwan-Foran Collection

The MacEwan family settled in for the debate. Grant believed mechanization of farming would increase production and yield. Alex, while he agreed with his son, was still very much devoted to his Clydesdales, and Bertha was quite forthright. She preferred horses to a noisy, gasoline-burping machine which controlled the operator, and not the other way round. Nevertheless, a Fordson tractor arrived on May 14, 1918 at the MacEwan homestead. Its cost was $795 delivered.

Eager to increase production and redress the problem of lost manpower, the federal government eliminated the import tariff on tractors under $800 in price and encouraged a buying frenzy by making 1,000 Fordson tractors — "The Great Production Fleet" — available to farm shipping depots across the Prairies.

The Fordson became a way of life. The churning of endless furrows took on new meaning. All of a sudden the channels were deeper and straighter. The operator no longer had to assert his personality over that of a horse. Moreover, the iron-horse did not have to be fed, watered or rested; all it needed was gas. Clearly, Grant MacEwan was captivated with the vehicle's comportment and capacity. "The Fordson's first job was breaking 15 acres on the southwest quarter for late oats. I ran the tractor and Dad cut scrub ahead of the breaking."

That year the once meagre seven-acre plot grew to 150 acres of wheat and 30 acres of oats. The labor-intensive work of breaking virgin sod, picking roots and stones, and bringing new land into furrow and cultivation, was now greatly reduced. Wrote MacEwan: "The Fordson's next job was breaking on the northwest quarter. We began to break on the east side of the quarter and while the brush was not the big kind, it covered the east side of the quarter. Furthermore, that part of the farm had about 25 acres of stony ground and we found the combination of bush and stones was very bad. Dad cut scrub and I did the breaking and handled the stones. Every stone that was touched by the plow was taken out and we finally took over 100 loads of stone off. We broke 50 acres on the quarter that year and did all our disking with the tractor."

Grant MacEwan's desire to follow his Grandfather Grant's wish for him to become a "free farmer" set him apart from other young men. He was always on the lookout for ways to expand his knowledge base and thereby improve his farming practice. During the summer of 1918, he attended a three-day course in weed identification and livestock judging in Melfort presented by John Rayner from the Extension Department of the University of Saskatchewan. His top marks earned him yet another honor, a spot at the Farm Boys' Camp at the Regina Exhibition. "The Fordson was idle for one whole week and thankful I was to be away from it," wrote MacEwan.

MacEwan, quartered at Connaught School with the other boys, was drilled beyond all reason in military movements, an activity the young pacifist detested. It was, however, a small price to pay for the knowledge he gained and he proceeded to score the highest marks in the weed competitions and near the top in horse and cattle judging. The crowning glory of the week occurred when the teen was asked to parade Beau Perfection 47th around the arena after the animal won the Grand Championship ribbon for Hereford bulls. Curtis Martin, head of the Curtis Cattle Company which owned the bull, was impressed by the lanky MacEwan who had performed small chores around the barn, and whose eye had silently selected his beast as the best.

The week concluded by giving Grant an axiom for life. He attended at talk given by W.J. Rutherford, the Dean of Agriculture at the University of Saskatchewan. "It was assembled in those buildings that I first saw and heard Dean (W.J.) Rutherford of Saskatoon. He talked for a few minutes on a topic I have not forgotten. A lot of water has passed under the bridge and a lot of topics and addresses have been heard and forgotten, but Dean Rutherford's text lingers green within my memory. It has lost none of its value and loftiness in the years. Few texts could be found more suitable for a talk to a bunch of boys and indeed I have used it myself a few times. It was this: 'The boy increased in wisdom and in stature, and in favor with God and man.'"

How could Grant increase in favor with God and man, yet hold firm his conviction that man should continually strive to be self-reliant and resourceful? The dean's words had challenged him to think beyond the fences which surrounded the family homestead. MacEwan returned to the Melfort farm with much to think about.

Ironically, the prosperity which the MacEwan's should have realized from their wartime crops and that Nature so cruelly foiled, came at the end of the war. Their earnings from the 1918 crop alone were $6,000 and this did not include additional income from surplus eggs, poultry, livestock and hay.

Dean W.J. Rutherford.
— MacEwan-Foran Collection

"Television has stymied conver-
sation. It has changed home
entertainment. I don't think it's
a development of recent times
that should bring us great pride.

Even the phonograph no longer
has a place. The phonograph
was a great instrument. It gave
people a chance to bring good
music into the home."

However, if 1919 began with optimism, it ended in sorrow. Alex and Grant expanded their herd in March with three purebred Aberdeen Angus cows, and by mid-April they were preparing the land for planting. By May they had seeded 198 acres of wheat, 40 acres of oats and 12 acres of barley, their largest crop since arriving in Melfort. They had only to wait, and perhaps pray, for the right amount of sunshine and rain.

But Nature began her cruel hoax on July 10. A ten-minute hail storm, with stones the size of hen's eggs, completely destroyed the standing crop. The previous period of drought was replaced with weeks of wet weather. To some extent, the moisture benefitted the slower to sprout grain seed. The yield was guessed to be between eighteen and twenty bushels per acre. Again, Nature intervened and on August 20, MacEwan recorded: "The wheat well advanced but rust severe." Alex and Grant plowed under half of the headless straw.

They quickly turned their attention to the oats and barley which would provide feed for the livestock. But a steady rain prevented them from threshing the crop, and on October 8, the area was blanketed with four inches of snow. "I went out on horseback to find the cattle but the storm was so thick I failed to locate them and got quite lost. . . " recorded MacEwan. By the next morning, eight-inches of wet snow covered their crop. Grant and Alex threshed whatever they could using sleighs. They pried the potatoes out of the icy earth with a crowbar, a shovel, and the old pickax Grant had bought in Brandon. The land produced a paltry $1,000 that year, and even Polly, the faithful milk cow, fell to bad luck. She dried up and was sold for slaughter. Life's deeds were unbelievably cruel to the family that fall. They were still reeling from their crop losses when word was received that Grandfather John Walter Grant — Grant MacEwan's namesake and idol — had died at the James Grant home in Brandon.

News about the Spanish flu epidemic replaced war mongering. Returning Canadian soldiers introduced the deadly virus to their homeland during the spring and summer of 1918. Its first major civilian outbreak occurred in September at Quebec's Victoriaville College when 400 students became ill, and for the next eighteen months, neither young, old nor healthy adults escaped the plague. Even animals were said to have been felled. Indeed, this outbreak killed more people, more quickly than any war or other disease in the short history of mankind. Somewhere between 15 and 25 million deaths worldwide — including some 30,000 to 50,000 Canadians — were attributed to complications from the flu, pneumonia being the most common.

The virus hit the MacEwan homestead on January 1, 1920. "John, the one-eyed horse died from influenza," wrote Grant. "We skinned him. The vet vaccinated the rest of the horses." In early March, the family received news that Alex, who had gone to Brandon to attend the winter fair, was in the Brandon Hospital with flu. The elder MacEwan was still a sick man when he returned home a week later. Within days Bertha fell to the flu as well. Fortunately, the family had by then, their first telephone. On January 10, Grant MacEwan telephoned Dr. Hawke to have him attend his parents.

Bertha and Alex continued to ail. On March 31, Alex hovered in and out of consciousness, his medication for the excruciating headaches, depleted. Believing little separated his father, and perhaps his mother, from death, Grant saddled a horse and started out for Melfort to fetch more medicine. But even the animal knew better than to be out in the late spring storm that buffeted the area. He returned the horse to the barn and walked the four miles both ways without thought for his own safety. ". . . the brute would scarcely face the storm, so I did the only other thing, I walked in and back and waded all the way over unbroken roads."

Nature has a way of compensating those who suffer her wrath. In 1920, the MacEwan family once again enjoyed the fruits of their labors. By April, Alex and Grant shipped ten steers with an average weight of 1,500 pounds to Melfort for slaughter. Next they planted 160 acres of wheat, 50 acres of oats and 50 acres of barley. This was followed by Grant's first-place win by his herd of four at the Melfort Summer Fair. And, in the third week of July, Willa MacPherson arrived at the family homestead. Her presence would irrevocably alter Grant MacEwan's future. He was, after all, a good-looking man looking forward to his own life, and love.

Alex MacEwan's sister had married an executive in the National American Biscuit Company and subsequently moved to the United States where Willa was born. When both of the girl's parents died during her adolescence, she went to live at the MacEwan family home in Guelph, and proceeded to visit whatever relatives would have her.

"But worst of all, kids and their parents have forgotten how to read, or they forget to read. I think reading is deteriorating, and if so, that is serious."

Alex MacEwan with one of his Aberdeen Angus bulls, 1925.
— MacEwan-Foran Collection

According to Grant MacEwan, "Mamie Argall taught me everything a boy should know about a girl. Willa was different." Three years before the arrival of his cousin, Grant had escorted Mamie home after successfully bidding on her

Grant MacEwan with Willa MacPherson in Melfort, 1920.
— MacEwan-Foran Collection

box lunch at a local social. Although the two teenagers shared a memorable evening, the encounter did not develop into a relationship. Willa's arrival, however, brought the memories of that one night back into sharp focus for Grant.

Willa MacPherson was a catch for any young man. She was attractive and intelligent, and she thoroughly enjoyed life making her fun to be around. Grant was smitten with his American cousin, as were the other bachelors in the district. The antics of his peers were, nevertheless, more than just a slight irritation for the eighteen-year-old.

MacEwan was caught betwixt pangs of jealously and questions about his future. These feelings multiplied when a neighboring couple, Mr. and Mrs. Jim Drury, who were rushing to Melfort to beat the stork, were forced to take shelter in the MacEwan homestead from an early November snow storm. They named their baby, born at the crack of dawn, John Grant MacEwan Drury. Six days later, Willa left for Ontario.

Christmas came and went. The wonderful sounds from Alex's present to the family, an Edison Victrola, filled the farmhouse. Wrote MacEwan: "It was a wonderful machine and was in operation constantly for days after its arrival." If music inspires the soul, and the soul is satisfied by work, Grant fulfilled both requirements during that winter. Much of it was spent chopping and hauling wood, or attending fairs. The death of poor old Bill, the horse with chronic indigestion, which had been a pivotal agent in the taming of the land seemed to signal the end of a phase of the family's fortunes.

Grant mulled over his plan to go out on his own throughout the winter and spring, and only after the planting was completed did he share his goal with Alex. He asked his father to give him a quarter section of land to which he would add a Hudson Bay quarter. Grant had enough money in the bank to begin with, and the proceeds of future crops, he reasoned, would pay off his debt for the land. Moreover, George was now fifteen years old and ready to take his place. The plan was simple, the need urgent. Alex's answer, nonetheless, was an abrupt no. "It was all without avail," stated MacEwan.

Highland pride prevented Grant MacEwan from questioning his father's decision or pining over what might have been. The summer was used to break more land, attend fairs and enjoy the prosperity this year's bumper crop would bring to the family. At the end of July, Alex traded in the old Fordson on a new one, and he also bought the family's first car. "The new Ford sells for $815.00 and the new Fordson $822.00," wrote Grant MacEwan. The old adage of "10 miles was a trip and 20 miles a day's journey" no longer held true. On August 4, 1921, Grant MacEwan drove his mother, George, and a friend of the family thirty miles north of Star City to pick blueberries, and returned the same day.

Within one short season, the world took on new proportions, and soon, Grant's quest for a future would take on new heights. He was leaving the farm — at least temporarily — to attend the Ontario Agriculture College. Interestingly, both the institution and Willa MacPherson were situated in Guelph. He had accepted Dean Rutherford's challenge to increase in wisdom. Grant MacEwan, like visionaries such as Horace Mann, would come to see schools as the means to produce economic change without disruption and chaos.

"I hope we will preserve the best of the past. That it will not exclude the computer, the telephone, or the radio — but it will put them in their places."

SECTION III

Grant MacEwan, B.S.Ag.
— McEwan Foran Collection

The University Years

Canada's pivotal role as a key partner in the Allied forces in World War I stripped the young Dominion of its previous innocence and launched it rather abruptly onto the world stage, a source of unease for many, a new challenge for others. The second decade of the new century buffered the horrors of global hostility and an economic depression which numbed body and soul. Inflation accompanied the postwar boom. Earnings of salaried workers such as bankers or teachers lagged in comparison to a steady rise in the hourly earnings of laborers. Insufficient agricultural and industrial products — the conflict had exhausted the country's cache — fuelled consumer demand and drove prices to an unprecedented high. A phantom prosperity enveloped the country.

The population of urban and rural Canada were, for a short time period, balanced: 50.48 percent of Canadians lived in the countryside and 49.5 percent were part of the developing urban sprawl. The lull in immigration caused by World War I ended, and once again trains carrying immigrants, hopeful for a new life, rumbled into train depots across the Prairies. Newcomers, though, were required to pass an English literacy test, a measure imposed to favor British immigrants. A wave of xenophobia swept the country. Fear and dislike for enemy aliens became fashionable.

Realism began to replace the romanticism that had whitewashed for so long the harsh truth about Canada's landscape and the life its pioneers suffered. A liberal approach replaced religious fundamentalism in Canadian churches. Naive missionaries, who knew little about the privation other countries suffered before their vets returned, travelled in search of the poor and uneducated, inspired by snippets of information about Albert Schweitzer and his humanitarian work. At home, an army of social fairies, intent on establishing a just society, began to assemble; and the Temperance Movement, propelled by women testing their newly enshrined right to vote, coerced politicians into banning booze visibly — if not in reality.

The dissolution on August 31, 1920 of the Wheat Board, which for three years had marketed the Prairie's golden grain to Britain and stabilized the price fetched by farmers, prompted agrarians to postulate that only an occupational party, one that was nonpartisan and nonpolitical, could understand or even begin to address their concerns. These seeds of discontent gave rise to the farm movement, its strength and credibility underpinned by such organizations as the Grain Growers and United Farmers. Members of the movement were no longer prepared to accept the status quo between their needs, and the aspirations and actions of established federal and provincial political parties, by and large made up of fat-cat type lawyers.

The twenties marked a time when grain-rust research crowned the previous developments of Marquis wheat by William Saunders and fertilizer by Frank Shutt. It was also when the discovery of insulin by Banting promised hope for diabetics, and the raw power of the atom was first observed by Ernest Rutherford. Canadian academics, the trials and tribulations of their research once scorned by less learned countrymen, basked in the success of their discoveries.

John Walter Grant MacEwan caught and rode this growing swell of economic and social change. His decision to leave the family farm in Melfort, Saskatchewan and to pursue a formal education in its science at the Ontario Agriculture College (OAC) in Guelph was presumably a knee-jerk reaction to his father's refusal to help him begin his own farm. It was this veto, however, that was solely responsible for the first career wave that MacEwan caught, rode and tamed.

Grant reasoned that OAC was perfect for him. Although both the University of Saskatchewan and Manitoba offered a two-year associate program which resulted in a diploma, only OAC offered an intermediate year and an opportunity for its top students to acquire a Bachelor of Science degree without formal attendance at a high school. During their intermediate year, students crammed four years of high school into six months and, with credit for some of the classes they took during their first two years, proceeded to the last stage of the program which resulted in a Bachelor of Science degree. It was an option tailor-made for boys like Grant who, through no fault of their own, missed going to high school. Dean Rutherford, who had so inspired MacEwan with his words, received his degree in this manner.

Grant MacEwan informed his parents of his decision on September 12, 1921. Three days later he departed for the East with twenty dollars in his pocket, the remainder of his

The Ontario Agriculture College (OAC) campus in 1921. — MacEwan-Foran Collection

"I hope I'm not through writing. I'm not sure — but if I am going to do anymore writing, I'll do it the old-fashioned way."

savings left in the Melfort branch of the Bank of Commerce. True to his frugal upbringing, he scoured the district for a method of cheap, if not free, transportation. When he learned a neighboring farmer, Malcolm McPhail, was shipping a carload of cattle to Toronto, Grant offered to be his herdsman, a rail requirement of the time. He carried his belongings — an extra shirt, pair of socks, and cheque for one hundred dollars from his father — in a telescopic valise. MacEwan recorded in his journal: "It was my first real break from the family ties and the departure was hard." He was nineteen years old.

A week later, Grant arrived in Toronto where he bought, at Eaton's, an ill-fitting suit and a hat that was a decade out of date. His six-foot-four-inch, long-limbed and lanky torso presented a constant challenge to clothiers. Moreover, the Westerner's fondness for bargains often contributed to his rather odd appearance. He visited his Grandfather MacEwan and renewed his acquaintance with Willa MacPherson within hours of arriving in Guelph, but any possibility of a social life was short-lived. The following day, September 22, 1921, he registered at OAC, paid sixty-three dollars for his first-term fees, and moved into 32 Upper Hunt where he shared a room with Wilf Weber who was pursuing a Bachelor of Science degree.

Although Grant MacEwan's farm background had prepared him for most of life's occurrences, he was more than slightly taken aback at the fervor of the freshman initiation. New entrants were required to parade up and down the streets of Guelph clad only in pyjamas, an attire unknown to the skin-sleeping MacEwan. He borrowed a nightshirt from his much shorter roommate and he recorded the following: "His nightgown on my long body resulted in more exposure than the streets of Guelph had seen to that date, but I got away with it."

The first year at OAC ignited in Grant MacEwan a passion for living life to its fullest and lifelong learning. Entries in his journals detail his attendance at lectures, movies shared with new friends, often female, and general merriment. The geographic and social restrictions that living in Melfort may have imposed were gone.

College provided MacEwan with an opportunity to serve on the executive of the campus YMCA, a movement to which his loyalty began on May 21, 1918 with a donation of ten dollars. Throughout his life, the frugal MacEwan preferred a clean but sparse room at the "Y" to accommodation in a luxury hotel — often to his host's chagrin. When Grant MacEwan Community College held a tribute dinner for their namesake in 1989, they thoughtfully reserved a room for him in Edmonton's Westin Hotel. College officials were, however, a might perplexed when the former Lieutenant-Governor observed: "Thunderation, the bed is big enough for an entire family." Only those who truly understood the persona of the man realized that he needed no ornate trappings to legitimize his success or position. His standard reply to those who criticized his choice of the YMCA was: "The sheets are clean and the roof doesn't leak."

Bertha and Grant MacEwan contributed one hundred dollars toward the cost of each term of the two-year associate program, and Grant, by living frugally, was able to take part in important activities such as inspecting cattle and attending local fairs. If he suffered any hardship, it was only in the quantity of clothing he owned. Shortly after his arrival at OAC, he scribbled in his journal: "Two pair of socks are hardly enough for a man."

While the college's professors were given the respect they were due, they were also part of the student fun. Wrote MacEwan: "The members of our year paid respect to St. Patrick by donning green ties. The annual freshman-sophomore fight began at 9:30 and lasted for one hour. It began at the entrance to Dr. Hugo Reed's classroom and Doc too had a hand in the melee."

Grant left OAC on the last day of spring term and returned to Melfort via train to Brandon and the James Grant homestead. The sun was just beginning to peak up from behind the distant eastern horizon when he walked into the Melfort yard in time for breakfast with his parents. One can only speculate who of the MacEwans was the happiest that morning.

MacEwan was back in the seat of the old Fordson performing the spring planting ritual within days of his arrival. He also planted seeds of various kinds that he brought from the East; college may have recessed for the summer but not his burning desire to learn. Grant performed his first public judging at the Tisdale Fair on August 14, 1922 and his father was none too pleased that judging was given priority over the task at hand, namely, harvesting. Alex may have even secretly hoped that Grant would quit the associate program

and stay in Melfort. It was, no doubt, extremely difficult for
the earthy, sod-busting Scot to accept his son's desire for a
college education over the school of hard knocks he attended
at the same age.

Grant MacEwan left Melfort on September 23, 1922 for
his second year at the Guelph college. He played herdsman
again for Malcolm McPhail, accompanying the latter's carload
of cattle to Toronto. He also met many individuals on this trip,
but one acquaintance provoked this entry in his journal.

". . . He carried no baggage other than what is in his pocket
and that is mainly a toothbrush and a gun. He is well-dressed
and told me that his clean clothes, when a change is needed,
come from somebody's clothesline on a Monday night."
MacEwan registered at OAC on September 30 and took room
and board at 126 Maidens Lane with Doc Paine from Orillia.

*Grant MacEwan, flanked by supporters, holds "house to rent" sign in front
of doors to Macdonald Hall, the women's residence at OAC.* — MacEwan-
Foran Collection

MacEwan was not an innocent bystander when there
were pranks to be played or mischief at hand. At the beginning
of his second year, he and Bill Reaves, both hungry for Ontario
apples, almost made good their craving one night after curfew.
They crept out of their second-floor rooms and picked from
nearby trees whatever could be carried in Reaves' pyjama
bottoms, the legs tied shut, and Grant's pillow case. The
mission's success was marred, however, when the pillow case
seam split, its contents spilling noisily down the stairs of the

slumbering house. On a subsequent trip for the forbidden fruit, both returned with a good supply but, " . . . a bunch of cannibals got wind of our expedition and came around and ate most of them."

By the time MacEwan entered college, he was using an improv-style humor in many of his journal entries. His sophisticated form of witticism was highly suggestive yet devoid of vulgarity, and self-described as "pioneer humor." After visiting Grandfather MacEwan's house for supper one evening, he wrote: ". . . reported the man from the prairies who wrote to Eaton's for prices on toilet paper. Eaton's replied advising him to look them up in his catalogue. The farmer wrote back that if he had a catalogue he wouldn't be needing any toilet paper." On another occasion he captured, in two sentences, a raunchy situation without one reference to sex. "Barber phoned to say that Granddad will either have to pull down the blind or his shirt when he goes to bed. He cannot get his wife to go to bed."

Grant MacEwan renewed his interest in sports, both as a participant and viewer, during his college years. Track and field, basketball, hockey and football caught his fancy, tested his metal, and conditioned his long, lean body into fine athletic form. During his first year at OAC, he played centre for the second-string basketball team. He recorded the coach's rules for players in his journal as if they would be commandments. "No smoke, no bulky foods like cabbage, only one glass of liquid at a meal, no pork, no gravy or greasy food, light meal at noon, eat slowly, no chocolate in any form, no pie or other pastry, no tea or coffee, and eight hours sleep a night."

Although most of the rules were already part of his modest lifestyle, it must have been a killer for him to give up pie. He had an insatiable desire for sweets, in particular, pecan pie with ice cream. As Lieutenant-Governor of Alberta, no conversation, however important, was allowed to begin unless the visitor or employee dug into the cookie jar that sat on the corner of the regal desk. Only when the Queen's Representative and his guest had finished munching did the business of State rate a discussion.

MacEwan attended his first Royal Winter Fair in Toronto in 1922. He was spellbound by the huge number of entries, sometimes as many as 10,000 animals to a classification. He had no way of knowing then that his career

"I sit in an easy chair when I write.
I rough out what I want to say, then I may rewrite it, long hand.
I may type it with two fingers.
I've done it that way all my life.
I like it.
I think when I'm taking time to write and type.
I think it's a process that's got to be preserved."

as a highly-respected agricultural man and livestock judge would be launched at this exhibition, or that he would someday be a valued member of their board of directors.

Notwithstanding that the term "associate" program somehow suggested its students got off with less work than their degree-focused counterparts, such was not the case. MacEwan's course load would overwhelm present-day university students. Notes were taken and exams written for horticulture, political economy, field husbandry, entomology, animal nutrition, drainage, dairying, Canadian literature, composition, agricultural economics, botany, farm engineering, animal husbandry and veterinary medicine and surgery. By the end of the first term in his second year he had an average mark of 67 percent and ranked fifth in a class of thirty-four. He was determined to qualify for the chance to transfer to a degree program, and he concentrated on that self-imposed goal.

Grant MacEwan may have lacked opportunities for boy-girl relationships during his Melfort days, but things were different in college. His male self-image was buoyed by the attention he received from the fairer sex. His journal entries suggest that he had a life beyond academics: "Took Isabell McConnell to a show. Rotten show but good girl." Some days later, however, Grant found himself in hot water when he

Grant MacEwan, back row, third from left. — MacEwan-Foran Collection

1924 FROLIC. O.A.C Memorial Hall. Dec 9th 1924

called Mrs. McConnell "a little brat" over the phone, having mistaken her voice for that of her daughter, Isabell. One can only speculate on the meaning of another entry: "The girl turned me down flatly tonight."

Following this rather rude rejection, encountered in early 1923, Grant MacEwan shaved off his moustache, "with regret." The removal of his cookie-duster, carefully cultivated to make him look more sophisticated, was symbolic of the personal struggle he was engaged in to define his identity and decide his future.

With the end of the two-year associate program in sight, he applied to the Civil Service Commission to become a livestock promoter in Alberta's Peace River country. It was his first stab, though unsuccessful, at a job and full independence beyond the confines of the family homestead. Indeed, one might even speculate whether this rejection, coupled with the conclusion of the program, was the impetus MacEwan needed to make a choice. He rationalized that his brother George, who by then was sixteen-years-old and finished with school, could fill the gap his absence created. Grant wrote his parents and told them that he had decided to pursue his Bachelor of Science degree, and that he would not be home that spring. Rather, he was going to remain in the East to earn his next year's tuition.

In addition to removing his moustache, which changed his outward appearance, Grant MacEwan also altered his identity when he changed the spelling of his surname. When his Grandfather George MacEwan arrived in the young Dominion of Canada from Scotland in 1857, he spelled his surname McEwan. However, in the spring of 1923, Grant departed from the traditional spelling and began to write it as, MacEwan. Possibly this deviation was no more than his quest for identity. Or perchance, was it a strident action by the proud descendant of Scottish lineage to differentiate his family's country of origin from poor Irish Catholics, whose names characteristically began with "Mc" and, likewise, were nicknamed Micks?

Nevertheless, an entry in his journal in early 1925, which he copied from a newspaper, may indicate his feelings for not only the growth on his upper lip, but perhaps the evolving role of the female. "Bishop Collins Benny advises every man to wear a moustache as the last distinctive badge of

"Like charity, or honesty — thrift was a virtue. Waste and extravagance were sins."

"I think reverting to a simpler way of life would have its advantages, not only to save our soil, our resources, and our environment, but for moral purposes. It just might be worth thinking about..."

masculinity that the women have left him. 'Wear one,' he says. 'That's all the women have left us. They cut their hair and wear men's clothes but they can't wear a moustache.'"

Having decided to pursue his degree, Grant MacEwan together with Ian McKay and Len Caveno, all classmates at OAC, organized a program of summer work. In the spring of 1923, the trio decided that MacEwan and Caveno would help McKay put in the crop on his family's farm, and in return the group could plant early maturing spuds on some of the land. It was also an opportunity for the three to test the advanced growing methodology they had learned during their last term.

With the potato seed selected and advanced by exposure to the sun's spring rays, treated with "formalin solution" and planted, the trio took to the road selling nursery stock for Howard Downham of Strathroy while their potatoes developed in size and dollar value. They criss-crossed southwestern Ontario in a 1918 Model A Ford that Grant MacEwan purchased for $175, selling trees and shrubs like Fuller Brush men. Grant soon discovered he had a natural talent for sales. Each week he rang up totals exceeding $150 and often more than $200 during a time in history when a loaf of bakery bread sold for five cents. At the end of June, the spud-growers received a minor setback. A journal entry reads: "Mr. Niel, who has been working on our potatoes at Woodville, is dead from sun stroke." The crop volume, although not as large as hoped for, resulted in a reasonable profit. Shrub sales, however, netted MacEwan enough to finance his intermediate year of studies and then some. He also managed to sell the old Model A — which had considerably more mileage than when he bought it — to his employer for $150. Grant's partners, though, lacked his chutzpah to close a sale, and thus barely met their expenses.

With more than a month of summer vacation left before university resumed, Grant took up an offer from a college acquaintance, Tubby Tolton, and his parents, to motor from Guelph to Winnipeg in their Columbian Six. The trip, which took the group through the northern United States, gave him an opportunity to study the Americans, swim in the Mississippi River and tour the famous Chicago stockyards. He arrived home on August 9, 1923 — just in time to help with the harvest.

Grant MacEwan registered for his intermediate year on September 27, 1923 and moved into 300 Mills Hall to find his worst fear realized. He scribbled in his diary, "I am going to room with J.J. Brickley from Marysville. He is a fat Irish R.C." Rattled but not fazed, the Presbyterian Scot was determined to find good in his nemesis. No doubt the following newspaper clipping, sent to him by his mother, affirmed his approach and reinforced the value of self-reliance and reliability — principles which guided him throughout life.

"Learn to be a man of your word. One of the most disheartening of all things is to be associated in an understanding with a person whose promise is not to be depended upon; and there are plenty of them in this wide world — people whose promise is as slender a tie as a spider's web.

"Let your given word be as a hempen cord, a chain of wrought steel that will bear the heaviest sort of strain. It will go far to make a man out of you; and a real man is the noblest work of God; not a lump of moist putty, molded and shaped by the last influence met with that was calculated to make an impression, but a man of forceful, energized, self-reliant and reliable character, a positive quantity that can be calculated upon."

Regular church attendance was a habit that was deeply embedded in MacEwan's character. Bertha MacEwan instilled in both Grant and George a lasting respect for their God and she taught them that a chat with Him could resolve most problems. His college years presented MacEwan with opportunities to experience varied styles of worship, often more gospel than fundamental in nature. However, he seldom missed a Sunday service, and he frequently attended lectures by missionaries who had tended to the suffering of lepers and the like. He also discussed, with his colleagues, his thoughts about his God, sometimes with dire results. During his second year of rooming with J.J. Brickley, once his nemesis and now his friend, the two became embroiled in an argument about the validity of a higher being. Wrote MacEwan: "My mate and I had a violent argument. He tells me he is an atheist. I tried to tell him that he has the same religion, the same social attitude therefore as the animals."

The tempo of MacEwan's involvement in campus activities increased that year to include Varsity football and Gladys Eaton, a domestic science student from Campbellford, Ontario. The two became a steady number at dances and games over the next two years, and Grant was often a visitor in

"I don't think that Christianity is the only religion in the world. I think there's good in all religions. I'd like to think we can develop a breadth of understanding and tolerance which would be greater than any we've known so far."

her parent's home. On March 21, 1924 he wrote: "I skipped classes this afternoon, had supper with Glad and saw her off home for Easter holidays." The relationship, however, was doomed to failure. Gladys, who was one year ahead of Grant, left Guelph to head up the home service department of Toronto's Consumers' Gas Company. In the intervening year, she abandoned her conservative look and behavior to join the rank and file of other young Canadian women in the workforce.

The Roaring Twenties was when young and middle-age ladies discarded their petticoats in favor of short, straight, untrimmed dresses. They exposed their arms, wore their flesh-colored stockings rolled down to the knee, and carried a handbag containing cigarettes, car keys, face powder and money. Their freshly-scrubbed faces sported plucked and pencilled eyebrows, painted lips and rouged cheeks, and the entire effect was precariously balanced on a pair of high heels. A cloche hat pulled down over their shingled or bobbed hair added to the rather dramatic look. "After she went to Toronto, she began to smoke," commented MacEwan years later. "She changed and we drifted apart."

Grant played jump centre on OAC's league championship winning first-string basketball team that year. He was a valued player and he found the games to be a source of fun and pride. An outbreak of mumps on campus forced the postponement of exams until the first week of January, and although worried, Grant did well.

OAC's 1925 first-string backetball team. Grant MacEwan (sitting, first left) is clean-shaven. — MacEwan-Foran Collection

The Melfort farm was now a successful and growing operation. Alex MacEwan's purebred Angus cattle fetched a premium price for breeding purposes, and business was so brisk that he had found it necessary to hire two farmhands. And George, the younger of the two sons, had enrolled in Agriculture at the University of Saskatchewan. Even Bertha's life as a farmwife was much improved. The hardship of recent years was but a memory now.

Providence, however, tested the family once more. On March 26, 1924, Grant MacEwan received a telegram from home: "George seriously sick, Dad." The next day, his father wired: "George died last night."

He left Guelph within four hours of the news. Grant's physics professor, W.C. Blackwood, who had grown quite fond of his student, promised him that he would take care of everything at the university. Friends packed up his belongings. Five days later, he helped to bury his seventeen-year-old brother. George MacEwan had died of spinal meningitis. "Mother and Dad are completely broken, their very life seems snatched from them." wrote MacEwan. When, many years later, Grant MacEwan's wife died of the very same illness, her sudden and tragic death triggered the release of his grief for George which he had set aside in order to care for his parents. He grieved not only for his spouse of almost six decades, but for the brother he had hoped to grow old with.

Grant's first concern after the funeral was to give his parents time to grieve and then to earn money for his last year at OAC. He took work with the nearby Rural Municipality of Star City as a weed inspector and was paid five dollars a day. True to his frugal upbringing, he spent little of his earnings. Thus, he was delighted to find a pair of discarded shoes on a right-of-way he was inspecting that were in far better shape than his own. "Providence seemed to smile upon me . . . ," he recorded. His earnings plus $150 prize money from showing cattle at the Melfort Fair was sufficient to finance his next year of studies. Professor Blackwood made good his promise. The university awarded him full standing for his intermediate year despite the fact that he never wrote the final exams.

Term fees for OAC were $73.75 — a full ten dollar increase over the amount Grant MacEwan paid for his first associate year. "That was a tough blow," he wrote on September 19, 1924. Inflation forced the already thrifty

George Alexander Grant MacEwan (April 16, 1906 - March 27, 1924) — MacEwan-Foran Collection

Sailing West

To a home that calls for me
To a home which yesterday numbered
four, and today but three. Yesterday morn
brought word of a brother's illness,
The message said "serious,"
A word which seldom enters the mind
of a boy at school,
But ere the second bell of that same day,
A wire said "Geordie has passed away."

A fair haired boy of seventeen,
And as pure as he was young,
Known for a smile that spelled innocence,
A beautiful song unsung.

Two thousand miles now lie between
My brother's body and me,
But if God is willing I'll view the boy
Before they have laid him down.

Then God speed the train
And deliver me safe and wound
To the home that stands unique,
The two boys' old playground.

I want to look once more upon the lad
Tho that is but half my hurry,
The other half is Mother and Dad To be
with them in their worry.

— J.W. Grant MacEwan,
March 29, 1924

"If there is a God in Heaven, and I choose to believe there is, then I think he's a God of Love and there's only one kind of love that would be acceptable to him, and that's universal love.

That means love for all living creatures.

I think that if we are going to have peace on earth, we're not going to achieve it by being kindly to our fellow humans and turning ugly to the animals. Or by silencing the guns of war and writing more peace treaties."

Brickley and MacEwan, who were rooming together again, to really scrimp. Hence, when they discovered two suits of the same size and color in a tailor's shop, they haggled with the owner until he agreed to sell them both suits for the price of one. "Mine fits!" wrote the long and lanky Westerner. One can only imagine how his short, fat counterpart looked in the half price garment.

It is difficult to determine whether the need or the love to make money drove MacEwan's enterprises. In one venture, he bought a supply of cushion covers with the Ontario Agriculture College crest, added a markup of seventy-five cents and hustled them to Christmas buyers. Shortly after, he and Harry Miller won the contract for the refreshment booth at the skating rink. Both undertakings turned a tidy profit.

Grant MacEwan returned to OAC in September 1925 after spending much of his summer investigating sow thistle in the Carrot River area. Once again, his pay of five dollars per day plus another $136 that he earned showing MacEwan cattle at the Melfort Fair was sufficient to finance his last year at college. Much of his energy during that fall was directed at winning a place on OAC's five-member livestock judging team which represented the college at the Toronto Royal Winter Fair and the Chicago International Exposition. It was considered not only a position of prestige, but a springboard to secure employment or invitations to judge at agricultural fairs, a highly lucrative profession.

He wrote: " . . . Throughout my college career my hopes have focused on the Chicago judging team more than anything else. . . . Today our senior class, every member of which is keen to make a place on the team, left Guelph in five autos to broaden our knowledge of types and to score among the top five if possible."

The coaches for the tour, Wade Tool assisted by Jack Steckley, Bill Knox and George Raithby, put the class through their paces. By day, students performed herd inspection and livestock judging, and at night they defended their judgements with "oral reasons" in their hotel lobby or room. In the first week, the group visited twenty farms and institutions renowned for their horses, cattle, sheep, and swine. One day, they judged at five places, and at one there were seven classes. Right after Jim Simpson, Herb Knox, George Cruickshank, Herb Hannam, Archie McGugan, Arnold Kennedy and Grant

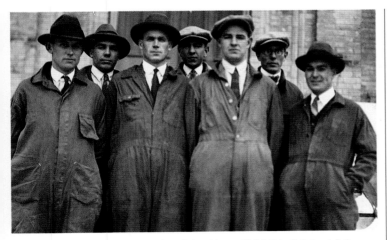

The OAC International Livestock Judging Team 1925-26: (left to right) George Cruickshank, Herb Hannam (alternate), Herb Know, Archie McGugan, Grant MacEwan, Arnold Kennedy (alternate), Jim Simpson. — MacEwan-Foran Collection

"I think we're going to have to develop a form of love where we don't talk about it on Christmas and then go out and shoot your fellow animals the next day."

MacEwan were selected, they set out on a second tour through western Ontario to determine alternates and regulars. MacEwan was named as a regular on November 11, 1925.

The OAC team won the prestigious Canadian Intercollegiate championship at Toronto's Royal Winter Fair, and Grant MacEwan had the highest aggregate score among the contestants. The agricultural section of Canadian and American newspapers carried some form of news about OAC's third-place win at the Chicago International Exposition. The *Melfort Mirror* edited a letter from Grant to his parents and published the following account on December 10, 1925: "We have been away nearly two weeks now, and it will be two weeks before we get back. We have had quite a trip. The competition capped the climax on Saturday. We got third place in the competition. Twenty-two teams from the American colleges and universities competed. Oklahoma got first and Illinois second. We had the high man in the competition — one McGuigan; Knox was fourth and MacEwan sixth. Our other two boys were about 23rd and 24th. We were all well pleased to get third in this competition and have three men in the first six. We get no money, but just the honor. It was a hard day and lasted from 7 am till 7 pm, almost continual; there being 100 in the competition including two girls, one of which was the high student in the competition at Kansas City Royal. We are certainly glad it is all over. We can think of something else now."

The Ontario team scored 4,416 out of a possible score of 5,000 — just 43 points behind the winning team, and the highest score ever made by a Canadian team. OAC produced the high man of the competition, with a score of 924 out of a possible 1,000 — again the highest score ever made in Chicago. MacEwan's score of 903 gave him his respectable sixth place position.

The article also contained MacEwan's earliest thoughts about the country and people that were soon to become a large part of his life. "The United States is a wonderful country, and I like the people as I never did before. For kindness and courtesy the Yanks have it all over Canadians."

This experience distinguished Grant MacEwan as an agriculture guru. When he graduated on May 28, 1926 with his Bachelor of Science degree, he did so with a firm job offer for the summer, and the promise of a job as a district representative. Bertha and Alex presented their son with a gold Waltham watch, and probably wondered if their son would actually settle down now and become a "free farmer" given that he had a degree and notoriety. And even the new graduate pondered

OAC class of 1925. Grant MacEwan, lower row, right of center.
— MacEwan-Foran Collection

his future. "I left dear old Guelph for Saskatchewan," wrote MacEwan. "I wonder if I'm right. Here in Ontario there is a job at Gunns Limited buying cattle, and later in the year there is district rep work for me, and out West there is just home. I plan to return in the fall and accept the rep work promised me."

MacEwan returned home for the summer and joined the Saskatchewan Cattle Improvement Train, a three-week livestock improvement tour which gave advice to farmers. One of the other lecturers on the train was very enthusiastic about the value of ultraviolet light, and each day he found a secluded spot where "he could expose his carcass to the sun," wrote MacEwan. One Sunday afternoon, though, Professor Jackson's hiding place was exposed by two girls and "he lost no time in gaining the shelter of the bush." The professor found an old apple barrel, slipped into it and returned to talk with the rather startled lasses. However, his wooden cover collapsed in the middle of their conversation ". . . leaving poor old Jackson standing before the car with no other protection than the hoop which he continued to hold."

After the tour was completed, Grant showed MacEwan cattle at the Melfort Fair, and then accepted an invitation from John Rayner, the director of extension at the University of Saskatchewan, to judge livestock at the summer fairs in southeastern Saskatchewan. The Canora Fair, July 26-27, 1926, became MacEwan's debut as a paid, official judge, a career-inspired hobby that eventually put his name front and centre across the Prairies.

That summer, Canadians were treated to their shortest government ever, the "Three-day Wonder" administration of Conservative Arthur Meighen. When the Liberal minority government of W.L. Mackenzie King collapsed in June 1926 after the discovery of widespread corruption in the Customs Department, Baron Byng, the British born and appointed Governor General of Canada, appointed Meighen as Canada's new prime minister using an outdated procedure. The action not only infuriated the nationalist Canadian populace, it motivated political neophytes like Grant MacEwan to show their party stripes.

The marriage of Bertha and Alex MacEwan many years before involved not only the union of two people, but of two families which supported diametrically opposed political parties. The Grants were staunch Conservatives from the time of John A. Macdonald and the MacEwan clan were loyal Liberals. Grant, although he resembled his mother in appearance and personality, sided with his father and grandfather when it came to politics.

Grant MacEwan worked hard to see Malcolm McLean, the federal Liberal for their constituency, elected during the fall election of 1926. The excitement of the candidate's campaign intrigued MacEwan. On a national basis, the Liberals were returned to power with a majority. Perhaps it was Grant's political bias and efforts to see the Liberal candidate elected which caused the Conservative-leaning Ontario government to pass him over when they selected their new district representative, the job he was promised.

He accepted an offer of work with the Saskatchewan Live Stock Branch in Regina. Between hanging pictures and dining out with provincial ministers and their bureaucrats, MacEwan developed a dislike for the trappings of power, albeit he was delighted to have the opportunity to consult with Dean Rutherford about work matters. He coached junior rugby in his spare time but was discouraged that the "players in this city appear to believe that to play, one must drink, smoke, fight, swear and practise Sunday mornings, etc." His residence also was a source of misery: "If the lady whose bedroom window faces mine would either pull the blind down or go to bed early it would be all right, but no, she won't do either."

Next he joined a Better Farming Train for sheep and swine which toured the northwestern part of the province. He returned to Melfort on December 17, 1926 with a young Collie pup under his arm that an appreciative farmer had presented to him. On Christmas Day, MacEwan persuaded his aging parents to spend the winter on the West Coast, and he promised to "hold the fort." He had his work cut out for him to draw feed and water for sixty head of cattle, horses and a house full of hens, particularly given it was a very harsh winter. The Collie dog and a young bull calf — which was too small to weather the outside temperatures — were his only soul-mates for the next few months. The thermometer seemed stuck at below minus 40 degrees Fahrenheit and blizzard after blizzard blanketed the landscape with snow. As for the calf, he wrote: "His house manners are the worst in the world."

The only warmth felt that winter was between the hands of an applauding audience. The congregation of Pleasant

Scotty. — MacEwan-Foran Collection

Valley Church challenged the cabin fever imposed on them by Mother Nature, and staged the play, *In Hot Tamale Land.* MacEwan was appropriately cast in the leading role of Ezra McWhackle, a pickle king. Their first performance in Pathlow drew an audience of almost two hundred, and a subsequent presentation packed the Melfort Theatre with three hundred pleased patrons. MacEwan and the rest of the cast spent the evening after their second show in the Ark Cafe so they could be the first to read the Melfort Moon's review. Indeed, it appeared as if the farmboy from Melfort had developed an instinctive appreciation for Shakespeare's observation: "All the world's a stage, and all the men and women merely players . . ."

Shortly after the elder MacEwans returned from their vacation in Vancouver, Alex suffered an attack of appendicitis, and Grant was forced to continue tending the farm. Short stints at one job or another between working the family land no longer satisfied his yearning. University had not only whetted his appetite for knowledge, it had expanded his horizon and increased his desire to see and do more than the prairie homestead could offer.

After speaking with Dean Rutherford, some months before, Grant MacEwan applied for, and received, a fellowship at Iowa State University. The dean, who was both an OAC man and had lectured at Iowa, may have had something to do with the award. Change and challenge were becoming common denominators in MacEwan's life. A entry dated September 16, 1927 simply says: "Once more I leave old Melfort and all the friends there. Today I am on my way to Winnipeg and from there I go to Ames, Iowa."

His program of study included eight hours a week in meat lectures, two hours in experimental methods, and five in comparative physiology. Additionally, he included biometrics and breeding in his course load. By early October 1927 he was settled in and was rooming with Milton Staples, an OAC '24 man. He found one person in his study group of particular interest. Maurice McSpadden was the nephew of movie-star Will Rogers. Some years later, MacEwan and his new bride came to meet and travel with the actor on a bus just before the plane crash that took his life.

By studying south of the border, he was afforded multiple opportunities to explore American churches, music and culture. MacEwan listened to sermons at the Methodist,

"Let there be peace between humans and humans, humans and non-human creations — in other words, God's other non-living things which are biologically just as wonderful as I am, and have the same desire to live I have. Without it — we will not be able to support the world's population."

Presbyterian and Catholic churches. About Aimee Semple
McPherson, a noted evangelist of the time, he commented:
"She is one in a million, chucked full of ability and most
fascinating. She is only human, however, and her tactics are
open to criticism, no doubt. Somehow her manner simply gets
you. . . It was a sight never to be forgotten, a hundred humans,
some crippled, some moaning, move over the stage. . ."

Grant was also more than duly impressed with the
head of the college, and it would seem that he adopted many of
the administrator's principles as his own. "Hughes," he wrote,
"is a real man with real principles and a broad outlook. I like
him . . . I attended a morning service at which President
Hughes spoke. In enumerating his blessings he said, 'first of
all, I am thankful for faith in a personal God and for the power
of prayer. That may seem unscientific but it's like listening to a
radio which is giving music from Australia. I can't believe it
possible, but it works.'"

In mid-December, MacEwan heard "The Messiah" for
the first time. Soon after, he travelled to the Mayo Clinic in
Rochester, New York to be with his mother, who was under-
going treatment following surgery. Days later, he heard Knute
Rochne speak and he recorded from his speech: "The
Agricultural Colleges of the country are the last strongholds
of rugged American manhood . . . The leaders of tomorrow
are coming from the rural communities; the people of the
cities are soft."

MacEwan's speaking career was inaugurated in
January 1928 when he addressed the Cosmopolitan Club about
Canada. Two weeks later, he was the guest speaker at the
downtown Lion's Club and he entertained them with his
renditions about Canada and Robbie Burns. His passion for
these topics helped to carve his reputation as a humorous and
witty after-dinner speaker in years to come.

With his year at Iowa State quickly coming to an end,
Grant MacEwan faced the dilemma of who would he work for,
what would he do? His thesis — a study of the nutritional
value of visceral organs based on a record of performance of a
colony of white rats he had been feeding — had attracted
some attention, but not the right job offer.

In April, the first of several offers arrived.
Saskatchewan's deputy minister of agriculture, F. Hedley Auld,
offered him the position of Chief Assistant to the Live Stock

"My objective has been to help establish an order that seems to approach peace on earth."

Commissioner at a beginning salary of $2,100 and a promise of $3,100 after "some years of experience and service." MacEwan responded that although he would like a larger remuneration, he would consider the offer. The deputy minister wrote back that he understood but was unable to "enlarge his offer."

The next bid came from the University of Chicago Meat Packing Institute which suggested a fellowship to pursue an advanced degree or a salary for full-time research. This proposition afforded MacEwan the freedom to design his own research, and a future. It also prompted the first bidder, Saskatchewan's department of agriculture, to up their ante when they learned the Yanks were after their boy. A third letter from Auld stated: ". . . I am recommending (to the Minister) that we give further consideration to the question of salaries." The deputy minister also scribbled on the bottom of the letter a rather paternalistic and non-bureaucratic postscript: "We want, in Saskatchewan, your services if we can make you an attractive proposition but we want more than that — to be sure that you are choosing the right line which will ultimately prove the best."

MacEwan accepted Saskatchewan's offer albeit with some reservations. He had just posted his letter of acceptance when he received the following telegram over the telephone. "Are you in position to consider offer assistant professor Animal Husbandry at U of Saskatchewan. Wire collect. W.J. Rutherford." It was the type of offer that he had dreamed about and had hoped for, but how could he renege on his letter of acceptance to the deputy minister? He found both the answer and support for his decision when he flipped over the program for Iowa University's Dedication Day Prayers ceremony which he had used to write the message on. The quote, "More things are wrought by prayers than this world dreams of," from Tennyson's *Morte d'Arthur,* met his glance, and ultimately determined his career for the next two decades. MacEwan wrote another letter to Auld, gracefully extraditing himself out of his acceptance, and sent a letter of decline to the University of Chicago.

Grant MacEwan was awarded his Master of Science on May 25, 1928. He was initiated into the Alpha Zeta Honors Society "for students in the upper two-fifths of their class and judged on their scholarship, leadership and character"; the Gamma Sigma Delta Honors Society for graduate students

"I'd like to believe the Author of this statement — 'In as much as you've done it unto one of the least of these my brothern, you've done it unto me' — was recognizing the fact that all living things are God's children. Just as much as I am one of God's children."

John Walter Grant MacEwan

Wilson Chapter
May 3, 1928

Grant MacEwan was seen to have "scholarship, leadership and character" — MacEwan-Foran Collection

"who have shown research ability in Agriculture and related departments"; and the Phi Kappa Phi Society for "outstanding graduate students." Iowa State profoundly influenced the rest of his life. His short-term goals were replaced by a long-term ambition. MacEwan left Ames not only wiser, but a more complex individual.

On June 12, 1928 he wrote: "I left dear old Ames and a lot of fine Iowa friends this morning at 7 o'clock. . . The Iowa people are hard to leave. Now that my stay with them is past I conclude they are the friendliest and most courteous people that I have ever mingled with." The scholarly Saskatchewan farmboy returned to the United States many times during his life, both as a respected livestock judge and as a guest speaker to highbrow audiences. His renditions of the colorful characters that roamed the plains and tilled the soil in the "Last, Best West" entertained many a service club and professional organization, elevating Canada's profile in a way never done before.

Professor Grant MacEwan

Section IV

"Arrived once more at home at Melfort," wrote Grant MacEwan on June 15, 1928. The acquisition of his MA from Iowa State revealed a strong and single-minded approach to self-imposed goals. Not only did his postgraduate degree allow him to bask in the respect Canadians were cultivating for their academics, it identified him as an emerging and important player in the country's then largest industry, agriculture.

He reported for work at the University of Saskatchewan on July 2, 1928 and soon met up with his mentor, Dean Rutherford, and Professor A.M. Shaw, the head of the animal husbandry department. MacEwan was scheduled to give three lectures per week plus perform general extension work including livestock judging at fairs throughout the province.

Professor Grant MacEwan (circa 1930) — MacEwan-Foran Collection

Shortly after his arrival, an older man wandered into his office, extended his hand and introduced himself. "My name is Murray. If you need anything, let me know." The president of the university, Walter Charles Murray, grew fond of his new lecturer who, like himself, believed agriculture underpinned both the direction of the university and the economic well-being of Canada.

The University of Saskatchewan sat up on the east bank of the South Saskatchewan River, high enough to provide a splendid view of the city of Saskatoon. Some twelve sand-colored limestone buildings rose out of the flat prairie landscape. The area was graced with neither trees nor shrubs, and the wind swept between the Gothic structures, alternately fluffing and flattening the long, dry grass. The washboard gravel road — or the streetcar line that paralleled it — was the only access in and out of the learned community.

The university was established in 1903 by Sir Frederick Haultain, then premier of the Northwest Territories. He had envisioned the institution as free from all government, sect or political influence and governed by its graduates. This same puritan, albeit naive, philosophy of people before politics, guided his actions to achieve self-determination for the Northwest and provincial status for the territories.

When Grant MacEwan joined the faculty, Haultain was its chancellor. The ensuing relationship between the two had a profound influence upon the young professor. Years later, as the mayor of Calgary and Lieutenant-Governor of Alberta, MacEwan systematically divested himself of his Liberal affiliations and truly put people before politics. He was troubled, though, that Haultain remained an unsung hero, and in 1985, MacEwan wrote *Frontier Statesman of the Canadian Northwest — Frederick Haultain.*

Much of MacEwan's first summer was spent acquainting himself with his future colleagues and judging livestock at the numerous fairs which were part of the prairie economics and social life. In mid-July he judged beef cattle at the Yorkton Fair and left via the Qu'Appelle Valley in the car of one of the organizers. One of the other passengers, being a very sociable type of fellow, brought along a supply of beer of which he consumed with great gusto. Wrote a sober MacEwan: "On the way up the valley our motor was working its hardest and the climb was steep. 'Hell men, why don't you coast?' asked the beer-drinking passenger, and with that leaned over and turned off the switch." Only the quick action of the driver and the handbrake held the vehicle on the crest of the hill. Seconds later it was resoundingly bumped by an oncoming car. That and another passenger's efforts to spit tobacco through the glass in the doors, concluded MacEwan, "made the trip quite interesting."

He travelled to fairs in Melfort, Moosomin, Mortlach, Belle Plaine, Stoughton, Bethune, Turtleford, Richard, Landis, Watrous, North Battleford, Glenbush, Assinaboine, Maple Creek and Duck Lake that summer. The last-mentioned he described as the "World's Worst Fair" with its ". . . Indians, French half-breeds and scrub bulls the best displays." And when the animal husbandry professor queried a young boy about the age of two Shetland ponies, he was informed, "These two buggers is twins." According to the wee lad, the animals had different mothers, but they were born on the same day!

The memories of his own hardship motivated the new professor to take pity on a Saskatoon bag lady. He described her in his journal as "ill-clothed and the very picture of poverty." According to him, she could have easily pulled her shoes over her feet and up to her knees without trouble.

Wrote MacEwan: "I stopped her and told her that if she would come with me I would get her a pair of new shoes. At first she was sceptical but at last we crossed the street in the direction of Hudson Bay Company store. I proceeded first through the revolving door and when I was part way through she began to come through on the other side of the axis. I was trapped and she continued to shove against the door which refused to go backwards. I signalled through the glass and finally won that round."

The scene became even more humorous inside the store. Grant asked for useful footwear and the old lady insisted the shoes be high. With none to be found, he hinted to the clerk that she substitute a pair of boy's boots, but the old gal " . . . scented an irregularity and in a haughty manner, she got up and left us." He thanked the clerk, tipped his hat to the spectators that had gathered, and slunk away red-faced and thoroughly embarrassed. He later conceded in his journal: "Moral — Have as little as possible to do with women."

MacEwan began teaching on September 27, 1928. In addition to seventeen hours of lecturing and whatever time was needed to prepare lessons, he also agreed to coach the agriculture college boys' rugby team. Judging, demonstrations and talks to agriculture societies and organizations were also spliced into his timetable. As well, the future vegetarian established a reputation for his ability to cut and identify cuts of meat, a feature of many exhibitions "for the ladies attending." He was known to be able to kill, pelt and hang the animal before the grizzly details of the slaughter sunk in with the audience.

He gave freely of his time to the associate students who required additional coaching for judging competitions. In one journal entry he wrote: "I gave the boys some special coaching which appeared to be rewarded. Everett Whewell was the individual winner in the competition." As an associate student, MacEwan had benefitted from the kind and generous support and coaching of many an OAC professor. As a teacher, he made a similar if not greater investment of time and energy in his undergraduates. He viewed their successes as his own.

Graduation came and went, and the 1929 round of summer fairs began. Grant MacEwan hopscotched across the prairies, judging livestock of every class and description. He was also invited to the Regina Farm Boys' Camp, this time as a coach and judge. Only a decade before, he had himself attended this camp. It was here that he first met Dean Rutherford, and paraded Beau Perfection 47th around the arena after the animal won the Grand Championship ribbon

"In 1932, I was on staff at the University of Saskatchewan. My academic friends were always going to England to study and improve their positions. They went on scholarships. I went on a cattle-ship.

But it suited me alright."

for Hereford bulls. One might wonder if it was déjà-vu for the farmboy from Melfort. Certainly, the dean's words from then had come true, and Grant MacEwan had ". . . increased in wisdom and in stature." It was only a matter of time before he would achieve " . . . favor with God and man."

MacEwan was, without dispute, one of the most-liked instructors to pass through the University of Saskatchewan. Rather than lecturing, he chatted with his students. He would hike himself up on a desk in front of the class and engage them in a two-way discussion, all the time swinging his long legs. It was a pose that thousands would come to identify him by. Long after he had departed from academia and finished his time behind the political podium, he returned to sit on a simple table to tête-à-tête with admiring audiences.

If he suffered the scrutiny of probation during his first year at the University of Saskatchewan, the outcome far outweighed the process.

University of Saskatchewan Hockey Team, 1929-30. Grant MacEwan, Manager (top row, second from left).

In a letter dated August 7, 1929, President Murray wrote: "The executive at its meeting yesterday resolved to increase your salary to $2,800 for the year 1929-30, $3,000 for the year 1930-31, and a promotion to Junior Professor with an initial salary of $3,200 from July 31, 1931." Perhaps the fact that Iowa State had offered him a full professorship and ample perks prompted the initiative, or maybe it was because the university's school of agriculture had never enjoyed such a high profile.

President Murray knew that an associate professor who could judge at sixteen fairs and seven other gatherings, give twelve formal talks and lectures to the public, publish scientific articles, lecture and participate in student activities, and still have time to socialize with faculty staff was an asset worth protecting. MacEwan had earned his spurs.

Professor Grant MacEwan was also a skilled horseman and he kept a good mount in the university's barn. According to Rusty Macdonald, a friend and previous biographer, "He was so incredibly handsome and looked so dashing on his horse that girls would swoon when he rode by and tipped his hat at them." Certainly, it would be a curious sight by today's standards, to see an instructor trotting across a campus and tipping his hat to a generation of feminists.

MacEwan began to fly between fairs to save time. In August 1929, he flew from Radville to Regina in one hour, a journey that would normally take six to seven hours by car. He was fascinated by the garden-like look of the farms from the air, although one aspect of the trip caused him some concern. "I was worried about the gasoline gage ahead of me which registered empty long before we reached Regina." The pilot emphatically stated, according to MacEwan, "that the measurement device was prone to exaggerating."

Later that summer, he purchased — for $950 cash — the first of many properties that he would own during his lifetime, a quarter section located on the White Fox River some fourteen miles from Nipawin. That purchase was followed by a quarter section in the Resource district south of Melfort. The asking price was $1,600; MacEwan paid $1,200 cash. And on August 29, 1929, *Western Producer* published his article, "Feeding Dairy Cattle." This marked the beginning of a long and symbiotic relationship between one of Western Canada's most prolific writers and the now-defunct prairie publishing

"I saw the slums — Glasgow, Liverpool, London — in the 1930s. I wanted to see them not that I knew I would enjoy it."

Alastair Ewen, 1939.
— MacEwan-Foran Collection

house. Professor MacEwan also established a rapport with the *Saskatchewan Farmer*, the *Free Press Prairie Farmer*, the *Family Herald*, and numerous other publications which became the beneficiaries of his early articles.

On October 29, 1929, stock prices plunged on the Montreal and Toronto Stock Exchanges creating panic on the trading floor and in boardrooms across the country. Only one week before the American economy had, for all intent and purpose, collapsed. Assurances from Prime Minister W.L. Mackenzie King that Canada was in fine financial shape did little to improve the canvas of human and animal suffering that journalists painted via the telegraph wires. From east to west and west to east, newspapers reported the growing number of unemployed. Owing to the paucity of the previous year's harvest, farmers lacked feed for their livestock. Stories of animal starvation emerged from the countryside.

Few countries were affected more severely than Canada by the global depression. Its four western provinces, which were almost exclusively dependent on primary-product exports, were hit the hardest. Drought and shrinking external markets for wheat forced the prairie economy to collapse. During the first four years of the economic turndown, the nation's Gross National Expenditure declined by 42 percent. By 1933, one in five Canadians were on welfare. Within two years of the depression's onset, Saskatchewan's total income plunged by 90 percent and 66 percent of its rural population was on dole. Relief camps — where so-called volunteers were accommodated, clothed and fed until they found work — popped up across the landscape.

The Dirty Thirties — which played similar scenes on both sides of the 49th parallel — inspired American author John Steinbeck to document the suffering of the time in *Grapes of Wrath* and *Of Mice and Men*. The works of Canadian authors Farley Mowat, W.O. Mitchell and Margaret Laurence, children of the time, were strongly influenced by their memories of this decade. The inspirational works of the Group of Seven became a mere memory of happier times for most. The radio became the main source of entertainment and serials such as *The Romance of Canada* — produced and directed by Tyrone Guthrie and aired on Austin Weir's CNR station in the early 1930s — romanticized the hardships endured by earlier explorers and pioneers.

Grant MacEwan gave his first radio address on November 19, 1929 over the Regina broadcasting station CKCK. The station had a permanent link in the Administration Building in the office of seventy-six-year-old James Clinkskill, a founder of the university. Clinkskill, who was in his office at the time, dozed off and his loud snorts punctuated MacEwan's script, causing him to lose his place.

On September 16, 1930, Grant MacEwan met his one and only male soul-mate, a strapping Scot by the name of Al Ewen. The two men developed the type of friendship most individuals dream of and few achieve. "Al was the only person who could put Father in his place," disclosed Heather MacEwan-Foran, Grant's daughter. "They had a very special relationship."

Grant MacEwan was designated to pick up the new assistant professor of animal husbandry. He proceeded to the King George Hotel at the appointed time, enquired at the desk for his charge, and even had a Chinese bellboy call out his name. All was to no avail, and Mr. Ewen was not to be found. Finally MacEwan and President Murray, who had arrived to assist with the search, approached a gentleman who had been watching with interest the increased activity in the lobby. It turned out that the Aberdeen native had heard the numerous announcements, yet his Highland ear prevented him from discerning his name, first in a western twang and then in a Chinese lilt. MacEwan sized up his new counterpart and wrote in his journal: "He is a big burly Scot, one who would never win a beauty competition, but an interesting and capable type."

Phyllis Cline MacEwan, 1935.
— MacEwan-Foran Collection

Since his earliest days at OAC and then Iowa State, the good-looking bachelor had never lacked for female accompaniment to dances or parties. Gladys Eaton, of all the women he befriended (and certainly the list was lengthy), was the closest to a steady girlfriend he permitted himself. It was a relationship, however, that turned out to have no basis after graduation, and the two went their separate ways although they did continue to correspond.

Grant MacEwan met his bride at a Halloween dance in 1931. He had accompanied another teacher but quickly became intrigued with a woman dressed as an Arabian dancer. All evening, her big, brown eyes stared at him from behind a silk veil. Eventually, he approached the lithe figure and asked her to, "Take off that mask so I can get a good look at your face." After meeting the distant relative of the famous country western singer, Patsy Cline, MacEwan wrote ". . . she was a very good looking kind to know." Just as his father had tumbled for the dark-haired, beautiful Bertha Grant with her fun-loving nature, Grant found himself bewitched by this stunning young woman.

It was helpful for their developing relationship, to say the least, that Phyllis sang in the choir of Knox United Church where MacEwan played an increasingly active role. While he had been raised in a strict Presbyterian home, he was more attuned to this moderate style of ministry and had sided with the Unionists during the 1924-25 debate. Furthermore, he knew the church clergy, Reverend James MacKenzie, from his OAC days; the pastor's previous parish had been in Guelph.

In addition to his multiple nonacademic interests, MacEwan had an inquiring scientific mind. Together with Professor Shaw and George Valentine of the Matador Ranch, he travelled through southwest Saskatchewan and southern Alberta during May 1930 in search of heifers for a proposed breeding project. The experiment brought four herds of cows, Hereford, Shorthorn, Angus and Galloway together on the ranch and put bulls of one breed to them each year. The calves were then moved to the University for feeding at weaning time. By the time the four-year experiment was completed, the 1,000 foundation stock had increased to between 3,500 and 4,000 animals.

MacEwan became a front-and-centre player in the project with the university, the provincial department of agriculture and National Research Council forming a partnership. The activity took the born-in-Brandon and schooled-in-Melfort academic to Alberta. With a critical mind and a sharp pen he scribbled down his first impressions of the province he would someday call home. "The country gives you the impression of vastness. Even the people, 'the cow men,' constitute a unique group. They are by birth or adoption sons of the country, he-men, and as natural as the wide open spaces below the canopy of heaven can make. They are kind and hospitable, they are businessmen who do things in a big way. They are gamblers and the stakes are big ones. They do not count their lands by quarter sections, but by thousands of acres, and by similar figures do they count their cattle and sheep. They have all had their severe reverses and losses. . ."

"The Old Country cities have their different sides. One side is very attractive and wonderful. Unfortunately they have poverty and degradation which makes you feel ashamed of society."

Two years into the project, the first experimental calves were ready for the international market. Because the United States had imposed high tariffs on Canadian meat, the British market was selected. It was decided that Grant MacEwan would accompany the shipment of livestock to the world-famous Smithfield market. Taking his usual few belongings, he set off on the two-month excursion wherein one month was used to explore his ancestral home. On July 29, 1932, he wrote: "Scotland is great. The country is one continuous picture, dotted with sheep, Ayrshires and Clydesdales. It is but little wonder that such a unique country has produced the best horses, the best cattle and the best men in the world . . . " This comment was in sharp contrast to his impression of the Scot's southern cousins. He wrote: "It is quite evident that there are too many Englishmen in the world. They beat all for dogged conceit." His visit to the slums of London was one of the most difficult emotional experiences of his life. Years later on a CBC program, he commented that, "This was not just a tragedy of human suffering but an example of our society's failure to look out for its weakest and most vulnerable members."

S.S. Silksworth in berth at Port Churchill, Manitoba, 1932.
— MacEwan-Foran Collection

Looking down from the hills of Inverness where Glen Urquhart meets Loch Ness, MacEwan's heart was in his hand when he wrote: "I stand tonight on the hills not far from Glen Urquhart from which old James Grant, son of John Grant came in 1773 and landed at Pictou, Nova Scotia. It is a bonnie, gripping, wild and lovable country and surely nothing short of dire persecution would ever divorce a man from it." By the end of his vacation, he had toured over thirty cities, attended some thirty agricultural shows, inspected herds on farms, visited twenty-eight historic sites and managed seventeen or so interviews about farming methodology, nutrition and economics.

He returned to Canada via the Hudson Bay Route aboard the *SS Silksworth*, a grain ship. When the freighter pulled into the Port of Churchill, Manitoba on August 29, 1932, Grant MacEwan became the first person admitted to Canada by Customs and Immigration via Churchill.

Many of MacEwan's activities at the University of Saskatchewan constituted an effort to reduce the inevitable "town and gown" gap that develops in university towns. He crossed the invisible barrier between the two by being active

"Let's dream of a time when peace will come to all of God's outdoor community.

Wildlife, water and air and soil, and iron ore and oil — you name the rest."

in both communities. He became a member of the local Kiwanis Club, and on occasion, he pumped up a set of bagpipes at the local St. Andrew's or Burns' Society. Traditionally, these organizations had little if any appeal for academics and it was a refreshing change for their members to see the human side of academia.

MacEwan also served as a director of the Saskatoon Exhibition, and eventually its president, and somehow found time to help establish the Saskatoon Riding Club. His service to the community and his climb to notoriety, however, engendered the occasional enemy in addition to an ample supply of wannabe friends. According to writer Rusty Macdonald, a rather astute lady by the name of Muriel Evans, accused Grant MacEwan of using the riding club as a "stepping stone."

The effect of the 1930s Depression on universities was not unlike that which has occurred on campuses during the early 1990s. Budgets were frozen and then reduced, programs were severely restricted and often cancelled, building ceased, salaries were often rolled back, and many academics were forcibly nudged out the door. There is no evidence that this time period had a negative effect on Grant MacEwan's career. Rather, he maneuvered through this period unscathed, and for a variety of reasons, his career accelerated during this decade. Moreover, he gained the benefit of increases from promotions, even though his colleagues' salaries were frozen, and he enjoyed job security because the agricultural department was seen to provide an essential service for drought-stricken farmers.

Early into their friendship, Al Ewen and Grant MacEwan recognized that there was a shortage of agricultural textbooks that focused on farming in Canada, and they set about to fill the gap. The exercise not only brought the already-close friends closer, it highlighted their differences. Grant MacEwan was over six-foot in height, slim with an almost graceful, if not purposeful, stride. He had regrown his moustache and though frugal in his choice of apparel, he presented a striking image. Al Ewen, on the other hand, was of average height with a chunky build. His square face had a bulbous-like nose that suggested previous contact with a set of knuckles. It was not surprising, therefore, that when MacEwan informed an inebriated Ewen that it was time to go home after a dance — the ex-boxer took a swing and flattened the teetotalling, tall professor, sending him swiftly across the floor on his backside.

Despite the altercation, the friendship between the two grew even closer. The men were working late one evening during August 1931 when Ewen proposed that they should make a raft and float down the South Saskatchewan River from Saskatoon to the Forks where the North and South branches meet. He reasoned there was no time to think about it and that they should set out the next day because the fall term would be quickly upon them.

Grant MacEwan on raft which he and Al Ewen built, August 1931.
— MacEwan-Foran Collection

The following morning MacEwan and Ewen met at the riverbank where they sawed and lashed poles together and stuck a large, wooden crate on top for shelter. Although it was a journey of only 100 miles, their experiences, sometimes life-threatening, forced Grant MacEwan to depend upon someone, something he had not done for a long time. At the Fenton Ferry where the channel narrows and deepens, their raft crashed into the oncoming current and upset. The men and their gear were tossed into the raging water and only their athletic prowess and luck saved them from drowning. Further downstream, they righted the raft, recovered most of their possessions and continued the journey.

There was considerable humor associated with the trip which MacEwan captured in his journal. "I suggested that if I were to sing in my most melodious tone that some of the

Farming

"Farming is a messy business - so uninteresting - and cows . . ." So said one whose chief pleasures in life are choir practices, bridge parties, golf and late nights. Perhaps farming is like that somewhat, but it's pretty much in the way you look at it. Hasn't it been that vocation which has made men, provided leaders, and imparted the best judgement and foresight to leaders in finance, administration, politics and other walks of life?

Granting that farming is fraught with certain hazards and hardships, one may refuse to take the least stock in the theory that it is uninteresting. As one who was born and reared on the farm, known something of its hardships, of pioneering and privation, the writer may advance the contention that the city dweller has no monopoly on the interesting things in life.

"It is unfortunately true that some farming folk are not getting all they should out of their work. Their work is irksome, tedious, monotonous, unfruitful to them. Perhaps they have always been too close to that work to obtain the happiest picture, so close to the work in the fields that it has meant only long hours and heavy toil, so constantly close to the cow that she means only manure to fork and teats to pull.

"There are compensations on the farm which are frequently under-rated. The joy of working as a partner with nature in her great laboratory, and the joy of caring for living animals which are growing, yielding and responding to the skill of the operator are compensations of no mean calibre.

"The compensation of hunger is food, the compensation of thirst is water, and of fatigue — rest. It can scarcely be questioned that there are some city dwellers who do not know the great joy of eating because they are never hungry, and they don't know the real joy of sleeping because they have not had sufficient experience with real toil.

"The finest compensations in the writer's life were not the circuses visited, theatres attended, or bridge parties endured, but rather the simple compensations of natural life. The long drink of cold, grimy, soot- colored water which was squeezed from the muskeg mud after a nine mile walk under a 30-pound pack and an

natives might offer us some breakfast," he wrote. "The Scot's partner's observation is that they would be liable to come out with a gun and give us some buckshot." In another entry MacEwan speculated that, "Probably my partner clothed just as Nature clothed him is enough to scare even a team of horses." He concluded that it was a great holiday, simple, thrilling and cheap. The entire six-day trip including the raft and provisions cost the travellers twelve dollars each.

Grant MacEwan began the long and arduous process of developing the public-figure side of his character during the Great Depression. His ability to judge livestock, crops, and on occasion, babies, placed him in hot demand with the prairie people. His straightforward and folksy approach, and his reputation for frugality, earned the respect of farmers whose crops and livestock withered before their very eyes while hard-nosed eastern bankers, devoid of sympathy, repossessed their once-flourishing farms.

Meanwhile, his public and academic image began to mesh. He gained publicity and acceptance for the "Cash Captive Bolt Humane Killer" — a revolver which he brought from Britain that made the slaughter of animals a kinder process. MacEwan also accepted the challenge of becoming the Dean of Men at Qu'Appelle Hall. He moved into the dean's suite and proceeded to form discussion groups which fleshed out contemporary thought about alcohol, gambling, religion, and working one's way through university.

The mood of the country turned ugly during 1933. While the relief camps provided shelter and food for unemployed men, they were also an environment for activists and their followers who agitated for social reform. An entry on April 27, 1933 in MacEwan's journal reads: "In company with Prof. Ewen, Chief of Police Geo. Donald, and Inspector Sampson of Mounted Police, I inspected a detachment of Mounted Police Force horses stationed in Saskatoon in anticipation of trouble with the unemployed." A week later, Inspector Sampson was killed and three other officers injured when the RCMP and city police clashed with some 300 unemployed protestors in Saskatoon.

Loss of hope and frustration was quickly turning the Prairies into a hotbed of violence. Farmers and the unemployed city dwellers found little solace in their present politicians. But Grant MacEwan was a man of their own heart.

He was approached for the first time to accept a political nomination in 1933. A delegation of Melfort locals wanted him to run in the upcoming provincial election for the Liberals. In as gracious a manner possible, he refused. Although he considered it an honor to have been asked, he sensed the timing was wrong.

Late that summer he went on a walking tour of Northern Saskatchewan, accompanied by Dr. P.M. Simmons, who worked for the federal department of plant pathology. The hike took them north to Candle Lake through heavily wooded forests, muskegs, tiny grain fields cultivated by "settlers of Central European type," and into the heart of the last known frontier. "The country is rare and wild and beautiful," wrote MacEwan. "It's great. It's certainly fine to be a millionaire and just enjoy this to the full. We found a most welcome waterhole in a muskeg . . ." His older and less agile companion, however, was not as inspired by his firsthand experience with Mother Nature and he quipped to MacEwan that there would be ". . . a packsack for sale cheap when he gets back to Saskatoon."

Writing was now a serious companion to MacEwan's life. It allowed him to experiment with thoughts and concepts that would have been foreign, if not controversial, to conversations of the day. He used his journal to record the day-to-day happenings in his life, and he wrote about a variety of subjects using poetry or essay format. He also pasted news clippings of the day to its pages.

An ominous entry in MacEwan's journal at the end of the year suggests the wide-spread suffering which he was witness to. "The year 1933 ends amid unhappy scenes. Trouble has loomed large in 1933. It was the fifth year of the Depression which has not yet released its grip. Poverty, unemployment, famine, drought and grasshoppers featured the year. The international political arena has been equally unsettled with war talk in Europe and in South America and the Orient. We welcome the new year with high hopes."

His reputation as a professor spilled into the pulpit. He was known to be both deeply religious and a pragmatic philosopher, and he was invited by clergy, weary of witnessing parishioners' privation, to give addresses which gave hope to packed congregations. In May 1934, the popular professor was the star performer at the Hughton and Elrose United Churches where he attempted "to discuss Agricultural, Social and

August sun was the most welcome draught ever to come to the writer's lips. It was liquid which the average person would not consider washing his feet in, but under the circumstances, it was so cheering, refreshing, and reviving that the pleasant thought of it will remain long after the outstanding social events of city life are forgotten.

"It may still be contended that a cow is beautiful, that food to a hungry man is sweet, that water to a thirsty man is the most welcome thing in the world, and a good bed to a tired man is the nearest approach to Heaven itself. It may be contended too that for those souls who find nature more uninteresting than contract bridge, the farm holds broader understandings of the way of life, finer appreciation of things and fellows, and the most genuine of compensations. There are those who can sincerely say . . . 'There is nothing more pleasant for me than do chores on my own farm.'"

— written by Grant MacEwan in church on October 22, 1933

Grant MacEwan and Al Ewen, Candle
Lake trek, August 1934.
— MacEwan-Foran Collection

Religious problems of the rural people, placing each in its proper relationship." It was a message he further refined and delivered to many gatherings over the next few years.

MacEwan was exposed to much embarrassment in early 1934. He received a call from a reporter at the *Saskatoon Star Phoenix* who wanted to know if he knew a girl by the name of Harriet Brigham of Oklahoma City. When he acknowledged the friendship, the reporter asked, "Are you engaged to her?" According to a wire story by Associated Press, the lady had just received a letter — dated January 1932, two years before — from J.W.G. MacEwan, a professor at the University of Saskatchewan, in which he asked her to marry him. "It was bolt from the blue to say the least," scribbled the bachelor. "I immediately communicated with the city editor and pleaded that the story be suppressed before it was printed. The whole thing looks like the most malicious plot or set of circumstances I have ever been mixed up with." A few days later, the rattled academic received a letter from his would be financée — who had been a graduate student at Iowa State at the same time as MacEwan — admitting to the folly and asking for forgiveness.

Grant MacEwan returned to Candle Lake with his soul-mate during August 1934. The trek may have been a physical adventure for Al Ewen, but for MacEwan, his sabbaticals in the wilderness were becoming a necessary counterbalance to the demands of public life. While Ewen was preoccupied with their dwindling food supply, MacEwan strode further into the bush in search of some higher meaning between man and his world. "I have thought so often today of the hymn, 'Peace perfect peace, in this dark world of sin,'" he wrote. "It all contrasts so obviously with the environment we labor in day by day."

The relationship between Phyllis Cline and Grant MacEwan had by now developed to a point where she was no longer prepared to continue as just a friend. Phyllis was the daughter of a rail stationmaster whose lineage could be traced to the Black Forest of Germany. The oldest of two girls, she was born on August 10, 1909 in Hamilton, Ontario and later educated at the University of Manitoba and University of Saskatchewan as a teacher. Classes of the time averaged thirty to forty youngsters, and the combined stress of teaching and making her students mind, often forced the fragile Cline to seek rest and refuge at her parent's home in Churchbridge, Manitoba.

Over their five-year courtship, the two young people enjoyed common Depression entertainment such as dances, church activities, walks in search of archaeological relics, movies or skating during the winter. Each visited one another's parents. The monetary restrictions that prohibited many a couple from marrying during the economic downturn did not apply to Grant MacEwan and Phyllis Cline. He was a well-established academic and she came from a comfortable background where money was neither salted nor frittered away, rather it was used to provide enjoyment and security. The Clines had seen to it that their daughters, Phyllis and Gertrude, had pleasant holidays, nice clothing and a good education.

The idea of marriage had not yet dawned on Grant, and he was probably more than slightly shocked when Phyllis mentioned to him that there were other men interested in her. He quickly became an attentive suitor, and on June 30, 1935 he wrote: "Phyllis and I decided finally to be married about July 26." Unlike most couples of the time, Grant had the resources to buy his future wife a diamond engagement ring. On July 8, he wrote: "Phyllis Cline got her Bluebird reg. number 70193."

Their wedding was one of the social highlights that year amongst the middle and upper-class of Saskatoon. Some fifty people attended the garden ceremony on July 26, 1935, including the federal minister of agriculture, the Honourable Robert Weir. Unfortunately, MacEwan's mother was unable to attend. Recurring asthma attacks kept Bertha in a Melfort hospital.

The couple was married by Dr. John L. Nicol, an uncle of the bride, in an outdoor service at the Forestry Farm, the home of another uncle, James McLean. Esther Wright, who had introduced the couple at the Halloween dance, was the maid of honor, and Al Ewen was the best man. The wedding enjoyed press coverage in the *Saskatoon Star-Phoenix* and the *Winnipeg Free Press*. It was a who's-who function where the names of the guests and who they represented were given top-billing. The University of Saskatchewan was represented by "the venerable chairman of the board of governors," James Clinkskill, the same man whose snoring provided the backdrop music for one of MacEwan's radio broadcasts.

"My religion is trying to take care of these treasures that my God entrusted to me."

The Cline-MacEwan wedding, July 26, 1935.— MacEwan-Foran Collection

The young couple departed by train for a honeymoon at the West Coast. The rail portion of the trip ended at Rosetown, where they spent their first night in the one and only hotel. The next day, they boarded a Greyhound coach to Spokane, Vancouver, Victoria, Seattle and back to Rosetown. There they caught the train for Saskatoon. Their mode of travel provided subject material for the campus gossipers who believed Grant MacEwan to be somewhat of a penny-pincher. However, Phyllis tried to set the record straight by explaining that her six-foot plus husband and a wife was more than a train berth could accommodate.

Grant MacEwan was thrilled when his favorite movie actor Will Rogers boarded the couple's bus in Spokane. He had known the star's nephew Maurice McSpadden from his days at Ohio State and this made for easy conversation between the two men. Rogers bid the newlyweds farewell in Vancouver to catch a plane to Alaska. The actor, who was best known for his statement — "I never met a man I didn't like" — was killed days later when his flight crashed near Point Barrow, Alaska.

One of Grant MacEwan's greatest strengths was his management of time. He realized early in his career that reports, letters, or even manuscripts could be written easily enroute to a destination, particularly if you travelled on a bus or train. Driving your own car prevented you from writing or reading, and being a passenger meant you had to make polite conversation with the driver at the expense of doing nothing.

Moreover, travel by bus or train, maintained MacEwan, "took the least charge on the environment."

He learned to combine vocation and avocation together with ease. If he was out in the field collecting agricultural data, then he took an extra couple of minutes to look for arrowheads or to document the historical significance of the location and its personalities. The newly married Phyllis MacEwan, however, was no doubt miffed when her husband chose to concentrate on his and Ewen's textbook, rather than her, during their honeymoon journey.

Phyllis quickly learned about the extent and type of demands placed on her husband by the public, and the incredible standards of performance that he set for himself. In their first year of marriage, there was one forty-day stretch when Grant was out every night. The couple was also required to discharge certain duties because they were part of the faculty. One such function was the regular Sunday afternoon tea where members took turns as the host and hostess. These gatherings were supposed to provide a favorable environment for academics to exchange ideas. But it ultimately became the gossip hour which prompted MacEwan to write, "A Sabbath desecrated by silly social superfluities."

The couple took up residence in the upper floor of Mrs. MacCallum's home near the college, and within a year they bought their first house. Grant MacEwan paid $4,240 for a two-story stucco house at 313 Bottomley Avenue North, one-and-a-half blocks from the university. Phyllis set about in short order to decorate the home and become the supportive wife of a respected university professor. Only twenty years before, Grant's home had been the bluff at the Melfort farm with the sky as his ceiling and the poplars, his walls. During those years, his father and mother, with his help, had re-established themselves. He had acquired an education and a career, and he now had a loving wife. For the most part, only the tragedy of his brother's death had marred this time period.

His future career as a historian and writer were profoundly influenced by a chance meeting with Arthur Silver Morton. MacEwan met the University of Saskatchewan history professor on October 8, 1935 when he attended a meeting of the Saskatoon Archaeological Society. Morton, whose *History of the Canadian West to 1870* became the bible of Canadian history, gave a speech about the "Migrations of the Tribes."

"I can't think of any higher challenge than the idea of conserving the treasures of Nature.

That means God's gift to not only the race, but to the world.

I think conservation is a moral matter."

They struck up a friendship, and three years later the twosome combed northeastern Saskatchewan for sites of old forts and trading posts.

Morton's habit of being formally dressed in a white shirt, tie and jacket complete with a silver-mounted cane — whether he was wandering through the bush in search of past civilizations or giving a university lecture — made him a peculiar looking partner for the young, casually clad animal husbandry professor. "He is one of the most impractical of men but he knows the story of the West as nobody else and it is a rare privilege to sit at his feet and listen," wrote MacEwan. The old geezer, however, was both hard of hearing and oblivious to time or direction and would wander off without notice. MacEwan's job of being a companion was nothing short of a nightmare and he eventually threatened to tie a cowbell around his mentor's neck.

Grant MacEwan's and Al Ewen's first jointly prepared manuscript titled *Science and Practise of Canadian Animal Husbandry* was accepted by Thomas Nelson and Sons on May 14, 1936. It was a proud writer that recorded in his journal on February 25, 1937, "The authors . . . received their first royalty returns today." A cheque for $36.58 was received by each. They collaborated on one more title before MacEwan went it alone.

On October 14, 1935 the federal Conservative government of R.B. Bennett was annihilated, and Liberal leader William Lyon Mackenzie King was installed as the new prime minister. The change in the administration was felt at the University of Saskatchewan where Dean Shaw from the College of Agriculture was appointed to the newly established Canadian Wheat Board. While President Murray took over his duties in title, in reality it was Professor MacEwan who performed the day-to-day activities of the former dean.

Suddenly he found his days packed with committee, agricultural, staff, and faculty meetings in addition to conferences, convention greetings and his own commitments to judge livestock. A short entry summed up his feelings: "It appears now like an apprenticeship in Hell." The next two years were particularly difficult for MacEwan who was kept busy pushing paper rather than travelling the judging circuit and collecting arrowheads on route. It was an experience that left him with few fond memories and a realization that, perhaps, he was not yet ready to accept a senior administrator's position.

One of President Murray's last duties before his retirement was to formally fill the agricultural dean's chair. Although Grant MacEwan had done an admirable job, he had only a masters degree and hence was passed over in favor of Dr. L. E. Kirk. Instead, MacEwan was appointed on April 19, 1937 as the manager of the university farm and the new director of the School of Agriculture which was responsible for the two-year associate program. These positions, in retrospect, did more for his profile than being a dean behind a desk. With the federal Liberals back in power, and their knowledge of his political inclinations, MacEwan was regularly invited to agriculture meetings in Ottawa. The new minister of agriculture, James G. Gardiner, had future plans for the professor.

By 1937, more than 1.2 million Canadians were on relief. While this represented a small improvement over the year before, the conditions across the prairies deteriorated. Drought suffocated all growth including grasshopper reproduction. In his new position as manager of the university farm, MacEwan was responsible for ensuring sufficient feed was grown for all of the animals, whether service or experimental. "The year has been the worst, agriculturally, in Saskatchewan history," he wrote. "Prices continue to be ruinous and the rainfall at a record low, the average wheat yield in the province will stand at less than two-and-a-half bushels per acre. Here at Saskatoon, there was no rain when rain was needed with the result that from 1,000 acres of crop we did not harvest a bushel of grain." The only yield they recovered was 200 loads of Russian thistles. They threshed absolutely no feed for their precious breeding and experimental livestock.

MacEwan had observed during his travels, though, that animals which ate Russian thistle seemed to be able to stave off starvation. With that knowledge at hand, he recruited every student he had ever helped, and together they began one of the most intense and important research projects of the decade. "We did everything with it," wrote the professor. "We pounded it, chopped it, pulverized it — even boiled it. We cut it green, we cut it late, we hammered it, we ensiled it, we mixed it but it was still unpalatable, laxative and low on feeding value." Even wife Phyllis was brought into the project. She was asked to prepare the tender shoots of the thistle as salad, so that her

Phyllis Cline holds "That" (1936).
— MacEwan-Foran Collection

husband could assess its taste from a human's viewpoint. Neither were overly keen about its flavor or texture.

With his only concrete observation being, "the animals — mainly cattle and sheep — are eating the stuff and maintaining weight fairly well," the professor took to the airwaves to encourage its use as a feed substitute. His advice spread like wildfire, and many a farmer and newspaper editor cast Grant MacEwan into the role of a Messiah who was instrumental in saving herds of valuable livestock from the grip of starvation.

On the home front, the couple became foster parents to two young skunks which Grant had found during a walk at the Jail Farm on June 17, 1937. The animals — which they dubbed "This" and "That" — created quite a stir on campus, particularly for those who questioned the professor's proficiency at deodorizing his new charges. When the male died a few months later, an entry by MacEwan in his journal speaks of his reverence for all living creatures. "He had become quite a part of the family and while only a skunk, perhaps he could bring about as much credit and glory to his Creator as the average human of the present age. Attachment is a funny thing." The remaining skunk burrowed out of its pen the following spring and was never to be seen again.

The strain of seeing suffering farmers and starving livestock began to take its toll on MacEwan's devotion to institutionalized religion. He wondered what kind of God would make people and animals suffer as they had during the Depression. On January 1, 1938 he wrote: "My resolve on this New Year's Day, 'to sing the church hymns for their meaning and to make the devotional part of church service count in 1938.' Goodness knows, the minister's contributions are not proving what they should in changing troubled lives."

From here on, MacEwan began a gradual drift away from the formal structure of the church. It did not signify a weakening in his belief of a higher being, but rather, an opportunity to more fully explore the interdependency between living creatures. He would come to question if one life form was more important than another or, indeed, if personal prayer was more powerful and meaningful than a structured weekly worship service.

MacEwan and Ewen sent their second book to Thomas Nelson and Sons on March 12, 1938. The two men had written

"I think it's about time we took water more seriously than we have before. The MacEwans got their view of water when they went back to the land in 1915. No fence, no cultivation, no well. We bought a house for $25 and two horses for $50. We borrowed a plow and broke the land. Dad bought an auger and added extensions as he dug deeper. Ten, twenty, thirty, thirty-five feet."

the 400-page manuscript titled, *General Agriculture*, in less than four months. The title received wide acclaim and both authors were celebrated for their second contribution to the Canadian agriculture community. Later that spring, after so many years of drought, the faith of Western farmers was restored when they received 36 hours of rain. "Hope springs eternal," wrote MacEwan. The university farm averaged twelve bushels per acre graded number two during the fall harvest, twelve bushels more per acre than the year before.

Phyllis MacEwan gave birth to the couple's only child on May 3, 1939. Wrote the proud father in his journal: "Heather MacEwan born at 11:45 p.m. Length 23", head 14-1/2", hair black and lots of it. Disposition good. Proof that a good sire pays." Five days after the baby's birth, Phyllis returned home by ambulance. She preferred the tranquillity of her own home to the antiseptic atmosphere of the hospital, and she cut short the usual two-week stay. The baby was christened at the Forestry Farm by Dr. Nicol, who had also officiated at their marriage four years earlier.

On September 2, 1939 Britain declared war against Germany. Once again the slogan "Food will win the war" guided MacEwan. His friend and co-author Al Ewen, however, joined the Saskatoon Light Infantry in June 1940 and left him to administer the animal husbandry department. Despite the additional workload, he managed to compile *Breeds of Farm Livestock in Canada* during 1941. It was a technical book which traced breeds, histories and the influence of livestock bloodlines in Canada. It was the first book he wrote by himself, and although it was a valuable contribution to those in the field of animal husbandry, it had little appeal to the general reading audience.

Like all human-beings, Grant MacEwan had his share of quirks. One was his fondness for sleeping in his skin, a habit that had caused him minor embarrassment when he was a freshman at OAC. The other was an inclination to sleepwalk. When he was at the University of Saskatchewan, both idiosyncrasies combined and left the professor in a train aisle, dazed and nude.

MacEwan had been returning from Maple Creek, Saskatchewan on September 4, 1940 via a CPR passenger train to Regina after a horse show and ram sale. Bone tired, he squeezed into an upper berth and left his size twelve boots

"I will never forget the night that Mother came into the house and woke us kids. 'Get up. We think we've hit gas!' she said. Well, it wasn't gas. It was water that wasn't fit for humans or animals. We ended up having to haul water from a neighbor's well and most of it slopped over the side of the barrow as we pulled it home on the wagon. It was a discouraging thing."

"Water makes the world go around, more than any of us have ever realized. There is no scarcity of water in the world."

at the edge of the lower compartment for the porter to collect for the ritual polishing. At some point during the night, he found himself standing in the middle of the train aisle in his birthday suit. And because the porter had collected everyone's footwear, and all of the curtains to the berths were pulled shut, MacEwan was left with no clue as to where he belonged. Only sheer wits empowered the au naturel professor to peep into each upper berth until he found a vacant one. Many years later, when MacEwan was appointed Lieutenant-Governor of Alberta, he received a cryptogram from the president of the same rail company suggesting he travel with "adequate cover-up." The writer addressed the letter to "Shorty" and signed it as "Baldy."

Phyllis and Grant came from diametrically different backgrounds which, in most circumstances, complemented their relationship. She was fragile, artsy and a pleasant hostess; he was athletic, pragmatic and somewhat formal. She had enjoyed material possessions and travel as a child; he had bedded down in a flea-infested granary and slept under the stars for a time. On December 22, 1940 he wrote: "Phyllis reminds me that I'm short of shirts. I have five that I know of and I immediately think back to the time when I had only one shirt and two pairs of socks and was never stuck. She is not ready to agree that such experiences of youthful days are something warranting thanksgiving. Her own youth was much different from mine. While I struggled as a poor but hopeful youngster, she was the proud owner of a fur coat and a team of Shetland ponies, and was able to winter in California. Somehow, I feel convinced that the child that does not have too many luxuries and who is required to struggle a bit, has a great advantage later on, has a finer sense of values and a different form of sympathy. Perhaps I'm wrong, but I must be shown." This was the first indication spending may have been a source of friction between the two.

Grant MacEwan sold his White Fox, Saskatchewan property and reinvested the money into an Alberta property on January 4, 1941. He purchased half of 23-22-3 W5 at $12 acre from F.G. Lenn Renfrew Motors; this land came to be known as Priddis. Later that year, he bought another section of land near Longview, Alberta, from George Wambeke, for $10 per acre. However, it was the Priddis property, he wrote, that "... still fulfils my dream as one offering good soil, trees, scenery, water and a good climate for the writing life of which I dream."

In the meantime, he leased some of the land to the Renner family for pasture and made a separate agreement with Hugh McNair of Midnapore to summer fallow and seed grass on the cultivated land. Land was, after all, a tool to increase one's investment. His dream to live at Priddis and to write, however, remained just that — a dream. The property sat unoccupied until the 1970s when daughter Heather and her husband, Maxwell Foran, built their home there.

The lean professor was developing a reputation for being an excellent orator. Normally, he spoke about livestock, but in 1937 he was asked by J.A. Thompson to give a banquet address at the Moose Jaw Milk Producers' Association. The grand old man of the dairy business expressed to MacEwan his belief that government help to farmers during the Depression could constitute support for a welfare state, a thought he loathed. He suggested no reference be made to cows or dairying during the talk and thereby the subject could be avoided. Instead, he recommended the professor speak about the role of individualism in the building of Western Canada. Although the capitalist-thinking dairy man died before the speech was given, MacEwan made good his promise and spoke about the history of farming in the west, a topic in which he was well versed.

This marked his speaking debut in an area for which he became famous. Shortly after this speech, he bought his first typewriter, a $38.50 Remington portable from Eaton's. And the following year, he prepared and read the script "How Horses Came to Western Canada" over CBC radio. The public relations side of his personality began to evolve.

MacEwan's interest in history and his perception that Canadians yearned for stories about the country they loved, encouraged him to proceed. His popularity as an agricultural giant greased his entry; there was no need for him to gain name recognition. He filled the increasing requests for speeches with topics such as "Place Names," "The Romance of the Horse," and "Yesterdays and Tomorrow in Agriculture." CBC radio and numerous newspapers and publications courted the budding historian and author, and although they offered a paltry remuneration, it helped to form the financial foundation for the investment portfolio that eventually made him independently wealthy.

"Seventy percent of the world's surface is covered with water but ninety-seven percent of that amount is in the oceans and is salty beyond use. Two percent is in the world's glaciers. That leaves one percent in underground water.

Water is indestructible.

We talk about saving water. There's a billion and a half cubic miles of water in this world, the same amount today as there was 100 years ago. But it's a shifty thing, a treacherous thing. It leaves when you want it and that amounts to the same as a water shortage."

Grant MacEwan gives reasons for judgement at a stock show in Climax, Saskatchewan on April 8, 1941.

In 1942, CBC asked MacEwan to prepare four programs of his own liking. The "Sodbusters" series became a characterization of the fearless men, like his father, who eked their homesteads out of the untamed frontier. The shows were an instant hit amongst Canadians who, until then, were bored by facts and starved for stories. The program was renewed in 1943 and again in 1944. No doubt the timing of the presentation was everything. The Dominion was at war and nationalism was at an all time high. The series was subsequently published by Thomas Nelson and Sons in 1948, and although the author felt it should have been more severely edited for book form, it met with instant success, and most importantly it positioned MacEwan as an author to be reckoned with.

Grant MacEwan purchased his first automobile on June 28, 1941 and as would become his habit, he listed the engine, serial and license number in his diary. The two-door Plymouth sedan, for which he paid $1,327.59 plus $37 for insurance, made travelling with their two-year-old daughter somewhat easier. On the family's first trip together, which turned out to be Heather's first trip to Melfort, Alex and Bertha MacEwan made known their plans to sell the homestead.

Would Grant want the land? Although emotions ran high and the memories of working the land beside his father, and of sending brother George to Cody's General Store for Cane Mola were still crystal clear images of bygone days, his answer was no. From a practical standpoint, the land had never revealed a steady supply of good water, a natural resource the younger MacEwan considered vital to any agricultural operation.

Auctioneer Robert Barr of Milden presided over the sale of the farm on September 25, 1941. Grant wrote: ". . . The pure bred cattle were sold primarily, and the horses he refused to sell, the latter must be destroyed humanely or remain on the farm where they have worked." Jack Gammie, a neighbor to the north, assumed the property, moved into the house, and kept his promise to Alex that the horses would be allowed to graze for the rest of their days. Bertha and Alex MacEwan, who had come to the district with so little, and had worked so hard, moved to White Rock, BC. At a going-away dinner for the couple, the community wished them well and thanked them for leaving ". . . their son, Prof. Grant MacEwan to help educate at the University of Saskatchewan young men from all over the Province."

Entries in MacEwan's daily journals ranged from one- to five-word staccato-like bullets of information to entertaining and descriptive accounts of happenings, people and places. Where once his activities centered around Saskatoon, diary accounts paint a picture of his growing importance. By the early forties, his circle of influence included all of the prairie provinces, British Columbia and Ottawa. And while the names of acquaintances and average people continued to appear, the frequency of meetings with the elite and powerful increased. A peek between the pages would have confirmed for the more senior administrators of the university, that their animal husbandry professor had outgrown his position and was biding time by accepting new challenges.

Other entries such as: "Went to Melfort and found Mother again sick and in bed." were spliced between career achievements: "I was on CBC at 10:30 tonight with talk "Some Homestead Memories. $20.00" and world events: "Italy entered the war against the Allies." Revenue Canada could have easily accounted for all of MacEwan's sundry income by scanning the pages, for he meticulously recorded the rent he received for pasture land and payments for his avocation. His journals were also a register of research for future books. Stories which later

"It's the misfortune of many people in this world today, to have a shortage of water. Africa and other Third World countries have famines of two kinds, water and food."

"I think we could do a lot to relieve the famine of water. California's population has grown sensationally and they have always been behind in their supply of water."

appeared under titles such as *Fifty Might Men* or *Sodbusters* began as handwritten sketches of personalities who were dinner, train or bus companions.

Grant MacEwan entered his forties as an expert in his field, a published author, a respected livestock judge, and a loved husband and father. He owned a car and properties, and had established a savings account and a growing portfolio of blue-chip stocks and bonds, unbeknownst to his spouse. But it was his ability to quickly master routine, and his need for challenge and change that prompted him to accept the presidency of the Saskatoon Exhibition, previously a full-time job for an unpaid volunteer.

His first assignment as president was to plead with Ottawa for a relaxation of the rail restrictions that had been imposed to assist the movement of troops and equipment across the nation. MacEwan's appeal met with limited success. "No special trains for fairs, but free use of regular freights." His final report to the board of directors revealed a net profit of $27,000 — not only a record in the exhibition's history, but quite an accomplishment given that the country was preoccupied with the conflict in Europe.

MacEwan's popularity as an agriculturalist and his ability to get things done did not go unnoticed. For some time, political leaders of provincial and federal parties, and of every stripe, had observed him in action. In 1933, he had turned down the first invitation to represent the provincial Liberals, led by J.H. Gardiner, in Melfort. He sensed the timing was wrong and he had put off the solicitation by saying that he was happy in his position and that it offered him a challenge "for the present time."

On November 21, 1943, Gardiner, who by then was the federal minister of agriculture in Mackenzie King's Liberal government, made another pitch for the professor to enter the political arena, this time as the federal Liberal candidate for Saskatoon in an election that was still two years away. The Minister, still hoping he could secure a commitment from MacEwan, appointed him to the Board of Review for the Prairie Farm Assistance Act which assisted farmers whose crops had failed. This appointment suggested the government's desire to cement their relationship with the academic.

In January 1944, the leader of newly formed Progressive Conservative party, John Bracken offered to Grant

MacEwan the leadership of the Saskatchewan party. Bracken, like MacEwan, was a graduate of OAC, and had also completed his postgraduate work in the United States. He had headed up the Manitoba Agriculture College until politics lured him away, and he was fully aware of MacEwan's reputation. If the party was to take hold in Saskatchewan, he knew he needed the professor and was prepared to make any concession including renaming the movement to "The Agrarian Party."

Two months later, provincial Liberal leader W.J. Patterson also came calling. The legislature had been prorogued and the province was scheduled to go to the polls in June. "Same question: 'Will you go into politics?'" MacEwan wrote in his journal. He politely refused all requests and escaped the humiliating defeats that each of the constituencies he had been asked to represent suffered.

Grant MacEwan had misgivings about being a party man. He tended to side with Frederick Haultain, who believed that Canada could be a better place without the negative behavior that accompanies partisan politics. As a statesman, this conviction would serve MacEwan well, but as a future provincial politician, it amounted to suicide.

Despite a schedule which was so busy that MacEwan spent more time away than at home, he found time to visit Priddis with his uncle John Grant. The eighty-four-year-old widower wanted something constructive to do, so on April 13, 1944 the two men walked over the Priddis property and selected a site "up high with lots of scenery," for a log cabin. On June 6 — just seven weeks later — Grant, who had been in Calgary to speak at the Feed Manufacturers' Association, stopped by to see how the old man was doing. He found him, ". . . completing chinking of log house."

By the time Phyllis and Grant had celebrated their tenth wedding anniversary, she had her own life outside their marriage. She used the time her husband was away to visit with friends, play with Heather or read. She even renewed her interest in drama and performed the leading role in "Old Cinderella" for the Saskatoon Little Theatre Club.

Phyllis MacEwan, for the most part, was not a jealous wife despite Grant's frequent absences and long list of female acquaintances. However, when Sally Rand, a well-known fan dancer and entertainer, asked Grant to visit her Montana ranch and proffer advice about its management

"They could build desalination plants. They've considered hauling icebergs from the shores of the Arctic or Antarctica. If they could haul it to California, I suppose they could have water for a long time."

"And here were are in Canada with one of the largest supplies of fresh water in the world."

and livestock, a resounding "no" was heard from Phyllis. MacEwan, always the gentleman, assured his wife that the beautiful entertainer really did have "a good mind." Years later, Phyllis was impressed with a television interview Sally Rand gave and remarked to Heather, "Your father was right. She does have a good mind!"

Young Heather MacEwan looked forward to Christmas Day each year as a child, and later as an adolescent and young woman — not for the number of presents because her parents were careful not to spoil her — but because it was the one day in the year that her daddy reserved just for her. The two would skate or toboggan, and in the evening the family would enjoy a sumptuous meal prepared by her mother. Both father and daughter would discuss what they were going to do "at Christmas" during the later half of each year, and the child would hold the memories of the day close to her heart for the next six months until the planning began again.

She recognized early on that her father was a busy man with important duties that took him away from the family, sometimes overnight and frequently for a stretch of three to four days. There were no presents when he came home, but stories about where he had been and who he had met, and sometimes he would produce an Indian arrowhead for her to admire. As much as she idolized her father, it was her mother who attended the childhood rituals of Christmas concerts, dance recitals, and doctor's appointments. While Grant MacEwan was a better than average provider for his family, his constant drive to achieve was not without cost.

The fun and enjoyment of the Christmas of 1944 was overshadowed by the death of Bertha Grant MacEwan. A sorrowful son wrote in his journal: "Wire from Dad advising Mother passed away last night. 'Will leave with body on tomorrow night eight-fifty for Melfort. You arrange with Melfort undertaker to meet train and prepare grave. Dad.'" She was buried on December 30, 1944 at the Mount Pleasant Cemetery beside her youngest son, George MacEwan.

Eleven months later, Alex MacEwan died of cancer of the colon. The old gent had taken ill in Ontario and had been rushed to the Toronto General Hospital for surgery. Grant caught a flight out of Saskatoon and arrived at his father's bedside well after midnight. When a night nurse suggested he lie down on one of the vacant beds in the ward, he did so and fell soundly asleep. His slumber was rudely ended the next morning when a nurse, who believed him to be a new patient, shoved a thermometer in his mouth! An entry on November 14, 1945 reveals the strong bond that had developed between the two men. "My father passed on to his rest today. He would be 76 at his next birthday. He was a good and sensible father."

Within a two-year span of time, most of the individuals who had played a vital part in shaping Grant MacEwan's life, died. Marion Grant, his maternal aunt; Dean Rutherford, who had inspired him to pursue a university education; Dr. Morton, who had given him the avocation of history; President Murray, who had encouraged his career; and now both of his parents. One can only wonder how the disappearance of this circle of strong support affected him. Despite his crusty exterior, some of MacEwan's journal entries indicate the pain he felt. When Walter Murray died, he wrote, "It was the passing of one of God's gentlemen. I loved the old man."

In January 1945 the Royal Bank of Canada appointed Grant MacEwan as a member of their board of directors in a fence-mending exercise between the institution and agriculturalists. The bank had severely damaged its relationship with prairie farmers during the Depression when their callous financiers foreclosed on farmsteads and tossed out the starving families. While Professor MacEwan had accumulated some bank shares, others had also stockpiled the blue chip stock. MacEwan, however, had the profile which the Royal Bank needed if it was to reposition itself as a bank for western farmers.

Its new director was seen as a calming force, and later as a watchdog in Alberta where the Social Credit government had established the Alberta Treasury Branches in an effort to curtail the involvement of eastern banks in the financial affairs of Albertans. The appointment was also the first indication to those in the know that the folksy and frugal prophet of the prairies had accumulated more than accolades in his portfolio. The announcement was made in the financial section of the *Globe and Mail,* and it took the new administration of the University of Saskatchewan by surprise.

President Murray had retired in 1937 and had been replaced by J.S. Thomson, and L.E. Kirk became dean of agriculture when Malcolm Shaw was appointed to the Canadian Wheat Board by the federal Liberal administration.

Grant MacEwan with his Palomino mare, Pepita, 1946. — University of Calgary, Special Collections

Grant MacEwan judging Arabian class in Chilliwack, British Columbia.
— MacEwan-Foran Collection

While the previous hierarchy had valued MacEwan's skill at reaching out to the people and walking the land, the new administration was research-oriented and had little interest in meeting or talking with farmers. Moreover, the professor's acceptance to manage the Saskatoon Exhibition and be its president — albeit both were volunteer positions — was out of step with the new regime.

When Dean Kirk criticized the populist professor ". . . relative to assignments in agricultural work outside the university and the province," MacEwan returned the rebuke and recommended the dean "review carefully the substance . . ." of his 1945 annual report. He also pointed out that he had taken no holidays since his honeymoon, a decade previous, and that his absences related to university work amounted to just over four weeks. Although Kirk tried to bring MacEwan into line with the institution's new philosophy, he reluctantly accommodated the work style of the folksy, handshaking, back-patting farmer-turned-professor.

During this same time period, MacEwan tangled with many of his agricultural colleagues when he disagreed with them about renaming their professional association. The loosely formed group, who had previously called itself the Canadian Society of Technical Agriculturists, insisted they were "agrologists" not "technicians" and that they should be reorganized along the lines of a self-regulating professional body. Always the farmer's son, MacEwan predicted the society's lofty new name and trappings of power would destroy the harmonious working relationship between farmers and academics.

Legislation to make the organization self-governing was passed by the government of Saskatchewan in 1946. Three decades later, the University of Saskatchewan awoke one morning to find their agrologists too busy in their labs performing research for farmers who neither wanted nor needed it. It would seem that MacEwan's foresight outmatched the institution's hindsight.

A short entry dated May 8, 1945 reads: "Official VE Day (Victory in Europe Day)." Combat in the air and fields of Europe was drawing to an end and Canadians had much to be proud of. Their men on the ground and in the air had become an integral part of the offence which had bravely defended the democratic principles Canadians abided by. Moreover, agriculturalists across the West had maintained a steady supply of food to the front, and although rationing had been imposed on the home front, the supply of food far exceeded the meagre years of the Depression.

The desire of the federal Liberal party to bring Grant MacEwan aboard heated up in September 1945. The minister of agriculture, James Gardiner, who was also the previous provincial Liberal leader, learned that the newly formed Canadian Council of Beef Producers was trying to woo MacEwan to Calgary as its manager. In a confidential letter to the professor, the minister suggested that the government was prepared to abet his entry into Saskatchewan politics. Gardiner wrote: "You have been in my mind for many years as one who would add greatly to the strength of Liberalism in the province of Saskatchewan if you would associate yourself with it actively. . . I am sure that if you still have desires to enter the political field now is the time to do it, and that we could make the arrangements in Saskatchewan which would be necessary to your taking part."

Gardiner was under tremendous pressure from his federal colleagues to position a strong ally at the helm of the provincial party which was scheduled to select their new leader in August of 1946. He wanted John Walter Grant MacEwan — professor, historian, writer, broadcaster, speaker and, decidedly, a household name in the province of Saskatchewan — to become the party leader.

In May 1946, MacEwan was wined and dined first by Walter Tucker, the Liberal member for Rosthern, and then by Jimmy Gardiner. His answer remained the same, "Thanks, but no thanks." However, on August 1, 1946, the *Regina Leader-Post* not only profiled the known contenders for the leadership, it stated: "Prominently mentioned some time ago and known to have substantial backing is J.W.G. MacEwan, professor of animal husbandry at the University of Saskatchewan, who is known from one end of the Province to the other and who is personally acquainted with thousands of Saskatchewan's agricultural population."

MacEwan realized that if he attended the leadership convention he risked the possibility of being drafted by friends and elected before he could say no. He also knew that if he stayed away without a good excuse, he risked alienating the political party which he someday hoped to represent. The dilemma required a creative solution.

"I don't think the majority of Canadians like the idea of shipping water to the United States, or even selling it."

On the eve of the Liberal's convention, Grant MacEwan informed his wife that he would be away for a few days, but failed to disclose his whereabouts. And Phyllis MacEwan, who was accustomed to her husband's frequent absences, thought nothing was amiss until a fellow parishioner quizzed her during Sunday worship about the state of her husband's health and current hospitalization. Extremely distressed, Phyllis proceeded to the hospital where she found her spouse — his posterior positioned atop a rubber donut — committing a colorful account of his hospitalization to paper. The gutsy, straight-shooting professor had opted for what he believed to be the lesser of two evils; a haemorrhoidectomy instead of politics.

Forever the author, MacEwan described the medical procedure in *Baseline Operations,* which, due to its rather descriptive content, was never published. His first paragraph politely alludes to the fact that politics may have been, indeed, a preferable decision. "Haemorrhoidectomy is the highbrow name for a below-brow operation," wrote MacEwan. "Pile-ectomy would convey the meaning more clearly for most of us. It is one of the penalties imposed on man for coming out of the trees and walking on his hind legs too soon. Still, most people choose the surgery instead of a return to arboreal bliss. If the decision had to be made a second time, however, some of us might be found sharing quarters with the robins."

Grant MacEwan achieved the dubious honor of being the shortest serving Lieutenant-Governor of the Kiwanis International for western Canada. He attended the 1946 western convention in Winnipeg in his position as president of the Saskatoon club. Convention organizers had persuaded the popular speaker into giving the after-dinner address, "What Every Kiwanian Should Know About Western Canada." The Kiwanians, like the Liberals, recognized a leader when they heard one, and on August 20, 1946, the assembly elected Professor Grant MacEwan to its top-ranking position.

During the next 24 hours, however, Kiwanian Lieutenant-Governor MacEwan was interviewed and he accepted the deanship of the College of Agriculture at the University of Manitoba. The president of the University of Manitoba, Dr. A.W. Trueman, and the vice-chairman of the institution's Board of Governors, had placed a call to the hotel where MacEwan was staying and asked if the three might meet. After the meeting, the professor consulted with wife Phyllis who encouraged him to accept the position. His Kiwanian colleagues, accepted his resignation with grace and held another election during the closing hours of their convention.

Grant MacEwan returned to the University of Saskatchewan on August 22, 1946 and began the task of emptying his desk of eighteen years. The University of Manitoba confirmed his appointment in a press announcement that same day. According to writer Rusty Macdonald, the president of the Saskatchewan institution, Dr. Thomson, concluded his speech at the faculty's farewell dinner for the departing professor "by reciting Baroness Orczy's poem from The Scarlet Pimpernel."

The Second World War had put Canada's previous problems of federalism and sectionalism into decline. Even Quebec's age-old irritation against compulsory conscription was placated by Mackenzie King's holding out against compulsory service until the last years of the war. No doubt his outward sensitivity to the cultural and religious dogma of the French province helped the Liberal leader to score one more victory in the general election of 1945.

In 1947, citizenship was established giving a separate status apart from being a British subject to Canadians. Soon after, the payment of family allowances was instituted and a new swell of immigration from Britain and war-torn European countries began in earnest.

"But we Canadians pump oil and gas from our wells — which are becoming rapidly exhausted — sell it to the United States and beg for more sales. But water — no. That's sacred. That's our trust."

During Grant MacEwan's first five decades of life, the Dominion had attained nationhood. He witnessed boom and bust, and played an active role in its development both as a private citizen and as an influential academic. From the time of his birth in 1902, communication was established across the Atlantic, flight competed with land travel as a means of transportation, telephones linked families with distant relatives and friends, automobile highways connected the settled and remote parts of the country, and banks collaborated and established an organized clearing house for the country's monies. Towns and cities dotted the map from British Columbia to Newfoundland and from the edge of the 49th parallel to the Arctic. Canada had become a self-sufficient nation which had earned worldwide respect and admiration. In 1948, MacKenzie King retired from political life and Louis St.

Laurent was chosen to succeed the man who was reported in later years to be a spiritualist who enjoyed regular contact with his departed mother and other deceased relatives and friends.

The development of name recognition, so necessary in achieving entry into political circles, soon became a by-product of MacEwan's years as a professor, dean, author, speaker and community volunteer. Certainly, his appointment as the Dean of Agriculture and Home Economics at the University of Manitoba could be viewed in a practical or political vein. By then, he was recognized as a skilful and practical administrator, but more importantly, he had developed a superb set of public relation skills. There are numerous indications that he was used as a magnet to attract the much-needed enrolment dollars of government-sponsored World War II veterans to Manitoba's financially floundering agriculture program. But once again the role he was recruited for was switched midstream when the leadership of the university changed.

On August 25, 1946, just five days after accepting his new position, MacEwan returned to Winnipeg with Phyllis and bought, " . . . Ross Caver's house at 814 Somerset Ave, $7,900 cash." The real estate tycoon sold his Saskatoon house for which he had paid $4,240 in 1936 for $8,500 cash on September 13, 1946. Five days later, the MacEwans moved into their Winnipeg home. In the space of barely three weeks, Grant MacEwan had gone from the lower echelon of academia to a deanship and relocated his family from Saskatchewan to Manitoba.

Grant MacEwan's journal entries — which during his early years had contained expansive accounts of people met, places visited and events attended — became progressively shorter during his years at the University of Saskatchewan, and even briefer when he moved to Manitoba. Each day contained a notation about a speech, radio program, banquet or judging appearance. The weeks had no beginning or end and the Sabbath was frequently just another work day.

It would be impossible to surmise how many miles Grant MacEwan travelled or how many people he met over the next five years. Public appearances fed the inner needs of the man, and daughter Heather and wife Phyllis jockeyed for time with the head of their household. When nine-year-old Heather fell ill with the measles in 1948, and pneumonia threatened the youngster's well-being, Dean MacEwan was forced to cancel previously arranged engagements, "with regret." The family physician had prescribed penicillin for the deathly-ill child. The "silver bullet," however, was still being administered intramuscularly, and given that neither a home nurse nor hospital bed were available, it fell to Grant MacEwan to administer the antibiotic. The agriculturalist's animal husbandry training had included the giving of hypodermics. It must have been quite an ordeal for the normally frugal father who was known to dispense to his child a weekly allowance of ten cents with the caution to "save half." He bribed Heather into cooperating by giving her twenty-five cents for every injection that she "was good."

"I know kids today. They expect honesty."

Despite Grant MacEwan's impossibly heavy schedule of public commitments, it can be said with certainty that he maintained contact with his relatives and longtime friends. Brief notations in his journal indicate that whenever the dean was in a town where a relative or acquaintance resided, he made an effort to see or talk with them. In 1947, nearly four decades after he had sat in Miss Bertha Pilling's Brandon classroom, MacEwan's relationship with his ex-teacher was such that she bought his 1941 Plymouth when he purchased a new Buick. Not only was the transaction recorded in his journal, but the entry also included the serial numbers of the engines and chassis for both cars. Mileage was recorded to be "25,000 plus."

His appointment was reported in numerous publications including an editorial in the British Columbia farm journal *Country Life* titled, "Now it will be Dean MacEwan." The editorial described MacEwan as the "ablest and best-known judge of cattle and horses in Canada" and an authority on the problems of breeding and raising cattle. Moreover, the announcement heralded his dedication to agriculture and noted ". . . he pays no attention to the sacrifices of time and energy he has to make." Other reports suggested that the new dean's role was to create a positive working relationship between academia and the farmers of the province.

It was no other than Dean Grant MacEwan dressed in a western outfit, Stetson and riding his Palomino mare, Pepita, that led the College of Agriculture and Home Economics in the university's freshman parade that year. Over

2,000 students followed him through the streets of Winnipeg. The tall, lean farmboy-turned-professor-turned-dean was an instant hit with the undergraduates. "MacEwanmania" had hit the University of Manitoba.

Heather and Grant MacEwan lead the University of Manitoba freshman parade through the streets of Winnipeg, October 1949.
— MacEwan-Foran Collection

The faculty members MacEwan inherited, however, were another matter. His staff lacked purpose and were adrift. He reasoned that a project which captured the attention and talents of his agricultural staff was needed to rejuvenate the department. The dean appointed Dr. Norman James, a bacteriologist, to re-examine the entire curriculum with a view to making it possible for applicants who lacked the formal academic requirements to be "admitted for reason." No doubt MacEwan was still thankful for the allowances made on his behalf while he was at OAC. During MacEwan's tenure at the University of Manitoba, the entrance requirements were relaxed to allow applicants, without the full requirements, to qualify for admission. Moreover, the institution became more involved with the province's farmers.

With the agricultural side of his department humming satisfactorily, Grant MacEwan turned his attention to the home economics section for which he was also responsible. After discovering its long-installed but thoroughly capable section-head, Dr. Grace Gordon Hood, was close to retirement, he refrained from stamping his more active management style on the rather passive department. Time would produce a new personality and the possibility for new programming.

Phyllis and Grant MacEwan worked as a team to see a sense of purpose and comraderie restored to "their" faculty members. Rusty Macdonald, MacEwan's first biographer, wrote that "the Dean's parties" — which MacEwan paid for from his own pocket — were held to bring ". . . the staff and their families close together." He described these affairs as being a once-a-year celebration with music and dancing, games, food, and singsongs and held at a downtown hall or sometimes on campus. Apparently, Phyllis MacEwan and the president of the university, Dr. A.W. Trueman, would often be found "at the piano leading the singing, performing alone or in a duet."

It would seem from the outset that Grant MacEwan had solid support for his style of management and goals. Trueman — who was both the university's president and chairman of the Board of Governors, and F.W. Crawford, who was the comptroller and secretary of the board, and coincidentally, the son of Alex MacEwan's neighbor when the elder MacEwan farmed in Chater, were highly supportive of their new star. However, a recent appointment to the Board of Governors, Harold Fry, questioned Grant MacEwan's motives for maintaining a rather expansive speaking itinerary. From October 1946 to September 1947, the dean gave over one hundred speeches in and around Manitoba, and eleven to centres outside the province. Fry, a reasonably well-known farm journalist and editor, speculated with his colleagues that perhaps MacEwan stood to gain more personally from this exercise of taking academia to the farmers than did the university. He questioned whose reputation was being established, Dean Grant MacEwan's or, that of the University of Manitoba's faculty of agriculture?

For the most part, MacEwan ignored his adversary and looked for other ways to forge a relationship between the farmers and the institution. He discovered a lack of communication existed between the college of agriculture and its corresponding provincial department. Although his overtures to the deputy minister, H.H. Evans, reaped little in results, MacEwan found the head of Manitoba's Extension Department, Norman McKay, to be receptive. Establishing a working link between the two entities, however, would take more than just a little time.

MacEwan lost one of the two champions who supported his efforts when President Trueman accepted an

"Canada needs the vigor, the honesty and the imagination of youth."

offer of employment from the University of New Brunswick. The new president, A.H.S. Gillson, an academic fixated on research, was openly critical of MacEwan's lack of speed in making agricultural research an important underpinning of the program. Interestingly, the criticism had a similar ring to one heard in MacEwan's last year at the University of Saskatchewan. While it was true that the money to sponsor research was in short supply, could it have been that Grant MacEwan preferred taking science to the people rather than collecting qualitative and quantitative reports to fill the pages of his annual report?

In early May 1950, the waters of the Red River caused the most extensive and disastrous flood damage in Manitoba during the current century. Between May 1 and May 13, Grant MacEwan made five brief entries in his journal. Apparently there was insufficient time to elaborate. "May 1 - Red River rising ominously; May 7 - Floods threatening; May 8 - Took University offices at Broadway because Pembina Highway cut; May 12 - Evacuated family to Saskatoon. Floods increasingly serious; and May 13 - Water 30.1" above datum."

In Winnipeg, the Legislative Buildings were named Flood Control Headquarters. Under the leadership of Brig. R.E.A. Morton, over 15,000 men, women and children worked to build dikes and top up those already in existence. More than 100,000 Manitobans were forced out of their homes, and military troops from as far as Calgary and B.C. were airlifted into the flooded province. The damage exceeded $26 million.

Just as it had fallen to MacEwan to preserve the University of Saskatchewan farm's livestock during the famine years of the Depression, it fell to him to save as many of the University of Manitoba's farm stock from drowning as possible. He secured a boat and crew at the Municipal Hall and made the precarious voyage. Seemingly, the vessel's mariners had tipped up one too many rums while waiting for a passenger. At the Central Office Building he waded through waist-high water to the barns. With the help of others, the pigs and some cattle were herded into boxcars which stood on the university spur line. The remaining cattle were evacuated to Brandon by rail, and the sheep were shoved into the loft of the horse barn. MacEwan not only pulled and pushed animals into safety, he worked with the city engineers to keep the sewers open and contain the contamination.

On May 29, Premier Campbell appointed Grant MacEwan as a member of the three-man Red River Valley Board. Its task was to survey the disaster area, assess the damage to individuals and recommend the amount of compensation to be paid. Politicians, claimed MacEwan, made no attempt to coerce the board to award more funds to one constituency than another. It would appear that the disaster brought out the best in all, including politicians.

Grant MacEwan was the type of candidate that all political parties wish they could recruit. He had no skeletons in his closet, he had name recognition, the average citizen found a commonality with him and he had the intelligence and foresight required to assume a position of authority. Shortly after the dean arrived in Manitoba, a story broke in the *Winnipeg Free Press* saying that he would seek the Fairford constituency seat in an upcoming by-election. This flurry of political gossip in 1948 resulted when Premier Stuart Garson became the federal minister of justice and Douglas Campbell became premier of Manitoba and head of its coalition administration. Accordingly, Campbell wanted to stack his end of the administration and had tried to lure MacEwan into becoming his minister of agriculture. The headline was squashed by a statement from Premier Campbell's office but not before the report set the university administration and board of governors into a tizzy.

Not only did the ides of March 1951 bring sunshine and warmth to the prairie provinces, it brought another attempt by the federal Liberal administration to enlist Grant MacEwan as a would-be candidate. On March 17, 1951, MacEwan wrote in his journal that he ". . .visited Brandon quietly to receive invitations to take Liberal nomination for the federal by-election. Mr. G.R. Rowe, sec., Frank Taylor, Rivers, pres., Tim Bass of Cecil Hotel, sparkplug." A resolution was moved by H.O. Bell, seconded by W.A. Wood, ". . .that we invite Dean MacEwan to attend the Liberal convention on the understanding that all here present will support his nomination."

In politics, secrecy has no meaning. Despite MacEwan's best efforts to keep his impending candidacy out of the newspapers, the Calgary *Albertan* published the following editorial on March 28, 1951. "J.W. Grant MacEwan, dean of the agriculture and home economics program at the University of

"I also think that we need, more than ever, the experience of older people."

Manitoba, and one of the best known and best liked
agricultural men in the whole of Canada, has been invited to
take the Liberal nomination in Brandon. . . .a livestock judge,
an after-dinner speaker, an author, historian, traveller, as well
as a teacher and agricultural scientist, he is without doubt one
of the most competent men in the country, a man of unlimited
capacity and good judgement. If he could be induced to enter
politics he would add greatly to the reputation of the party he
sided with. The story is that Rt. Hon. Jimmy Gardiner will not
last much longer in cabinet and that Mr. MacEwan would take
his place as minister of agriculture."

While the many discussions between the dean and
Prime Minister Louis St. Laurent suggested that MacEwan
would play an important role within the Liberal cabinet if
elected, there were no promises. The discussion about Grant
MacEwan's possible entry into the political arena, however,
provoked the administration of the University of Manitoba to
issue an ultimatum. On April 12, 1951, the board of governors
of the university passed the following resolution. "That if and
when the present Dean of Agriculture accepts the nomination
as a candidate at an election for a seat in the House of
Commons in the forthcoming by-election in the constituency of
Brandon, he shall immediately submit his resignation."

Perhaps Grant MacEwan felt there was no room to
back out this time, or perchance, it was the change he wanted
and needed. Certainly, he had performed miracles in making
the University of Manitoba a welcome name in barns and show
rings throughout the province, and country. And where he had
used the excuse of a haemorrhoidectomy to avoid a previous
provincial draft, the same reason could not be used again. On
April 19, 1951, Grant MacEwan accepted the nomination to
become the federal Liberal candidate for the upcoming
Brandon by-election. He submitted his resignation to the
administration of the university immediately.

President Gillson accepted MacEwan's resignation
gracefully. He eloquently phrased, in a letter to the resigning
dean, the feelings of most Westerners: "I have long had the
feeling that your future career might lie away from the
University, but I have refused to think about it until the
present time. However, now that another career is opening
before you I would like to say how indebted I am to you for the

close cooperation which you have given to me at all times since I have been at the University. It is clear that we shall all miss you, but we are confident that not only will Higher Education have a new champion in Ottawa, but that the point of view of Western Canada will be stated with emphasis and clarity." Twenty-three years of university work had come to a close and Grant MacEwan was about to catch a new career wave — politics.

"They seek him here, they seek him there,
those Frenchies seek him everywhere.
Is he in heaven? Is he in hell?
That dammed, elusive Pimpernel!"
— The Scarlet Pimpernel

SECTION V

Grant MacEwan (circa 1950).
— MacEwan-Foran Collection

The Politician & Statesman

The House of Commons welcomed Louis Stephen St. Laurent, a fluently bilingual lawyer from Quebec City, as its twelfth prime minister on November 15, 1948. Prime Minister Mackenzie King had recruited the Quebecker in 1941, and when he retired, St. Laurent became his chosen successor. The grandfatherly appearance and mannerisms of the new prime minister had a soothing effect on the Canadian public. During the previous two decades, the Depression had bared the nation's cupboards and emptied bank accounts while the Second World War had ripped loved ones away from family and friends, often leaving their young souls on far-off beaches. St. Laurent's intelligence and patriotic spirit succeeded in winning the respect of both friend and foe alike.

On June 27, 1949 the federal Liberals were led by St. Laurent to their then largest majority ever. The party secured 193 seats while the Progressive Conservatives under the leadership of George Drew won 42, the CCF 12, Social Credit 10, and independents five. It was then that Lester Pearson, C.D. Howe, Douglas Abbott and Brooke Claxton made their first appearance in parliament. On the global stage, Canada became a NATO partner, supplying forces to fight in Korea on behalf of the United Nations. At home, the government extended old-age pensions; enacted hospital insurance; approved equalization payments among the provinces and welcomed Newfoundland as a formal partner of the Confederation.

The end of the 1940s and beginning of the 1950s heralded a new stage in the development of the onetime British colony. King George VI gave his assent on December 16, 1949 to a statute before the British Parliament which gave Canada limited power to amend the British North America Act. On August 10, 1949, the four-engine Avro made its maiden flight at Malton, Ontario. And on June 15, 1950, the *Cité Libre*, edited by Gérard Pelletier and Pierre Trudeau, appeared on newsstands. The magazine counselled Quebeckers "to throw out the thousand prejudices with which the past burdens the present, and to build for the new man."

By 1951 the political overtures by the federal Liberal government grew into a crescendo that was impossible for Dean Grant MacEwan to ignore. Their bid for the dean was particularly appealing in that the excitement and need which World War II veterans brought to the University of Manitoba campus had faded. Moreover, the importance of farming as a pivotal industry in the Canadian economy had begun its decline.

Grant MacEwan's entry into the federal political arena by way of the 1951 Brandon-Souris by-election was thought to be a foregone conclusion. The idea of defeat had never entered the minds of the "wannabe" politician or the smug Liberals who had recruited the candidate. The dean of agriculture and home economics at the University of Manitoba confidently resigned from his position and accepted, on April 19, 1951, the challenge to run in the by-election. MacEwan had everything a successful member of parliament needed. He not only had name-recognition and respect, but he belonged to the new crop of learned individuals. His populist manner, however, scored less votes than the native son he contested, and the dean was resoundly trounced by Conservative Walter Dinsdale.

During the course of the campaign, Grant MacEwan became painfully aware of the follies that characterize politics as well as its symbiotic relationship with the media. An advertisement in a Brandon newspaper to announce a radio program starring MacEwan bore the headline, "Mr. Pile Sufferer" — no doubt a crude reminder of how he had turned and run from a previous political proposition. And when the radio program went off the air in the middle of the candidate's chat, some listeners were bold enough to suggest that the other party must have cut the wires. Even MacEwan's own clergyman joined the salvo by first noting his presence in a pew, and then by delivering a sermon based upon Luke 3:5 which included the passage ". . . and the crooked shall be made straight."

Mail to the candidate brought messages of congratulations, concern and condolences. In his book, *Poking into Politics*, MacEwan recounted one of the letters he received. "Dear Grant, I once thought you were too honest for politics but now that I know you better, I think you will do just fine." Other letters blatantly criticized elected officials, and went on to describe them as ". . . ignorant and stupid and most of the clever ones are rogues."

MacEwan quickly discovered that his lofty ideals about how the country should be governed was of little concern to

"Politics has always had its shortcomings."

"Politics has always had its tests, always had its scoundrels, but there were saints as well as sinners in public life."

the voting public or pollsters. Rather, his opinion about unions and drinking ranked right up there with his personal preferences for cigarettes, whisky and underwear. He also learned that his days in academia had impaired his ability to assess the background of "nice" people. Following a dance at the Polish Hall, where he had been instructed to ". . . greet every woman as though she were a queen," he kissed the hand of one of his dance partners. Upon his departure he asked a friend about her identity and was promptly told, ". . . she's the one who is picked up now and then for running the bawdy house on the next street."

On June 25, 1951 a total of 19,613 voters cast their ballots for the next member of parliament for Brandon in a by-election. The Progressive Conservative candidate, Walter Dinsdale secured 11,124 of those votes. The Liberal candidate, John Walter Grant MacEwan, was massacred.

The yearly remuneration of Members of the House of Commons at that time was a sessional indemnity of $4,000. In addition, they received $2,000 as an annual expense allowance, paid at the end of each calendar year. This allowance was not subject to income tax.

Surely it was not the pay which had drawn MacEwan to politics, for as dean he had earned a substantially larger salary and enjoyed job security. Perhaps it was his belief that every citizen should give back some of one's time toward service for his country, or maybe it was his desire for change that caused him to shuck the security of the past for an uncertain future.

The swells of success that MacEwan had been riding crashed around his ears. Not only had he lost the by-election, he had been forced to forfeit his prestigious position as dean of agriculture in order to accept the nomination. This was surely a watershed for a man who had shunned failure and enjoyed perpetual mastery in whatever he undertook. Never had this man been dealt such a bitter blow to his career, nor had his future ever looked so bleak as on the morning after his defeat. MacEwan was, after all, forty-nine years of age and he had no imminent prospect for employment. The pages of his daily appointment book remained blank for the first weeks following his defeat.

It was a period of abyss for the farmboy from Melfort. It was also when Grant MacEwan finalized the text for *Between Red and the Rockies* which he dedicated "To Heather who was shaking the table much of the time when her daddy was writing this story." At least his avocation was on firm footing.

When Mr. MacEwan — now minus the title of "Dean" — learned that the managing director of the Calgary Exhibition and Stampede office, H. Charles Yule, had resigned, he enquired about the possibility of future employment. The position, he was informed, had been promised to Saskatchewan's deputy minister of agriculture. The fact that a one-term bureaucrat was worth more than a failed wannabe Liberal member of parliament became a harsh reality for Grant MacEwan.

On February 14, 1952, the *Western Producer* announced Grant MacEwan would become its new agricultural editor. The position was short-lived. An outbreak of foot-and-mouth disease amongst Canadian livestock prompted MacEwan to write a story about the disease and its consequences. The closure of the American border to cloven-hoofed animals forced the Western Section of the Council of Canadian Beef Producers to take aggressive action in order to shore up the subsequent downward spiral of price paid for beef.

On April 17, 1952 the Beef Producers asked Grant MacEwan to consider the position of manager with a purpose of mounting a public relations and product promotion campaign for Canada's beleaguered beef and cattle industry. The Calgary-based job came with a salary of $6,500 plus a $500 allowance for moving. MacEwan would administer a minimum yearly budget of $15,000 which would cover the costs of a secretarial staff, rent, travel, publicity, and other office expenses. Additionally, the Council was more than willing to allow Grant to continue his judging of livestock. The agreement was open-ended and if for any reason the arrangement did not work out, neither of the parties would be forced to complete the three-year contract.

The MacEwan's 814 Sommerset Avenue house was put up for sale and although the Winnipeg real estate market was in a slump, Grant managed to recoup his 1946 purchase price. There was no fanfare when the former dean left Manitoba — the province of his birth — only two entries in his little black appointment book: "Friday June 27, 1952 -

"I think the scoundrels have had a better run in politics than the saints have."

Loaded out. Saturday June 28, 1952 - Left Winnipeg at 11 a.m." The MacEwans arrived in Priddis on July 1, 1952, ". . . where they had land and where opportunities for writing appeared attractive."

It was, perhaps, somewhat ironic that Grant MacEwan's arrival in the province he chose to call home occurred on the anniversary of the country he had worked so hard to serve. But even more bizarre was the fact that both father and son had met personal defeat in the same city. Where Alex MacEwan had been lured off the land by Brandon's then buoyant business and real estate market, Grant had been persuaded to abandon his university post and jump into the polluted pool of politics. Both men had desired change, failed and were forced to begin again. Both had moved further west, Alex to Saskatchewan and Grant to Alberta. In each case, their respective wives became a significant force in the rebuilding process.

The log cabin which Grant MacEwan's Uncle John Grant had built in 1944 became the family's home for the summer. Just as Bertha had turned the crude shack into a home for her family, Phyllis made the rustic cottage comfortable and treated the experience as an adventure with one minor exception.

One evening, when the family had left for an invitation in the city, their car became marooned in muck. Rain had turned the dirt road to the property into a quagmire. Grant, who was convinced he could push the vehicle out of the mud, instructed Phyllis to "hold the wheel." With a similar brute strength that Alex MacEwan had used to break the virgin sod, Grant tried to budge the Buick out of the gumbo. "Mother was convinced Father would have a heart attack," recalled Heather MacEwan. "He finally gave up and we slept in the car that night." The next morning, Bob Renner, whose parents had leased the MacEwans' fields for grazing for many years, pulled the car out of the mud with his tractor. Renner then took the dirty and dejected family to his farmhouse for breakfast. Soon after, the MacEwans moved to a bungalow in northwest Calgary.

MacEwan was a natural for his new position. He was familiar with most of the Council's members, he knew more about the pedigrees of the cattle than their owners, and he had known the editor of the industry's magazine, *The Canadian*

Cattlemen, for many years. It should have been the perfect working situation but it wasn't. In December 1953, United Grain Growers assumed responsibility for the publication and MacEwan's thrice-per-issue contributions disappeared. Moreover, there was little support or money for the public relations campaign; the outbreak of foot and mouth disease was now just a news event of the past. The purpose that Grant MacEwan needed to give his work meaning began to vanish. By the spring of 1955 he was concluding this chapter in his career.

In Alberta, Grant MacEwan caught the last of the great career surges which carried him to new heights and challenged his talents in a way never done before. The Stampede City was entering a period of unbridled growth and what was seen by many to be an era of lurid expenditure. Council needed a conscience and the Civic Government Association determined that voice would be Grant MacEwan.

The former dean was apprehensive about tossing his hat in the political ring again. The Brandon loss was still a fresh and bitter memory, not so much for the experience itself but for the manner in which the university had discharged him. Moreover, MacEwan's decision to enter the old boys' club of civic politics seemed somewhat out of step for the man who, throughout his lifetime, had placed great value on self-reliance and maintained the highest respect for individual initiative. It was, however, his belief in the need for people to give of themselves for the common good which aroused his desire to serve.

But, how on earth, he questioned his boosters, could the voters of Calgary be convinced to vote for him? He was just a Manitoba farmboy who was raised, educated and made his career in the other two prairie provinces. And he had lived only fourteen months in the city. To his query came the response, "If people knew you better, they probably wouldn't vote for you. This is your chance."

Like the biblical admonition from Ecclesiastes — "To every thing there is a season, and a time to every purpose under the heaven" — MacEwan seized the opportunity. On October 14, 1953 he wrote in his appointment book: "Elected Alderman." His reputation for honesty was larger than life. According to MacEwan's book, *Poking into Politics*, a local editor even went so far as to praise the electorate for their wise choice.

"I want to be a Canadian first, I'll be an Albertan second, I'll be a Calgarian third."

Calgary city council. Grant MacEwan (front, right) .
— Glenbow Archives

Calgary enjoyed spectacular growth during the decade following the Second World War. Its population grew from 100,000 to 130,000 between 1941 and 1951. When Imperial Oil struck oil in 1947 at Leduc — there was no looking back. The discovery of the huge sedimentary oil reserve set off a flurry of activity throughout the province. In Calgary, the quantity and total dollar value for building permits went from 1,523 for $2.6 million in construction in 1941 to 4,136 building projects for a value of $25.8 million in 1951. And by 1958 there were a total of 7,228 projects with a value of over $100 million. The boundaries of the city pushed beyond the Bow and Elbow Rivers and consumed the rolling foothills and prairie grass. Demand for municipal services escalated as the suburbs spread.

The honeymoon between council and the media was predictably short-lived. MacEwan quickly discovered honesty had a lower priority in politics than the whim of lobby groups, and Calgary had more than its fair share of "Not in My Backyard(ers)." He wrote of the NIMBYs ". . . the petitioners wanted more industry but fewer smoke stacks to pollute city air, better transit service but lower fares, improved garbage disposal but no sanitary land fills within miles."

During the spring of 1955 MacEwan had mostly concluded his work at the Council of Beef Producers. To ensure the electorate had easy access to him, and to facilitate his writing, he rented an office in the McLean Block. Occasionally, he accepted a consulting contract. One of these arrangements saw him prepare a forecast of the prospects in the north-western United States for the Royalite Oil Company. The firm was interested in establishing a fertilizer factory.

MacEwan's futuristic report outlined the potential for the yet-to-develop fertilizer market in the northwestern American States and the Canadian Prairies. However, when Royalite received Grant MacEwan's invoice for services, there were probably a few quizzical looks. The alderman and part-time consultant billed the multi-national for $54.40. The fee included transportation, food, accommodation and the writing of the report. Royalite proffered their appreciation for what must have been their cheapest consulting contract ever and promptly sent a cheque to MacEwan for $103.40 — $53.40 as invoiced and an honorarium of $50.00.

Alderman MacEwan was neither a frequent speaker nor an aggressive debater. He can be credited, however, for making the motion in 1955 that established the University of Calgary on its present campus. In time, the public learned that they could count on their professor-turned-politician to side with motions for fiscal restraint. In 1958 when an annual levy of 10.2 mills was required to service Calgary's $2.8 million gross debt, MacEwan moved that council ". . . accept as its objective the complete arresting of this growth of debt in the next ten-year period, and that the first step in a direction of a pay-as-you-go policy be taken in preparing the 1959 budget." Although the motion was defeated seven to six — Mayor Don Mackay's vote tipped the balance — the rookie alderman had mastered a remarkable show of support.

Grant MacEwan served as a Calgary alderman from 1954 until 1963 with a short break between 1958 and 1959 when he was the leader of the Alberta Liberal Party. He had been elected to the provincial assembly on June 29, 1955 and for three years served as both an MLA and alderman. A workaholic who abhorred laziness, MacEwan reasoned to his concerned electorate that since he was neither the mayor nor a cabinet minister, he could — thank you very much — handle both positions! He wrote that "a backbencher on either the Government or Opposition side was appreciably less onerous than serving on a Council within easy calling range of every citizen . . ."

Alderman Grant MacEwan.
— Glenbow Archives

"If we're going to spread power around ten provinces, I don't know how we're going to escape having ten Balkan states in this country. I think someone is going to live to regret that decision, to dilute the unifying force, the federal government."

The 1955 provincial election had followed a bitter and aggressive campaign by both the Socreds and the Liberals. Grant MacEwan openly denounced the Social Credit government of Premier Ernest C. Manning for their right-wing policies that muzzled contemporary democracy. When the votes were tallied on June 29, 1955, the provincial Liberals led by J. Harper Prowse had won 15 of the 61 seats. The Social Credit's 52 seats were reduced to 37.

During the first session of the thirteenth legislature, Grant MacEwan urged the government to plant trees where cutting had occurred, to build future schools and roads based on population trends, not constituency patronage, and to improve the province's museums so that Alberta's rich history would be preserved in perpetuity. Albertans were well served by the conscience of the practical thinking backbencher.

MacEwan's years in provincial politics must have seemed like a flashback to his federal flier. He soon discovered the Alberta assembly also thrived on its fair share of enemies, moles and general warfare which is driven by partisan politics, something the new MLA came to deplore. Yet, once smitten by the political process, it is difficult to withdraw.

In the fall of 1958, Liberal leader Harper Prowse resigned and Grant MacEwan was pushed into the leadership arena. In Saskatchewan he had used the excuse of a haemorrhoidectomy to avoid the draft, but this time he was ready and willing. He won the party leadership on the second ballot and faced the impossible task of curtailing Ernest Manning and his Social Credit army.

Encouragement and advice flowed freely following his election. One newspaper, however, baited its readers with a catchy headline. Whereas the official media release following the leadership convention described MacEwan as a "lean and lanky westerner" — the weekly described him as a "mean and cranky westerner." The editor, a known conservative supporter, later apologized for the so-called typographical error.

Notwithstanding the popularity MacEwan enjoyed on the Calgary council, breaking the Socred's 23-year grasp on Albertans turned out to be his Waterloo. Between January 1, 1959 and June 18, 1959 the Liberal leader spoke at 101 meetings, did ten radio and eight television appearances, travelled 4,500 miles in one two-week period and knocked on 3,000 doors in his north Calgary constituency. But "Broadcast

Ernie" — a stodgy, Bible-thumping facsimile of his mentor "Bible Bill Aberhart" — was a match bigger than life for MacEwan. On June 18, 1959, the Alberta Liberal Party was annihilated. The party's fifteen seats in the legislature were reduced to one. Even the Liberal leader lost his seat.

Grant MacEwan, MLA and Leader of the Liberal Party of Alberta addresses the legislature. Premier Ernest Manning (front, right) listens.
— Alberta Public Affairs/MacEwan-Foran Collection

MacEwan, who occupied the helm for six short months before the election, had little time to assemble a slate of candidates or to prepare and sell a platform to the electorate. In addition, seasoned Liberals resigned and new candidates had to be recruited for more than half of the province's sixty-five constituencies. He quickly found out that enlisting women for candidates was less difficult than men. At least they didn't have to ask for their wife's permission. In the Peace River constituency, 41-year-old James Mann refused the nomination because he lacked his wife's approval. He pointed out, much to the humor of the assembled Liberals, that he didn't have ". . . to sleep with the Liberal Party" when all was said and done.

The campaign trail was far from dull. When MacEwan knocked on one constituent's door, the home-owner, who grouped politicians with baby-kissers, informed him the couple's first baby was not due for another week. "You can come back then," he said shutting the door. And when a sparrow found its way into the Liberal leader's Falher Hotel room, he surmised the Conservatives would use it by announcing: "MacEwan had a chicken in his room all night."

"We worked to win, knocked on doors, travelled far, kissed babies and made speeches, but lost the gamble," wrote Grant MacEwan. The cards were inevitably stacked against a Liberal win. Only months before the election, the Social Credit party had disproportionately weighted the rural vote by discontinuing the province's proportional representation system. The Socreds were fully aware that their support lay in rural Alberta, and that urban centres such as Edmonton presented a Red risk. Conservative governments which followed the Socred administration have continued to benefit from this political maneuver.

Disappointment and party politics must have by now seemed synonymous to MacEwan. His sojourn into this battlefield, however, gave the people of Alberta ample time to appraise the man who would soon become a household name. He resigned as the leader of the Liberal party in 1960 and once more pondered his future. Grant MacEwan was fifty-eight years of age.

Would Grant MacEwan flee to Priddis, his prized property on the Eastern Slopes and finally devote his life to writing? The idea was somewhat appealing, but not compelling. Would his family and his own privacy finally take precedence over his public? From the very beginning of his marriage to Phyllis, she, and later Heather, the couple's daughter, accepted that they were secondary to the family patriarch's work commitments.

Three months after MacEwan was drubbed by Manning, the former Calgary alderman re-entered civic politics and topped the polls. The same voters who had said "no" to him in June gave him a resounding "yes" in October. In his book, *Poking into Politics,* MacEwan complained that, "The people who voted against me in the provincial election now supported me with the biggest aldermanic vote in the city. It was not easy to understand."

His reputation as an alderman and a writer began to grow exponentially. The swell of positive public opinion not only praised his performance on city council — it supported his literary efforts with purchasing power. MacEwan became a book-a-year writer and an indispensable commodity for fledging prairie publishing houses such as *Western Producer Prairie Books* and *The Institute of Applied Art.*

"I don't see how, if we have the aspirations we've always had, that we can avoid that unifying central force, the Government of Canada."

Eye Opener Bob, published by The Institute of Applied Art in 1957, was a runaway success. Grant MacEwan brought Bob Edwards to life, the Calgary Eye Opener's venerable founder, publisher, and one and only reporter. The following year, Western Producer Prairie Books published *Fifty Mighty Men,* a collection of stories about men in Canada's vanguard. It became an instant best-seller. Edmonton's diminutive Institute of Applied Art was not to be outdone. It published *Calgary Cavalcade,* also in 1958, and then what may have been MacEwan's most profitable work, *John Ware's Cow Country.* His 1960 poignant account of the Negro horseman and rancher found a receptive readership. Ware, born in 1845 into the slavery market of South Carolina, had through a turn of events settled east of Brooks, Alberta, in 1890. It is not clear whether MacEwan chose to research and write about one of Canada's only black ranchers during the hype of the Civil Rights Movement, or if the timing of its conclusion and publishing was coincidental.

"We've got great compromisers in government today who'll trade, and their trades are not always good."

The book attracted considerable attention from film-makers in Canada, the United States and Great Britain. Soon after its release, Irwin Rose, a Montreal director, secured a 90-day option on the manuscript. In a letter to MacEwan, dated September 1, 1963, he wrote, "My partner in California is now negotiating with director John Ford and star John Wayne as well as the most highly regarded colored actor in the world . . ."

Western Producer Prairie Books published *Blazing the Old Cattle Trail* in 1962 and *Hoofprints and Hitchingposts* in 1964. While MacEwan compiled many magnificent stories about the movement of livestock for the title *Blazing the Old Cattle Trail,* no story is more remarkable than his account of the Eppard sheep drive. MacEwan, who had been personally acquainted the family during his days at the University of Saskatchewan, is not shy in describing the hardship and challenges the family faced in shepherding their flock of three hundred sheep from Estevan, Saskatchewan to Vernon, British Columbia.

It would be difficult to ascertain how much influence Grant MacEwan's conservation-based column, *Our Natural Heritage* — which began in the Calgary Herald on December 8, 1956 — had to do with his growing popularity. Basil Dean, the publisher of the Herald and MacEwan had innocently bumped into one another at a pre-Christmas reception. Since

"We've yielded here and there. We've said: 'I'll give you this if you give me that.' I think history is going to be pretty critical of our actions."

both men were straight-shooters and not cocktail sippers, their conversation turned to other more interesting subjects. By the end of the evening, the publisher, who had strong convictions about the exploitation of Canada's natural resources, secured a new columnist by the name of Grant MacEwan. Herald readers were treated to a total of 1,854 columns over the next 36 years.

MacEwan's column caught the swell of the environmental movement. Its message was simple: "We must preserve the best of the past and conserve our precious supply of natural resources." Again, timing was everything. The general public was becoming more aware of the environment and increasingly concerned for its well-being. Landmark works such as Rachel Carson's *Silent Spring* had exposed the risk of indiscriminate use of pesticides. Television brought nature-films into many homes and people began to realize that they were living in a rapidly shrinking world. Suburbia was quickly encroaching upon the little natural landscape that remained. There was an awakening to the dependence of human survival on the environment. In Grant MacEwan, the public found a protector and spokesman for Nature's storehouse.

The writing of books or a weekly column requires a tremendous amount of research before the first words are committed to paper. It was MacEwan's extraordinary ability to manage time that allowed him to juggle the demands of city council, his responsibility as a MLA and the leader of the Liberal party in addition to writing a weekly column and a book a year.

The accumulation of research for his writing became an effortless and inexpensive process. He assembled files of information on topics that interested him during his countless rounds of speaking and livestock judging engagements. In these rural communities he tapped into rich sources of historic data in addition to the colorful folklore that came to characterize his writing. His priceless ability to relate to people — young and old, rich and poor — turned probing interviews into pleasant conversations. By making his avocation into an extension of his work, he was able to avoid and control travel and accommodation costs, the most inhibiting expenses that a writer incurs. As his reputation grew and invitations came from further afield, MacEwan was able to extend his range of research. He began to model his behavior, consciously or unknowingly after the colorful characters he

wrote about, and, increasingly, the public placed him on the
same pedestal as the heroes he portrayed in his books.

*Grant MacEwan poses with Les Robson and Barbara Tussey at the Second
Annual All Morgan Show in Abbotsford, British Columbia, July 1964.*
— MacEwan-Foran Collection

During the time that MacEwan served as a Calgary
alderman and mayor, he listed his occupation on taxation
forms as, "Public service, writing and some radio." And while
some of his acquaintances probably wondered about the
financial health of the family, they need not have worried.

Grant MacEwan was financially independent by the
time he was forced to resign from the University of Manitoba
in 1951. On his 1952 T1 General Tax Form, he recorded his
total income to be $11,221.83. His position as general
manager of the Council of Canadian Beef Producers earned
him $3,249.96 — the remaining amount was earned from
writing, speeches, property rent, dividends, and bond and
bank account interest. Although one might be tempted to

Heather MacEwan poses for junior high graduation, June 1953.
— MacEwan-Foran Collection

consider his yearly income paltry by today's standards, the average annual earnings of a production worker for the same time period were $2,647 and $3,513 for a supervisory or office employee. He was earning three times the amount earned by other white-collar professionals.

MacEwan's income climbed to $23,878.86 by the end of 1965. His salary as mayor of Calgary accounted for $11,152.75 and the remaining $12,726.11 came from investments and writing royalties. Blue-collar workers of the day earned an average annual wage of $4,492 and white-collar professionals enjoyed a salary medium of $6,185. By all standards of measurement — Grant MacEwan was earning big bucks.

There was, however, a high personal cost to this self-imposed level of activity, and the price for his fame was paid for by wife Phyllis and daughter Heather. Christmas Day remained the single family day in the year when Grant MacEwan refused invitations from his public. But for the rest of the year, communication between MacEwan and his wife and daughter was fleeting at best. The family had no sooner moved to Calgary when thirteen-year-old Heather suffered from an appendicitis attack which required surgery. It was Phyllis who rushed her daughter to hospital while Grant proceeded to one of his speaking engagements.

When 91-year-old Grant MacEwan accompanied his daughter Heather to an elementary school music performance that was being directed by his grand-daughter, he asked Heather in a booming voice, "Were you ever in a school performance?" The pace MacEwan inflicted on himself prevented the sharing of precious moments and events that weave a family together. There were no family vacations, only a steady stream of engagements.

It could be argued that the societal roles of the time and day were different, and that head of the household's role was to provide adequate income to support the lifestyle of the family. This would seem not to be the case in the MacEwan family. While Grant MacEwan did work particularly hard and was highly successful in his endeavors, the spoils of his efforts were not spent on his wife or daughter. Rather, he imposed strict frugality upon Phyllis and repeatedly cautioned her against spending any money.

MacEwan recorded every nickel he spent in the little appointment book he carried with him. Purchases such as

"Heather's Easter Egg - \$.25" or "Brick Ice Cream - \$.25" or "Extra for groceries - \$5.00" were meticulously accounted for, and at the end of the month the expenditures were tallied. "I grew up believing we were poor," declared his daughter. "Father treated Mother and me as if we were spendthrifts."

The 1960s marked a turbulent time in Canada's social and political development. The scheduled hanging of 14-year-old Steven Truscott, despite his apparent innocence, rocked the Canadian judicial system and confronted society with the moral dilemma of capital punishment. The New Democratic Party — dedicated to a planned economy, full employment and a high standard of living, emerged under the leadership of Tommy Douglas. Universal medicare began in Saskatchewan, and the drug thalidomide was linked to a rash of deformed babies. Beatlemania and North Vietnam competed for airtime and the acronym FLQ made fleeting appearances in the mastheads of Canadian newspapers.

When the Cold War peaked in October 1962 with the Bay of Pigs crisis, Canadian forces readied themselves the best they could. The Canadian CF-101 fighters, however, were not equipped with missiles. Moreover, the nation's NORAD Bomarc-B missiles lacked warheads. The decision of Diefenbaker's Conservative government to cancel its order for the Avro Arrow CF-105 — a supersonic, twin-engine, all-weather interceptor jet aircraft — was once again an unpopular news topic.

In 1963 the federal Liberals under the leadership of Lester Pearson defeated John Diefenbaker's Conservatives to win a minority government. Canadian hearts swelled with pride on February 15, 1965 when the nation's new Maple Leaf flag was unfurled on Parliament Hill. Less than a month later, the House of Commons approved the Canada Pension Plan. Mike Pearson's Liberals won another minority government in November 1965, and the three "wisemen" from Quebec — Pierre Trudeau, Jean Marchand, and Gérard Pelletier — commenced their political careers.

In 1966 the federal justice minister, Lucien Cardin, revealed that a former Tory MP, Pierre Sevigny, had enjoyed an affair with an East German spy, Gerda Munsinger, during his term as Diefenbaker's associate defence minister. Although Expo 67 helped Canada to celebrate its centennial and newfound maturity, Charles de Gaulle's declaration of

Prime Minister Lester B. Pearson appointed MacEwan to Lt. Governor's post on December 20, 1965.
— Glenbow Archives

"I think 'Partyism' costs us too much — and has cost us too much."

"Vivé le Québec libre" during his visit to the event managed to create a diplomatic storm.

On April 20, 1968, Pierre Elliot Trudeau was sworn in as Canada's fifteenth prime minister. By the time the Sixties ended, Canadians had accepted no-fault divorce, decriminalization of abortion and homosexuality, policies of bilingualism and multiculturalism, lotteries and a new flag.

MacEwan became mayor of Calgary the first-time by default, and the second-time by election. When city mayor Harry W. Hays was elected as a federal Liberal in 1963, his resignation resulted in most of the Calgary council jockeying for the interim position. Everyone, that is, except Grant MacEwan. Oblivious to the antics of his colleagues and the factions they belonged to, and seemingly a non-contender in the next election, he was seen by the other councillors as a safe bet for a caretaker mayor.

Left to right: Harry Viner (Mayor, Medicine Hat), Maurice McManus (Lord Provost of Dundas, Scotland), Grant macEwan (Mayor, Calgary), 1965.
— Glenbow Archives

Grant MacEwan performed his custodial role dutifully and steered clear of the conflict and controversy municipal governments get mired in from time to time. His counterparts, however, had another thing coming. For when the autumn arrived and the civic election was looming, public pressure convinced MacEwan to enter the fray. The only other contender for the mayor's chair was Art Smith, a professional politician who had served as both a MP and MLA.

The local media, no doubt, had a field day in their editorial meetings deciding on how to portray the pragmatic-thinking, folksy and frugal MacEwan in contrast to the elegantly dressed, smooth-talking Art Smith. Ultimately, the rather undazzling appearance that MacEwan made against Smith in apparel was inconsequential, for when the votes were tallied he had defeated Smith by a margin of 13,000. The tide of public opinion for the most economical politician in Calgary's history was far from ebbing. The crest was still in the future.

On the domestic front, the MacEwans enjoyed good health and the addition of a son-in-law to their family. Daughter Heather had spent the summer and fall of 1962 and spring and summer of 1963 travelling the world in search of its best scuba-diving waters. By the time she arrived in Australia, she was short of cash but determined to complete the Indo-Asia leg of her trip. She met her husband, Max Foran, during a teaching stint in a Sydney school where he was the deputy headmaster. Max followed Heather to Calgary where the couple were married in December of 1963.

Few Calgary politicians were as well adorned by females as Grant MacEwan. Heather and Phyllis alternated in accompanying Grant to countless social events. Heather had inherited her mother's dark eyes and hair, and she made a striking companion; age had only served to make Phyllis more beautiful.

The new mayor's shiny black Chrysler Saratoga and police constable driver were more often idle than in use. The thirty-first mayor of Calgary preferred his own car to the city's, and a talkative taxi driver to a polite policeman. He was also enamored enough with the city's public transit that he actually used it, and he was definitely not opposed to hoofing it to an official event. *Calgary Herald* columnist Johnny Hopkins wrote that MacEwan was frequently seen loping from one meeting to another in Calgary's downtown "as though he wasz being chased by demons."

MacEwan's mornings began early. He was usually in the office by seven o'clock and sometimes a lot earlier. South-west Calgary residents were used to seeing the tall, lean figure hurrying down Elbow Drive to where he would catch a bus for downtown. His bulging briefcase would be swinging by his side and his coattails flapping. His pace forced his long, thin white hair to lie flat against his head.

Heather MacEwan, 1962.
— MacEwan-Foran Collection

Foran MacEwan wedding. Groom Max Foran, bride Heather MacEwan and Grant MacEwan in receiving line.
— MacEwan-Foran Collection

Grant MacEwan was making his usual early morning dart for the bus in October 1963 when a police patrol car drove past, made a U-turn and approached him again. The officer ordered him to stop and to state where he was going and why. The mayor replied. Still not satisfied, the policeman shone his flashlight on MacEwan's face and was heard to say, "Omigosh, it's the mayor!" His Honour politely refused the embarrassed copper's offer to drive him to work.

Mayor Grant MacEwan accepts replica of bus from Calgary Transit Service official. — Glenbow Archives

Although Grant MacEwan probably preferred the company of his friends the beavers to his colleagues on council, he turned out to be a skilled administrator and a hard-nosed negotiator. He also tried to keep his campaign promises. During his term of office, he negotiated for a $21 million fertilizer plant to be built within the city confines and worked to see the shortage of hospital beds reduced and better use made of Calgary's existing road system.

His pragmatic style of leadership served Calgarians particularly well when it came to the proposed CPR downtown relocation. Essentially the plan called for the moving of the rail tracks from the downtown core to the south bank of the Bow River. The agreement had been negotiated in principle by former Mayor Harry Hays, and was inherited by Grant MacEwan. By the time the topic was tabled before council again, the public had become concerned about the millions of dollars the city would have to contribute despite the potential tax yield from the project. Citizens were also fearful of the environmental impact on the river valley. The more council dragged out the discussion, the harder CPR negotiators pushed for a settlement. On June 22, 1964 the Calgary council voted to withdraw from further discussion. Mayor MacEwan had guided the proposal through the process and to its natural death without so much as a smudge to his reputation.

"Pay as you go" Mayor MacEwan faced his greatest challenge in the proposed relocation of the Calgary Exhibition and Stampede grounds. Once again the extra-curricular work of Harry Hays — former mayor, Calgary Exhibition and Stampede director, and the newly installed federal minister of agriculture — muddied the political waters and forced MacEwan and his colleagues to diplomatically back-paddle.

The relationship between Harry Hays and Grant MacEwan dated back to when both were young men and involved in showing livestock. During one of MacEwan's early appearances as an alderman on Calgary's city council, he accused Hays of stealing a bale of hay from him during a Depression fair. Both aldermen were engaged in a lively exchange when the straight-faced MacEwan, his blue eyes twinkling, interrupted the debate and declared, "Harry Hays, you stole that bale of hay from me didn't you!" Hays responded, "Yes, but I was so poor." With the debt acknowledged, both councillors returned to their original deliberation. Harry Hays became one of MacEwan's strongest political allies both as the federal minister of agriculture and later as a senator.

Calgary had acquired Lincoln Park, the 426-acre former air force base for $750,000 from the federal government's War Assets Corporation, largely because of MacEwan's finely developed skill to drive a hard bargain. To Harry Hays, the new federal minister of agriculture and former mayor of Calgary, and Don Matthews, the president of the Stampede Board, this southwest parcel of property was their preferred relocation site for the Stampede grounds. In addition, Commissioner John Steel's report to city council supported the Stampede Board's offer to purchase the land from the city for $759,000.

Residents in the proposed area, however, were less than thrilled with the possibility of sharing their quiet neigh-borhood with thousands of exhibition-goers and

Mayor Grant MacEwan and his council colleagues were labelled by one journalist as a "pinch penny civic administration." — Glenbow Archives

livestock stockades. Moreover, there were other practical options for the land including a residential development, relocation of Mount Royal College and an industrial park surrounding ATCO Industries.

MacEwan was forced to walk a narrow fence during this debate. He had longstanding friendships with members of the Stampede Board and he was well aware of the federal agriculture minister's wishes, yet he felt the other options made better financial sense. The matter was referred to the Planning Department and, in June 1965, the Calgary council unanimously accepted the department's recommendation that the land be developed around ATCO Industries and Mount Royal College. In his book *Alberta Was My Beat*, veteran journalist Fred Kennedy labelled the politicians involved as a "... pinch penny civic administration." Unquestionably, MacEwan considered the taxpayers' money a sacred trust, and he would no sooner fritter their money away than he would his own.

"One of worst things in politics is caucus. Our representatives go behind closed doors and they're sworn to secrecy, and what they talk about is never reported. I sat in caucus for awhile and my conscience bothered me. I thought it was undemocratic."

His term as mayor provided him with additional insight into the ways of people. And it supplied the writer in him with ample anecdotes to write about. In his book, *Poking into Politics,* MacEwan describes the telephone as one of "... the evils sent to test a Mayor's patience ... break his spirit and drive him mad."

When a caller demanded that MacEwan make the parks people roll the grass at Central Park, he asked the caller why and was promptly informed that "...some people have to sleep there." On another occasion a late night caller from Boston asked him to find "Tom ..." When the mayor queried the reason for the request the female voice replied, "He's the father of my baby and I can't find him to tell him what he should know."

The growth of public demand upon their elected officials was clearly a source of frustration to the self-reliant MacEwan. He wrote: "When a cat paused on a garage roof where it could be beyond the reach of belligerent dogs, the Fire Department was called to effect a rescue. When a boulevard shrub became the home of a colony of caterpillars, the Parks Department was urged to do something about it. When the garbage collector overlooked a can of refuse, a call of distress was relayed to the Mayor who happened to be sitting at an important meeting. And a man who remained too late at a party and missed the last transit bus, telephoned the mayor at 1:30 a.m., requesting the dispatch of a city vehicle to take him home."

During the span of his lifetime, Grant MacEwan witnessed the evolution of a cradle to grave social-net mentality of which he wrote ". . . gave people the idea that everything should and would be done for them." He was an ardent follower of Arnold Joseph Toynbee, the British historian who traced the rise, decline and fall of 26 civilizations. MacEwan, like Toynbee, postulated that the growing unwillingness of people to do things for themselves was symptomatic of a civilization in decline.

Grant MacEwan not only weathered Alberta's political storms as an MLA, alderman and mayor, he earned the respect of friend and foe alike. Even Mike Pearson's government liked what they saw in this crusty Westerner. And notwithstanding MacEwan had withdrawn from partisan politics when he became mayor, the federal Liberals were acutely aware of their debt to MacEwan for the Brandon by-election fiasco.

A telephone call from Ottawa on June 28, 1965 alerted the scholarly, bird-watching civic politician that a new challenge was taking shape. Mayor MacEwan put down his gavel of office on October 7, 1965 and once more became "Mister" MacEwan. On December 20, 1965 a press release from Prime Minister Lester Pearson's office announced the appointment of ". . . Mr. J.W. Grant MacEwan, B.S.A., M.S., as Lieutenant-Governor of the Province of Alberta, succeeding the Honourable J. Percy Page."

Grant MacEwan had been sitting on the desk of Heather, his elementary school teacher daughter, discussing the history of the West with her young pupils when he was called to the office to take a phone call from Ottawa. A few moments later, "Mister" MacEwan returned to the classroom as His Honour Grant MacEwan, the ninth Lieutenant-Governor of Alberta. According to *Calgary Herald* reporter Walter Nagel, the Queen's new representative told the students, ". . . In this bonnie province — this wonderful province — this appointment makes me very, very proud." Forgetting his normal thriftiness for an hour, MacEwan took Heather and her colleagues to the coffee shop across from the school and bought them lunch. Afterwards, he took the bus home.

Grant and Phyllis MacEwan, 1965.
— Glenbow Archives

Best wishes poured in from all over the world. Even the man who caused Grant MacEwan to leave Manitoba, Conservative MP Walter Dinsdale, sent congratulations. Another writer articulated what many of his friends pondered. "I keep wondering just how you will react to having a chauffeur, an aide de camp and all the golden cords and tassels. One thing for sure, there will never be any parking difficulties and your seat will always be reserved in church."

There was also considerable cross-correspondence between MacEwan's friends about his appointment. In one letter, which was copied to the new lieutenant-governor, the author predicted, "He (MacEwan) will fill it with dignity and tact and make a host of friends for the Queen as her representative, but more than that he will provide a volume of thrills for the impressionable Fair Sex whenever and wherever he makes an appearance."

Grant MacEwan studies his new hat of office, 1966.
— Provincial Archives of Alberta

Basil Dean, who had secured MacEwan as a columnist for the *Calgary Herald* and was himself now the publisher of the *Edmonton Journal* proffered ". . . you will bring not only dignity but urbanity and the kind of cultivated outlook which will give official functions an interesting new look." The publisher's prophesy would become a reality.

The new lieutenant-governor was sworn in on January 6, 1966 in the mid-afternoon. Chief Justice S.B.

Lt. Gov. Grant MacEwan signs his oath of office, January 6, 1966. Phyllis MacEwan stands in background.
— Provincial Archives of Alberta

Smith of the Alberta Supreme Court presided over the ceremony which was attended by the vice-regal's family, Dr. J. Percy Page, the retiring lieutenant-governor, and Premier Ernest Manning and his cabinet ministers, onetime political adversaries of MacEwan.

The $18,000 yearly salary of the office was augmented with a $15,000 travel and entertainment expense allowance payable from the federal coffers. Given that Alberta did not maintain a residence for the Queen's representative, the province was obliged to provide MacEwan with a $4,000 housing stipend.

News pundits used the re-emergence of this information to harangue Manning's Social Credit government about its anti-monarchist policies. In 1938, William Aberhart's Socred government had evicted John Bowen, the lieutenant- governor of the time, after he withheld royal assent to a number of controversial bills. While much of that legislation was ruled unconstitutional by the Supreme Court of Canada, the Socreds remained firm in their refusal in the years following to maintain a vice-regal residence. The fray became so heated after MacEwan's appointment that the City of Calgary threatened to purchase an appropriate residence for their beloved former mayor if the government continued to refuse.

Grant and Phyllis MacEwan distanced themselves from the housing controversy and purchased from their own funds a bungalow at 13845 MacKinnon Ravine. With the outdoors just a few steps from his back door and the legislature a healthy walk away, the new lieutenant-governor began to imprint his style on the office. However, within days of moving into their new house, the Manning government announced it had purchased 58 St. George's Crescent as the new residence for the province's vice-regal. The MacEwans lived in their own home for a year while renovations to the official residence were completed and then sold it.

In the *Calgary Herald*, opposite to the newspaper story describing the lieutenant-governor's new home, a smaller subtitle, "Generosity recalled by Herald Newsman," caught the attention of readers. Journalist Eric Erickson recounted how his family had lived in an old log cabin on Grant MacEwan's White Fox district property in Saskatchewan during the Depression.

The story bears an uncanny resemblance to earlier events in Grant MacEwan's life. When thirteen-year-old Grant and his father first viewed their Melfort farm, he recorded in his journal that the property had ". . . no fence, no house, no cultivation, but an abundance of trees." It was the generosity of the neighboring Sparrow and Poole families which provided the MacEwans with a refuge. Wrote MacEwan in his journal, "Jas Durnin, a farmer to the south of us, agreed to let us use his old bedbug infested, log building. . . We used it for sleeping quarters . . ." Those memories profoundly shaped MacEwan's compassion for other families experiencing need but demonstrating self-reliance.

The reporter's parents had arrived in 1929 at their land claim to find it located beside the quarter-section MacEwan had purchased for an investment. Because there were no buildings on the Erickson land, they asked if they might use MacEwan's cabin. It was in this one-room affair with a wooden slab roof, rough plank floor and two small square windows that the reporter was born on October 9, 1930.

When Erickson interviewed the new lieutenant-governor, MacEwan shared with him a story which had gone untold for over thirty years. Grant MacEwan had made a point of visiting the young family once per year. During the course of one of these visits, MacEwan's pants became soaked as he walked through the tall wet grass. He built a fire and hung his trousers over the flames and settled down to write in his journal. When he looked up again, his pants were aflame. He returned to Melfort minus one pantleg, the other singed.

Grant MacEwan brought this same pioneer generosity and practicality to his lofty new position. His humble past had mettled his character and sensitized his feelings for those truly in need. Typical Albertans were more in tune with the man than those who believed themselves to be important.

Grant MacEwan read his first Speech from the Throne on opening day of the third session of the 15th Alberta Legislature without the tassels and braids of the traditional Windsor uniform. The suit used by the former, and much shorter, lieutenant-governor J. Percy Page neither fit nor could be altered to cover MacEwan's six-foot four-inch frame. Rather, he presided over the event in formal day dress complete with a black silk top hat.

The public side of his new position provided Grant MacEwan with countless opportunities to speak. "Confederation was an act of necessity, born not in wedlock, but in deadlock," he told Alberta's professional engineers. The crowd collapsed in laughter when he concluded, "Every autocrat or statesman makes a blunder when he gets mixed up with a woman or a Scotsman."

"Politics should bring out frankness and honesty."

Heather MacEwan-Foran, Lt. Gov. Grant MacEwan and Phyllis MacEwan with Premier Ernest Manning at the opening of the Legislature, February 1966. — Provincial Archives of Alberta /MacEwan-Foran Collection

He also assured a gathering of Edmonton's doctors that, "There is no greater success story than the West which was an ugly duckling 100 years ago." At the Women's Canadian Club of Toronto, he bemoaned the lack of awareness by average Canadians for the country's unsung heroes. MacEwan compared Alberta's first squatter, Kootenai Brown, to Tom Sawyer. He likened the Hudson's Bay Company governor George Simpson to Julius Caesar. "He was a good administrator; he could fight, and he got along with the ladies." And he compared Jack Martin to Robin Hood when it came to robbing the rich to help the poor. "He was a rancher with 5,000 horses and he always helped the homesteaders, particularly when they needed horses."

Lt. Gov. Grant MacEwan inspects a pioneer home, 1968.
— Provincial Archives of Alberta

MacEwan sold the Alberta advantage at home and abroad. During the fall of 1966, Phyllis and Grant accepted an invitation from the State of Israel to tour the young nation. In his book, *Entrusted to My Care* — published that same year — the agronomist in MacEwan praised the soil restoration and reclamation efforts he had witnessed firsthand: ". . . the Jewish people have been making valiant efforts to restore the productivity of their depleted soils. . . . The wounds and scars created by shifting soils could not be healed or erased completely but tribute should be paid to the splendid efforts to safeguard and improve what remained." In 1967, Grant MacEwan was honored by Canada's Christians and Jews. Senator Paul Martin Sr. — himself a former recipient of the tribute — was one of the first to congratulate MacEwan. "May I extend my sincerest congratulation to you as a recipient of the highest award of the Canadian Council of Christians and Jews — the Human Relations Award."

The MacEwans, whose only other vacation together was their honeymoon in 1935, visited Athens, Rome, Madrid and London before returning home from their state visit to Israel. The first year of Grant's term of office ended with an announcement from the American Association for State and Local History. Their 1966 "award of merit" was being given to Grant MacEwan in view of his "exceptional contributions to the fields of western and agricultural history through books, lectures and articles."

MacEwan received more invitations than there were hours in the day. His declines, though, were gracious and personally pecked out on his own manual typewriter. To the Walsh Cattle Marketing Association, he wrote: "Your organization has commanded the attention and the respect of cattlemen across the nation. . . I know them as the aristocrats of the cattle kingdom, resourceful men, vigorous men, and men who have not lost their God-given individualities. It would be easy in the age of luxury and prosperity to lose forever some of these qualities which brought greatness to the Western soil."

Some of MacEwan's invitations and responses, though, required caution. In December 1972, a youth by the name of John Smith invited the lieutenant-governor to be his surrogate parent at the Youth Development Centre's Christmas concert. The Centre was the forerunner of the present Youth Detention Centre for young people in trouble with the law. The young man explained that the performance was produced by students for their immediate family. "But since I have no immediate family to invite I would like to take the opportunity to invite an important man like yourself to be my guest. . ."

Lieutenant-Governor Grant MacEwan responded as follows. "Dear John Smith: I thank you for the invitation which I would have accepted had I been free on that evening. I know it would be a pleasant experience. . . I can only hope that you have a fine evening together and I wish you and all around you a happy time." Given MacEwan's response lacked

Lt. Gov. Grant MacEwan (1966-1974).
— Provincial Archives of Alberta

"It amuses me — it bothers me to hear from people — 'If such and such fails, what are we going to do?' I've heard it from the highest level of government, 'If Quebec leaves Canada, we've no future.' That's inconsistent with the pioneer attitude. Nothing like that should keep us from having a future.

We started Canada with four provinces. Even if one were to leave today, we'd still have nine, or ten. And to think that we'd let something like that frustrate us is completely unthinkable."

the normal anecdotal storyline that accompanied most declines, one might assume that he was not enamored about the source of the invitation.

One year after Grant MacEwan was sworn-in as lieutenant-governor, Canada turned 100-years-old. In keeping with the mood of the country — a nation perpetually preoccupied with separation — his 1967 New Year's address challenged Albertans to "think seriously about the need for rededication to some high resolves about Canadian unity."

On June 29, 1967, in an article published in *The Albertan,* Lieutenant-Governor Grant MacEwan pleaded with Albertans to ". . . get to know their Canada better, know its history, its geography, its resources and its people." He cautioned the readers that "Canadian unity is not guaranteed. The possibility of a break in the Sea-to-Sea concept of the Fathers of Confederation must fill thinking Canadians with horror." One of MacEwan's greatest fears in life was the potential fracture of the nation he loved and wrote about; the land his Scottish forefathers had struggled valiantly to settle.

Throughout 1967 MacEwan travelled Alberta's highways and dirt roads into communities which had never experienced an opportunity to welcome their lieutenant-governor. No community was too small, no person so insignificant that MacEwan would not stop and chat. His official commitments also took him outside of the province. Canada's lieutenant-governors and their spouses were

Her Majesty Queen Elizabeth II is greeted by Lt. Gov. and Mrs. Grant MacEwan, 1973. — Provincial Archives of Alberta

summoned to Expo 67 by Her Majesty Queen Elizabeth II. The monarch and her husband, Prince Philip, wined and dined the royal representatives aboard the Royal Yacht *Britannia.*

MacEwan, who sat beside the Queen during dinner, aptly observed that she controlled the conversation by directing a litany of questions to her dinner partner. "Must have been her queenly training that taught her that," he asserted. His conversation with the conservation-minded Prince Philip was more to his liking. "He's a pretty straight-forward person. I bet he causes the Queen some concern from time to time." The two couples met again in 1973 at the Calgary Stampede.

In 1969 Lieutenant-Governor Grant MacEwan's outspokenness created a furore of national proportion. The St. John's School in Genesee, Alberta had invited MacEwan to participate in a ribbon-cutting ceremony and to say a few words. The boys' school emphasizes the development of physical and mental stamina through a variety of outdoor activities including trapping.

After the tall, stern-looking MacEwan congratulated the school's staff for their work with Alberta's youth, he launched into a tongue-lashing which was reported by news media across the nation. "I wish you would leave my furred and feathered friends alone," he told the unsuspecting audience. "It's a personal thing, I don't think it's right to catch animals in steel traps." Not only did his remarks provoke a storm of responses for and against the trapping of fur-bearing animals, his rebuke incensed the bishop of the school's sponsoring church body. It was one time that MacEwan's forthrightness necessitated damage control.

The candor with which Grant MacEwan approached societal problems must be applauded. His respect for and concern with his aboriginal brothers' age-old problem with alcohol prompted him to deliver another strong message. "Beat the booze," he told the Enoch Band in 1974. "Face and come to grips with it. It's your number one enemy." Only a white man whose titles included Chief Walking Moose of the Sagatawas or Honorary Chief Aka-tah-si (Owns Many Horses) of the Blood Indians could be so bold yet retain the band's respect. MacEwan advised the assembly to band together against the drug which has destroyed the lives of many of their brothers. Only then would they have control over their destiny.

Lt. Gov. Grant MacEwan and Chief Joe Crowfoot unveil Centennial display, 1967.— Provincial Archives of Alberta

Lt. Gov. Grant MacEwan sits on bank of North Saskatchewan River, 1968. — Edmonton Journal

Grant MacEwan became an affirmed vegetarian during the late sixties. It was a curious conclusion to an academic career which had focused on the yield maximization of livestock. MacEwan's adherence to vegetarianism and his respect for all living creatures suggest he was influenced by two key tenets of Buddhism — although he may not have been aware of it.

However, Rusty Macdonald, author of *Grant MacEwan: No Ordinary Man,* postulates that MacEwan's friendship with Chief George McLean, better known as Walking Buffalo, helped the former dean to redefine the structure of his spiritual life. During the 1953 Calgary Stampede, Grant MacEwan spent several hours in the chief's teepee. Macdonald quotes MacEwan as saying, "When I sat at his feet, I had the feeling that one of the ancient philosophers had come back to life."

The assassination of Dr. Martin Luther King prompted Alberta's lieutenant-governor to promote understanding and tolerance during a week-long Ontario tour which was sponsored by the Canadian Council of Christians and Jews. On November 26, 1968, Grant MacEwan told a joint luncheon meeting of the Rotary Club and the Chamber of Commerce that most national and international problems stem from misunderstanding or ignorance.

Chief Stephen Fox, Sr. of the Blood Reserve inducts Lt. Gov. Grant MacEwan as an honorary chief, 1967. — City of Lethbridge Archives & Records Management/MacEwan-Foran Collection

He reminded the audience that Canada was not free from acts of intolerance. "In particular, there is the Indian problem," he said. "Reserves are evidence of segregation." The loss of independence and resourcefulness by the people of Canada's First Nation during the first 100-years of confederation troubled MacEwan terribly. He reasoned that if aboriginals remained on their reserves, it could be equated to "self-imposed segregation." Should they leave, he feared they would be absorbed by the white society. Like a soothsayer, he predicted in 1968 that eventually violence would erupt between the two groups. The 1990 Oka crisis would seem to confirm his prophecy.

Lt. Gov. Grant MacEwan collects beaver-chewed logs to use for carving, 1968. — Edmonton Journal

During 1993 research interviews for this book, the ninety-one-year-old MacEwan contended that segregation, and its contemporary cousin, racism, is driven by greed. "Our ambition must be tempered if we are to live in peace and harmony," he said. He compared the disenfranchisement of visible minority groups such as Canada's aboriginals as a practice comparable to South Africa's former policy of apartheid — practices which run contrary to his belief that all of God's creatures should be equal. He also cautioned the writer that the rise of special interest groups with accompanying power bases threaten our unity, our oneness, the very interdependence that built this nation.

Be it Buddhism or aboriginal teachings that influenced MacEwan to accept all of God's creatures as his equal, his search for a religious structure had come to an end. The journey had taken him many miles and introduced him to many faiths including Catholicism and its eastern offshoots, Judaism, and Anglican doctrine. His formal relationship with organized religion had ended when he assumed the deanship at the University of Manitoba in 1946. Macdonald writes that MacEwan ". . . was repelled by the bitterness and division that sectarian rivalry often gave rise to." The lieutenant-governor's acceptance of a Universal Ruler prompted him to write his well-known creed in 1969.

It would be impossible to recount a complete repertoire of Grant MacEwan's human and humorous antics during his term as lieutenant-governor. Many are known by way of newspaper stories, others continue to circulate amongst friends and acquaintances. However, his chauffeur, Henry Weber, often found himself a player in the mirth.

The twosome were returning to Edmonton from a Calgary engagement when MacEwan asked his driver to pull off the highway onto a side road and open the trunk of the car. His Honour pulled out two sleeping bags, spread them out on the grass, and advised Henry that since this was probably the last opportunity of the year to bed down under the stars . . . he hoped the chauffeur wouldn't mind.

Phyllis and Grant were returning from an commitment when MacEwan suggested that an ice cream cone for everyone was in order. Henry dutifully pulled off at a service station and the threesome left the car to procure their treats. After Henry had driven some distance, the lieutenant-governor asked him if he planned on fetching Mrs. MacEwan from the service station later in the day.

On still another occasion, Weber diligently reminded his boss and family of an appointment which was quickly approaching. By the time Henry made it back to the vehicle, the lieutenant-governor had opened the car doors for the members of his family and, of course, the chauffeur.

Grant MacEwan possessed quirks which must have challenged Henry Weber's sanity and patience. It was not long into Weber's employment before the lieutenant-governor proposed the driver accept a wage rollback. The meagerly paid civil servant had timidly suggested to his boss, that given the long hours — MacEwan preferred to return home after an engagement even if it meant driving through the night — that remuneration for the overtime might be in order. His Honour Grant MacEwan was eventually absolved of any responsibility for making this decision by the government's human resources department. Henry's extra efforts were rewarded.

Grant MacEwan was besieged by requests for recipes, book forewords and any possible memento that the mails could carry to the asker. When Ontario's Victor Lauriston Public School wrote to His Honour with a request for one of his favorite recipes he responded: "The only thing to which I can lay any inventive claim might be labelled Misery Pudding, or Bachelor's Salvation. Strangely enough, it is more appetizing than the recipe would seem to indicate. The desperate male begins with three thick slices of well buttered brown bread placed in a pan. To this he adds 3 tablespoons of maple syrup and a cup of buttermilk. For a bit of extra special delight a handful of walnut chips can be added, and then, when the

Chauffeur Henry Weber stands with Lt. Gov. Grant MacEwan at Vermilion Firefighter School, 1967.
— MacEwan-Foran Collection

whole is thoroughly soaked and mixed, the feast can begin."
The recipe did not include any further instructions, and the
young cooks were left wondering whether to bake the
concoction or serve as is!

In March 1968, the headmaster of Paarl Boys' High
School in South Africa invited Grant MacEwan to provide the
foreword for a book the students were writing to celebrate the
academy's centenary year. His message to these young South
Africans is as relevant today as on the day he wrote it.

"Character is not a commodity you can purchase at a
corner store. It does not come from text books. It is something
forged on the anvil of life. I believe the potential for good
character is present in every young person. In each there is the
desire to be tested and challenged, an instinct to be heroic and
conquer over hardship. But unfortunately, periods of peace and
prosperity and luxury make it more difficult to bring out those
qualities of fine manhood and womanhood.

"The search for comfort, almost universally accepted
by adults of today as the reasonable aim in life, can be
destructive of much that is best in man — ability to think,
and willingness to fight for what one believes to be right.
Described in these pages is a school which will encourage
good thinking and good acting, and produce fine manhood
from the raw material of youth. The purpose is a vital one. It
will receive the endorsation and best wishes of responsible
citizens everywhere."

Solicitations for souvenirs and letters of admiration
came from all over the world, and sometimes the writer's
command of English provoked humorous moments for
MacEwan and his secretary, Patricia Halligan-Baker. One
unedited letter from a Bavarian admirer professed, " you are
doubtful one of the greatest and importantest politician
personalities in North America and the world." The writer
wondered if His Honour would send an Alberta flag or map.

Patricia Halligan served as Grant MacEwan's private
secretary for most of his term in office — although for six
months prior to her appointment — the lieutenant-governor
answered his own phone and typed his own letters. His choice
of Halligan-Baker, in fact, broke an age-old tradition of the
vice-regal being attended to by a male secretary. Eventually,
MacEwan had Miss Halligan-Baker perform the ceremonial
duty of carrying the Speech from the Throne into the

*Lt. Gov. Grant MacEwan presents Life
Saving Award, 1967.*
— Provincial Archives of Alberta

Lt. Gov. MacEwan at the Oxfam "Freedom from Hunger" walk, 1967.
— Provincial Archives of Alberta

Legislature. The relationship between the young woman and the elderly MacEwan and his wife grew, over the years, into a close friendship.

Pat Halligan not only faced the challenge of keeping up with the mountains of correspondence her boss received each day, but she quickly learned that MacEwan preferred a casual look to being all "gussied up" for an official invitation. It often fell to her to inform the lieutenant-governor that his clothing was less than suitable for a given event.

On one occasion, she sent him back to his house three times before he emerged in appropriate attire to which he exclaimed, "Thunderation woman!" Usually she collaborated with Phyllis MacEwan, and the vice-regal's appearance was, with the exception of his shoes, fairly presentable. Shortly after Grant MacEwan's retirement as lieutenant-governor, an MLA stopped by Miss Halligan-Baker's office and asked how it was going with her new boss, Lieutenant-Governor Ralph Steinhauer. She replied things were going well to which the MLA retorted, "Well I see this one polishes his shoes."

The MacEwans and Halligan-Baker shared a penchant for early Canadiana furniture. The three would frequent auctions together, sometimes bidding against one another. At one Saturday sale, Pat Halligan-Baker actively bid for a particularly beautiful maple sideboard. When the price exceeded her predetermined budget, she dropped out of the bidding. Some days later Grant spotted the same piece of furniture at another auction and bought it for sixty dollars. The following day, Henry Weber and Grant MacEwan lugged the heavy piece of furniture up two flights of stairs and set it down in Pat Halligan-Baker's suite.

The popularity of walkathons and runathons for charity took hold during the later half of the 1960s. MacEwan, with his well-known bent for fitness, led the way in countless Alberta marathons beginning with the 1967 Centennial March. "Miles for Millions" and Oxfam's "Freedom from Hunger" walk and the like benefitted from the lieutenant-governor's participation. Generally, the sixty-plus-year-old would finish long before contestants half of his age. "He would stride and I would run," recalled Inuit lawyer David Ward. "By the end of the course, MacEwan was still striding and I had been reduced to a shuffle."

Lt. Gov. MacEwan shows off new hiking boots while Phyllis MacEwan holds a bronzed pair at Miles for Millions, 1970. — MacEwan-Foran Collection

When journalists tallied the number of miles the vice-regal had walked and discovered it to be well over 1,000 — they stopped counting. In the same well-paced stride that had taken him from the Melfort train station as a university student to the family homestead in time for breakfast, MacEwan walked distances of fifteen, twenty and thirty-plus miles in the name of charity.

It was after one of those marathons that David Ward, then a radio talk show host, arrived at Edmonton's CJCA to discover a newspaper-wrapped package on his desk. Inside the paper wrapping was a log, its ends chewed by beavers. In its centre was an intricately carved beaver. The masterpiece was signed, "J.W. Grant MacEwan." Similar logs were whittled and presented by MacEwan to heads of state, government officials and guests. He was often heard to say, "The more I see of people, the better I like the beaver."

Entertaining people was a large component of the lieutenant-governor's position. The MacEwans evolved a style of function that closely followed the "Dean's parties" they had hosted at the University of Manitoba. Usually the invitations, which sported a cover sketch by Heather MacEwan-Foran, were folded sheets of mimeographed paper with a catchy limerick on the inside. One invitation read: "We hope you'll remember the day of our party, We'll be waiting for you with a welcome that's hearty. You know it's informal — Western too; The time is seven — we'll be looking for you. — signed

Lt. Gov. MacEwan poses with daughter Heather and grand-daughters, Fiona and Lynwyn, and an admirer holding one of his beaver log carvings. — Calgary Herald/Glenbow Archives

Lt. Gov. Grant MacEwan "the Queen's cowboy" leads the 1972 Calgary Stampede parade. — Calgary Herald/ Glenbow Archives

Phyllis MacEwan and Grant MacEwan." The get-togethers were mostly held at Edmonton's Mayfair Club, and all invitees learned by experience that dancing, stories, singing and games were part of the evening's entertainment. The guests were served hearty food like stews or baked beans, and lots of it, and dessert but no spirits.

MacEwan's increasing popularity caused many organizations to seek a formal relationship with the Queen's cowboy. Late in 1967, the new University of Lethbridge asked him to become its first Chancellor. Two years later, he was nominated to the board of directors for the Wawanesa Mutual Insurance Company in absentia. The lieutenant-governor, however, steered systematically clear of any relationships which had the potential the create a conflict of interest.

As the end of Grant MacEwan's term of office neared, the lobbying for him to stay began. Editorials sung his praises and citizens wrote letters to Alberta's premier and the nation's prime minister. Although the effort was not orchestrated it became, nevertheless, a concerted effort by individuals reluctant to part with the folksy and forthright man that said what was on his mind.

On December 15, 1970, Prime Minister Pierre Elliot Trudeau broke tradition and extended MacEwan's term of office. "While I cannot commit to future governments, I am pleased to confirm that your appointment has been extended and that you will continue to serve until the next federal election. I am of course delighted that you have consented to continue serving your country and the people of Alberta as lieutenant-governor of that province, a position which you have filled with a great deal of dignity and to which you have brought your personal touch. — Yours sincerely, Pierre Trudeau." Albertans were ecstatic.

During the first five years of his appointment, Grant MacEwan had travelled to almost every hamlet in Alberta in addition to spending time with the province's numerous cultural, business and professional groups. His travels presented him with ample research opportunities for current and future manuscripts. He wrote in the early morning or night or whenever he could eke out enough time to scratch down a few sentences. Finalized manuscripts were neatly pecked out by the two-finger typist and sent to the most likely publisher. If the author failed to hear from the company within a reasonable time period, he followed up with a letter of inquiry. Publishers who did not look after MacEwan's manuscripts in an appropriate fashion faced his wrath.

When Grant MacEwan sent his manuscript *Chief Walking Buffalo* to The Blandford Group in London, England, he was reasonably confident that they would publish it. The company had expressed interest in his earlier work and had invited him to submit manuscripts on a variety of subjects including Indian chiefs. Upon receipt of the manuscript and accompanying photographs, the senior editor wrote to MacEwan and told him that he liked the story. A few weeks later, an agreement was forwarded to the author for his signature.

After a year passed and MacEwan heard nothing from the publisher, he wrote to the editor. Several weeks later, Grant received back his manuscript, which had been damaged, and a letter cancelling the contract. It was a very angry MacEwan who wrote, ". . . You did not inform me that while you held the copy under a written agreement to publish it, you or your people scored, obliterated and mutilated page after page so that its presentation to any other publisher, as you suggested, would be completely out of the question. I am advised to ask you if this is your conclusion or what you propose to do about it." The manuscript was eventually published by Edmonton's Hurtig Publishers under the title of *Tatanga Mani*.

In 1966, the Institute of Applied Art published *Poking into Politics* wherein MacEwan confessed in its foreword his three loves in life: food, girls and politics. He wrote: "I hope to retain my awareness in all three subjects but intend to confine my writing to the only one on which I would speak with confidence."

Prior to the printing of this manuscript, the Queen's cowboy shared its contents with the politicians whose names were destined to appear in print. Later that same year, the same publishing house produced *Entrusted to My Care*. Its text clearly articulates the author's passionate concern for the environment and links for the reader events of history and corresponding happenings of the day.

During Grant MacEwan's term as lieutenant-governor — he not only finalized the text and made ready for publishing the material for nine books — he had at least another seven manuscripts underway. Twice per year, hefty royalty cheques

"History has utility as well as charm, and reflection is always good and useful."

Lt. Gov. Grant MacEwan's three loves: food, girls and politics.
— Edmonton Journal

Fiona and Lynwyn Foran.
— MacEwan-Foran Collection

"Dear Fiona and Lynwyn:

One of you is four years old today and there are a few things your Gramp wants to say. I'm glad you little girls are so fond of animals and all living things. Your mother, when she was small, was like that too. One of the first words she mastered was 'horse' and some time later she added 'daddy' to her vocabulary. I hope you never lose your love for the real wonders of Nature.

The so-called mechanical wonders suffer terribly by comparison but for some reason they capture the imagination of many people, young and not-so-young.

It wouldn't be so bad if there wasn't a corresponding decline in interest and respect for the great works of Nature, the Great Spirit's works, upon which we all depend. We could live without the moon rockets; we could not live or would not live very well without soil, crops, grass, trees, birds, animals, insects, clean air, clean water, oil, gas and metals - yes, and the wild grandeur which was Nature's pattern in putting them all together.

I hope you little people will grow up with respect and reverence for these treasures, partly because Canada needs people who will hold them as a sacred trust, partly because your own lives will be richer if you appreciate Nature's creations and are in harmony with them.

were mailed by publishers to his legislative office. If return correspondence was required, His Honour would type it himself on the manual Royal typewriter in his office.

On March 4, 1967 the MacEwans became grandparents with the birth of Fiona Foran, their first granddaughter. For Grant MacEwan, the happiness of the event was tinged by the death of former Governor General Georges Vanier the following day. It was a particularly trying experience for Grant MacEwan. He had, to some extent, mirrored his behavior after Vanier, who became well-known for his public speeches, his concern for the poor and simple folk, and for Canada's youth and families. "I loved that old man," said MacEwan on a CBC broadcast. "It was my privilege to sit with him during some of his last days."

The MacEwan's second granddaughter, Lynwyn, arrived on August 24, 1968. Four years later, the column-writing Lieutenant-Governor of Alberta wrote an open letter to his granddaughters which spelled out his worry about the world's deteriorating environment.

On Grant MacEwan's seventieth birthday, on August 12, 1972, he arrived in a hackney-drawn carriage to open the Canadian Derby in Edmonton. When he entered the royal box and stepped forward to receive the Royal Salute, MacEwan was puzzled by the silence that fell on the audience. Eighteen thousand people stood up and sang "Happy Birthday" to him.

That summer MacEwan decided to drop the selling price of piece of land he owned on Battle Lake just west of Wetaskin. It was not long before the agent informed him that the 4-H Clubs of Alberta was somewhat interested in the property but that the $150,000 asking price might be too much for the organization. MacEwan advised his agent to negotiate a price the club could afford. The land is rumored to have been sold for $100,000.

Grant MacEwan had become a living legend. The message he repeated over and over again was simple. Conserve the best of the past including our natural resources, show respect toward all of God's creatures, use your resourcefulness to live full lives and remember waste is a sin. On June 30, 1974, MacEwan concluded his term as Alberta's ninth lieutenant-governor — eight-and-a-half years after being appointed. He had travelled over half a million miles, attended more than three hundred engagements per year, and signed a total of 19,481 Orders in Council. He was 72-years old.

On June 30, 1974, Grant MacEwan concluded his term as Alberta's ninth Lieutenant-Governor.— Provincial Archives of Alberta

As young Canadians, you are shareholders in a fabulous inheritance. But like other inherited gifts, it can be squandered and some of it has already been frittered away. Now I wonder how much more will be lost before you little girls reach maturity.

The last passenger pigeon died when I was 12-years old, at which time there were still some kit foxes and pinnate grouse around. I'm wondering if your grandchildren will ever see a prairie dog or whooping crane or bighorn sheep.

Things are changing rapidly. Civilization is cutting more deeply into the fresh wilderness areas; natural landscape is being uprooted; more and more good earth is being overlaid with concrete; gas and oil are flowing rapidly from the non-renewable reserves; water and air are carrying increasing loads of pollution; grizzly bears and peregrine falcons and bald eagles are having a harder time to survive.

You will hear somebody say, cheerfully: 'Don't worry. When these things disappear, we'll find something else.'

I wouldn't be too sure. The chances are the person who makes that remark is one who is in the business of selling resources for cash and it would be well for you to use your own unprejudiced judgment about what is right and wrong in exploiting Nature's treasure.

I hope that when you little ladies grow up and have children and grandchildren there will still be a good deal of unspoiled Nature for you to love and enjoy. I hope that to you a stream will be much more than a handy place to dispose of garbage; I hope that the sight of a beautiful bird or animal will not bring with it the strange temptation to shoot and kill; I hope you will hate steel traps and cruelty wherever living creatures are concerned; I hope you will be the kind of people who would rather plant a tree than cut one down.

If you are completely at peace with Nature, I have every confidence that you'll be good citizens in other respects.

Sincerely, Gramp."

SECTION VI

"Preserve the best of the past," was an expression Grant MacEwan became known for. — Provincial Archives of Alberta

1974 - 1994 – THE CIRCLE CLOSES

"A verbal tip of my hat to the people in this House, people I admire very much." And with those words, Lieutenant-Governor Grant MacEwan bade a fond farewell on June 10, 1974 to the seventy-five members of Alberta's legislative assembly. "Nothing will give me greater joy than thinking back to my association with the members of elected bodies in this province," he told the packed chamber. "Thank you so much and God bless."

He tipped his black Homburg to old friends and waved to others. Members had ignored the rules of the House. Their salute began with the traditional desk-thumping and grew into a solid applause with friends and former colleagues jumping to their feet. Only the wail of the bagpipes was missing.

Earlier, the Queen's representative had sidestepped the rules himself and delivered a tightly-worded speech. Lieutenant-governors rarely address the Assembly but MacEwan had been talked into it by the House staff. Even at the last minute he had wanted to call it off because the vice-regal was sure the members and spectators in the galleries wanted to get home. The MLAs had already sat an hour past their usual 5:20 p.m. adjournment.

However, after giving Royal assent to 68 Bills, Grant MacEwan stood up, cleared his throat, and peered over the top of his glasses. He took his time in surveying both sides of the chamber, and he performed it in a manner that suggested each face he looked at held a special memory. He shoved his hands in the pockets of his trousers and began to speak.

"I am not sure if this is constitutional or not. But having reached the age and stage where there is inclined to be some licence for recklessness . . ." He proceeded to remind all those present that this was his last appearance "in this particular spot." The tone of his voice and demeanor was more like a university professor than a lieutenant-governor. MacEwan praised the members for their attendance to their duties and then moved on to the topic of change vis-à-vis, ". . . the preservation of traditions that have been passed on to us." He cautioned the audience to examine each one, and to ". . . preserve the best."

For the next two decades and beyond, Grant MacEwan wrote and talked about what he described as, "The best of the

past." His writing remained focused on the importance of the
West in the development of the Canadian identity by depicting
members of its vanguard. And his conservationist philosophy,
which often had set him apart and at odds with earlier
contemporaries, eventually earned broad public favor.
Moreover — his belief that human ambition was driven by
greed and must be tempered if the planet is to live in peace
and harmony — prompted him to walk yet another path, that
of being a humanitarian.

The 1970s had begun in Canada with the kidnapping of
British Trade Commissioner James Cross and Quebec Labor
Minister Pierre Laporte by members of the Front de libération
du Québec (FLQ). Prime Minister Pierre Trudeau responded
by invoking the War Measures Act on October 16, 1970, the first
time the 1914 statute was used in a domestic crisis. Two days
later, Laporte was found murdered. Terrorism, and the fear of
it, was at an all time high. In December 1970, Prime Minister
Trudeau extended Grant MacEwan's term as lieutenant-
governor "until the next election."

*Lt. Gov. Grant MacEwan says goodbye
to the Members of Alberta's Legislature,
June 10, 1974.* — Edmonton Journal

Canadian unity was thought to be further threatened
by the election of the separatist Parti Québècois (PQ) on
November 15, 1976. PQ Leader René Lévesque promised
Quebeckers a referendum on sovereignty-association which
fuelled fears of a divided Canada. Quebecer's "yes" vote for
unity in 1980 would be challenged again in the nineties with
the 1993 election of the Parti Quebecois as the official
opposition in the House of Commons.

The term "acid rain" began its appearance by 1971.
Suddenly, the quality of water in the Great Lakes became a
source of concern to Canadians living in the vicinity. By 1984,
fourteen-hundred bodies of Canadian water were said to be
polluted by acid rain and devoid of fish. The effect of excessive
amounts of sulphur dioxide in precipitation had taken on real
meaning for many Canadians. Environmental activists like
Greenpeace began to win respect and funding.

Scientific reports in the early 1980s confirmed that the
burning of fossil fuels was contributing to a "greenhouse
effect." By the mid-eighties, chlorofluorocarbons (CFCs) were
being connected to depletion of the earth's protective ozone
layer. Global respect was at the heart of the essay, *Sharing the
Continent*, published in 1982 by Canadian scholar Northrop
Frye. He wrote: "It seems to me that the capitalist-socialist

*Lt. Gov. Grant MacEwan with
Sherwood Park children, 1972.*
— Edmonton Journal

controversy is out of date, and that a detente with an outraged nature is what is important now."

In October 1973, the oil-producing Arab states increased, overnight, the price per barrel by 70 percent and they vowed to cut production by five percent per month. The global oil-pricing crisis sent Alberta's resource-based economy into a period of unprecedented and unbridled growth. Edmonton and Calgary became Canada's fastest-growing cities and the centre of commercial and residential construction almost overnight. The seventies oil-boom, though, became the eighties land-value bust. The combination of the federal Liberal government's hated National Energy Policy (NEP), high interest rates and a nationwide economic recession put many Albertans who had speculated heavily into bankruptcy. Land prices tumbled and unemployment jumped from four to ten percent.

Throughout the 1970s, eighties, and into nineties, traditional Canadian values, real or perceived, seemed to be under siege. Moreover, the 1972 launch of Anik A-1, the nation's first telecommunications satellite, fulfilled Marshall McLuhan's prediction that the world would become a global village, and Canada just another citizen. Good news stories such as Team Canada's win over the Soviets in 1972 and the myriad of scientific and technological discoveries and developments that followed were being overshadowed by print and electronic media accounts of other events and trends.

Reports emerged during the seventies that there were Canadian children who were undernourished, and who went to school without breakfast. During the eighties, the proud nation learned that as many as one million of its females were abused each year. By the nineties, the spread of AIDS and an accumulated debt and spiralling yearly deficit — with the potential to catapult Canada into bankruptcy — dominated conversations.

The Roman statesman, orator and Latin prose writer Marcus Cato wrote: "The agricultural population produces the bravest men, the most valiant soldiers, and a class of citizens the least given to all evil designs." But by the late 1980s, prairie farmers were under siege. The same agrarians whose proud ancestors had influenced the development of the West's culture, society, politics and economics were forced by low crop prices to seek outside employment, or to leave farming entirely.

Grant MacEwan's term as the ninth lieutenant-governor in Alberta's history was far from reckless, and certainly not conventional. Throughout his eight-and-a-half years in office, the former MLA and mayor of Calgary was a man for all people. His message was always clear and consistent: conserve the best of the past and show respect to all living creatures. The children in classrooms where he talked about the need to plant trees were as important to him, and perhaps more, than the rich and famous at formal functions. Young people represented, to MacEwan, eager minds and willing bodies to carry forth his convictions about conservation.

"We laughed more in my youth than we do today —notwithstanding the hardship, the absence of television and radio, telephones and automobiles, magazines and whatnot."

Lt. Gov. Grant MacEwan talks with elementary school children about conservation, 1970. — Provincial Archives of Alberta

Phyllis and Grant MacEwan try out the rocking chairs given to them by the city of Edmonton as a farewell gift, June 22, 1974. — Edmonton Journal

When Grant MacEwan was appointed to his post, he vowed to Albertans that he would not become a lieutenant-governor for the sole pleasure of Edmontonians. He took his office to every corner of the province. It was his achievement of this self-imposed goal, plus his forthright and folksy way of commenting on current and sometimes controversial issues, that identified him as a Western legend, and for Albertans, a hero.

His retirement, like his appointment, brought a tide of wishes for a happy and healthy retirement. On June 23, 1974, the Conservative provincial government led by Peter Lougheed, held a reception for the retiring lieutenant-governor. Journalist Ralph Armstrong of the *Edmonton Journal* reported: "The province had thrown the reception open to all Albertans. Not all 1,700,000 were expected but the caterers were ready for 8,000. . ."

Grant MacEwan amongst admirers at province sponsored farewell, June 23, 1974. — Edmonton Journal

The province also gave him a big, shiny, gas-guzzling car with all the trimmings. According to writer Rusty Macdonald, Grant discreetly whispered to Phyllis MacEwan, "whoever suggested that gift doesn't know me." The following day, the lieutenant-governor exchanged his gift for a smaller more energy-efficient model of car. He returned the difference to the government treasury.

During Grant MacEwan's term of office, much of the rivalry between the Edmonton and Calgary disappeared.

He admonished those who spoke disparagingly of one or the other in a grandfatherly manner. On June 22, 1974, the city of Edmonton held their own tribute and over 2,500 Edmontonians came to cheer the former Calgary mayor. "We've been told here tonight that you love the MacEwans," said the retiring vice-regal. "Well, the MacEwans love you back. . ."

Although Grant MacEwan was not Alberta's longest serving lieutenant-governor (John Campbell Bowen served for a total of thirteen years) his popularity rivalled that of a movie star or famous politician. Many people thought he had more authority than he did.

A week before his retirement, MacEwan received a letter from a young American who asked His Honour to officiate at his marriage. Marvin Dennis from Oregon wrote: ". . . About the first week in July a young lady and I have decided we would rather live together than live alone. . . It would be a great satisfaction if we could arrive in your fair city about the 4-5-6 of July, put up in a motel for a day or so and then on any convenient day drive over to Government House and have the Honourable J.W. Grant MacEwan perform a simple marriage ceremony . . ."

The lieutenant-governor wrote back, "Congratulations on the important decision to go into double harness . . . There is nothing that would please me more than to have a part in performing the ceremony, but that authority does not come with my office. . ." He concluded his letter by saying he was not sure where he would be or what he would be doing.

Alberta newspapers reported the Queen's cowboy was returning to the land. Put more accurately, MacEwan's goal was to spend time in his log cabin overlooking the Little Red Deer River near Sundre, Alberta. He had built the cabin just as the pioneers had at the beginning of the century. He furnished it in the same way, and wanted to work the land with implements from the time period.

MacEwan had built the cabin from recycled and secondhand telephone poles that he had gathered during his vice-regal trips throughout the province. "If Dr. MacEwan saw a pole," disclosed Pat Halligan, his secretary, "he would ask his chauffeur to stop, and he'd toss it in the trunk." MacEwan told *Herald* journalist Kevin Peterson that his abode was ". . . not very handsome, not very square and not very level, but log houses were never supposed to be level or square."

"I guess it's just as well we can't look ahead. It's fun to look back. We can all thank God for memories. We should make the most of them."

*Max Foran, Heather MacEwan-Foran
and Grant MacEwan at Priddis, 1973.*
— MacEwan-Foran Collection

*Max Foran, Heather MacEwan-Foran
and Grant MacEwan errect poles for
teepee at Priddis. Cabin built by
MacEwan's uncle John Grant (in 1944)
stands in background.*
— MacEwan-Foran Collection

There was never any question about Grant and Phyllis MacEwan not returning to Calgary. Their daughter, Heather, and her family lived there, and MacEwan's fondness for doing his book research at the Glenbow Museum was well known. Perhaps Grant MacEwan would finally get to live on his beloved Priddis property?

As a small child, the Priddis property had taken on an almost mystical quality for Heather. Even before the family left Manitoba, "living at Priddis" was a future goal, albeit, an elusive one. While Grant would talk about the solitude it afforded, Heather dreamed about living there. However, after her marriage to Max Foran and the arrival of their two little girls, the dream faded. Besides, the couple's home in Calgary's southwest district was comfortable and met their needs.

Where her parents would live on their return to Calgary was, of course, a question which interested Heather. During one of the family discussions, "and I don't remember who suggested the idea," recalled Heather, "but someone suggested Max and I should switch properties with Mother and Father." The idea took hold. Heather, Max, Fiona and Lynwyn Foran moved to Priddis in the summer of 1973 and Grant and Phyllis MacEwan moved into the Foran's home upon their return to Calgary in 1974.

On June 26, 1974, the University of Calgary (U of C) made a successful bid for the teaching services of the retiring MacEwan. "On behalf of the Board of Governors . . . I am pleased to offer you an appointment on the teaching faculty as a Professor (part-time) in the Faculty of Arts and Science's Department of History . . ." wrote the acting president, F.A. Campbell. MacEwan began teaching *History 436 - From the Red to the Rockies: Selected Topics in Prairie Canada* in the fall of 1974. His remuneration was set at $8,000 per two-term year.

The appointment to teach about the Prairies fulfilled Grant MacEwan's every hope. During his early years in the Brandon school system, the abysmal lack of Canadian content in history books had bothered him. As an adult, he had worked to correct the score by writing about the colorful pioneers who helped to build and shape the Canadian identity. His book *From the Red to the Rockies*, which provided a graphic portrait of the development of the West as an agricultural giant, became title and text for the course. It was the book he had completed after the Brandon-Souris by-election defeat.

MacEwan's classes were an extension of his everyday personality. They were structured yet informal. The students were inundated with information packaged in anecdotal stories to make it interesting. His courses were usually full to overflowing, and whether it was the professor's reputation or a requirement, students almost always wrote a note to him to explain absences from class.

Student Brenda Vickers wrote: "Please forgive me for not being at your class lately but I have had so much work that I have not had the time to come. . ." MacEwan underlined and scribbled a question mark behind her operative phrases "so much work" and "not had the time." Perhaps he was thinking back to his undergraduate course load and all of the requirements made on his time.

In addition to teaching at the U of C, Grant MacEwan agreed to give two lectures per week at Olds Agricultural College. The college, located 89 kilometers north of Calgary, was founded in 1913. Structured education for future farmers followed the American agrarian reform movement of 1880s and 1890s. The movement believed that the rural population had different educational needs than urban populations and, hence, several agricultural colleges were established in western Canada in the early 1900s. At Olds, the seventy-two-year-old MacEwan presented a course on the history of western Canadian agriculture. He also presented a program for seniors about western history, and like his other classes, both were filled to capacity.

Grant MacEwan dedicates memorial to Negro rancher John Ware.
— Glenbow Archives

Grant MacEwan gives convocation address at the University of Alberta, 1966. — University of Alberta Photographic Service

Throughout his term of office, and after his retirement, Grant MacEwan was recognized, awarded and honored by communities, universities and governments. The first institution to award him an honorary doctorate, his bachelor of laws (LLD) in 1966 was the University of Manitoba. It must have been, somehow, a bittersweet experience for MacEwan. This same university had forced him to resign his position as Dean of Agriculture and Home Economics in 1951 when he accepted the Liberal nomination for Brandon-Souris. After his defeat in the by-election, MacEwan had moved to Alberta and began his political career. It was uncanny that the institution that was so quick to discharge him for his interest in politics became the first to celebrate his appointment as Alberta's lieutenant-governor.

More honorary LLDs followed from the University of Calgary in 1967; Brandon in 1969; Guelph, his alma mater, in 1972; and Saskatchewan in 1974. He had achieved, finally, the title that he had lacked and which had prevented him from becoming the Dean of Agriculture at the University of Saskatchewan. At each of the convocations, he talked about the convictions which had guided his life in addition to a related theme that was becoming increasingly important to him — greed.

At the University of Guelph's convocation in 1972, Grant MacEwan recalled, for the guests, his return to the family farm after he graduated in 1926. "Our farm neighbors were still without cars, tractors, trucks, telephones, electric lights and radios," he said. "Plumbing wise, they had three rooms and a path."

The lieutenant-governor described how machines and gadgets and appliances began to command mastery over people — of how natural resources were converted into money for a higher standard of living — and of how all this newfound wealth was said to bring contentment. "But instead of bringing contentment," countered MacEwan, "these advances were accompanied by unrest, rebellion, protests, frustrations and people looking for more sleeping pills, more tranquilizers, more of the dope stuff to escape the easy life."

He suggested that air and water pollution were only symptoms — "the point of the iceberg" — of a society which had grown soft "physically, mentally and morally" because of its preoccupation with "wealth and luxury and leisure and machines." MacEwan urged the assembly to examine the emerging score between Nature and humanity, and concluded: "Our problems, at bottom are too many people demanding too much easy living costing too much in resources and environ-ment."

"I love to look back to my farm days. They weren't my worst days, they were good days. Somehow we found compensations."

At that time, Alberta was poised to begin a period of extraordinary growth due to the global oil crisis. His remarks, no doubt, raised a few eyebrows in his own home province, which derived most of its income from the export of its natural resources. It was not, however, the first time MacEwan appeared to be out of step with contemporary thinking. During his term as leader of the provincial Liberal party in the late fifties, Grant MacEwan had severely criticized Alberta's Socred government for allowing the sale of natural gas for ". . .44 cents a thousand cubic feet for gas at Grande Prairie in the Peace River district when Peace River gas is sold at the United States border for 22 cents a thousand cubic feet."

On February 11, 1959 the Liberal leader had openly accused the government of the day of being in a great rush to export and convert the province's resources into spending money. The following day, *The Albertan* published an "open letter to Grant MacEwan" in which it chastised the Liberal leader for wanting to "horde" Alberta's natural gas.

The newspaper felt, perhaps, that it correctly mirrored the thoughts of the population when it wrote: "Hasn't the

"You had to be resourceful to be a pioneer in Western Canada. You had to be versatile."

history of civilization, Mr. MacEwan, been that of the use of whatever resources were at hand at the time? Man's ingenuity has always outstripped his use of nature's resources, but if man had not used what was at hand for fear of running short in the future, he would still be back in the caves." Four months later, MacEwan and his provincial Liberals were annihilated by Manning's Socreds, and the province continued to sell-off its resources with little thought to the future.

In 1974, Grant MacEwan's convocation address to University of Saskatchewan graduands was sharper, and it openly introduced greed as the force behind many of the world's problems. "Greed," he told the assembly, "brought a bigger crop of troubles than anybody anticipated." He contrasted the "well-to-do North American maintaining a palatial home, a three-car garage, a private launch and possibly a private plane" to current news events of the day, namely, the famine in Ethiopia. "In the name of peace on earth, conservation of the non-renewables, pollution control and moral responsibility," MacEwan pleaded, "we must attempt to lift the poorer countries closer to our level or bring our level down closer to theirs."

By the end of 1974, MacEwan had accumulated five honorary doctorates; the B'Nai Brith Humanitarian Award; the Canadian Brotherhood Council Award; an honorary diploma from Grant MacEwan Community College which also honored him by naming the institution after him; and he was made an Officer of the Order of Canada.

One honour became a special source of pleasure and pride to MacEwan during the years following his retirement. "I was occupying an office in the Legislature Building about twenty-five years ago when two public-spirited Edmontonians, Barry Moore and Judge Ed Stack made an early morning call," wrote MacEwan in the foreword of *The History of Grant MacEwan Community College: The First Two Decades.*

"They didn't have time for coffee and a muffin but before leaving, Mr. Moore hinted that they had a plan. 'We believe,' said Mr. Moore, 'that Edmonton should have a community college to accommodate students who are no longer within reach of high schools and not qualified for university.' I was impressed and said so but his next remark left me momentarily speechless: 'We would like to call it Grant MacEwan.' I was puzzled and flattered and didn't overlook the

possibility that my guests were indulging in humor. . ."
Lieutenant-Governor MacEwan quickly queried his guests,
"This isn't one of them funny religious groups, is it?"

Judge Ed Stack was convinced that the new
institution, initially called Edmonton College, should be named
after an important individual. Glenn Ruhl, author of *The
History of Grant MacEwan Community College: The First
Two Decades* wrote: "Two names were submitted that held the
interests of the community in top priority. . ." The names were
Grant MacEwan and John Michaels, who had been, for years,
the newsboy on the corner of Jasper and 101 Street and eventually the owner of Mike's Newsstand.

*Grant MacEwan, namesake of
Edmonton's community college.*
— Alex Hill, GMCC Students' Assoc.

Stack felt that Grant MacEwan — who by then had
authored eighteen books, was the past mayor of Calgary, an
educator and conservationist, and was well-known for his
involvement and services to community groups — was the
right person and that his name would benefit the new
institution. On July 15, 1970 the Board agreed "that the
Honourable Dr. J.W. Grant MacEwan be selected because of his
availability to perhaps lay the cornerstone and otherwise
participate in the opening of the College."

Dr. MacEwan, in a letter dated July 24, 1970, granted
permission to the college to use his name. "I repeat my very
great delight in the proposal which you made on behalf of your
Board and I can only repeat that the adoption of my name in
connection with the College will bring me lasting joy and
satisfaction. You have my permission as well as my blessing."
When MacEwan was asked about his new honor he replied,
"I don't know why they did it and still don't. But I'm not going
to ask any questions in case they change their minds."

Often, foreign students, and some members of the
Edmonton community and visitors to the city even went so far
as to assume the college was established by MacEwan. For
them, there could be no other reason for a college to bear his
name. Meeting students from around the world, who chose to
study at the institution named for him, pleased the former
lieutenant-governor to no end. "It was a real thrill for him,"
said Dorothy Gray, an English instructor and an acquaintance
of MacEwan for forty years. During one campus visit, he
stopped to chat with two students from Nigeria. When he
learned where they were from he asked: "I guess you don't go
home for summer holidays?"

Grant MacEwan's favorite mode of travel - Greyhound coach.
— Edmonton Journal

A kinship developed between the college and Grant MacEwan. Certainly the institution's close association with this Western legend helped them to gain wide public acceptance. Although the institution's first premise was a converted grocery store, MacEwan made an outstanding effort to not only lend his name to the college but to create a presence within its structure.

In 1986 the college established "MacEwan Day" in mid-February to honor an employee who was deemed to have made an outstanding contribution to the institution during the previous year. Grant MacEwan would travel by Greyhound bus to Edmonton, leaving his Calgary home as early as five o'clock on the morning of the appointed day. A college administrator or student would be dispatched to retrieve him. If the bus arrived early, the eighty-plus-year-old MacEwan walked the seven blocks from the bus depot to the Seventh Street campus, leaving the designated chauffeur to spend several frustrating minutes searching for his well-known passenger.

The celebration began with a pancake breakfast and was followed by the presentation of the "MacEwan Medallion" to the awardee by Grant MacEwan. The bronze, coin-shaped medal, some four inches in diametre, with MacEwan's profile minted on its front dangled from the recipient's neck during the rest of the day as he or she accompanied the elderly MacEwan on a stroll of all the campuses. At the end of the day, MacEwan boarded another Greyhound bus to return to Calgary. It was often ten o'clock or later before he arrived home.

At the 1987 Grant MacEwan Day, the college made arrangements for a chuckwagon drawn by a team of heavy horses to take their namesake from the Seventh Street campus to meet then Lieutenant-Governor Helen Hunley. The wagon pulled up in front of the Alberta Legislature where the eighty-four-year-old MacEwan hopped down from the rig in time to lend assistance to the college's much younger president, Gerald Kelly. The former vice-regal then climbed several flights of stairs as if he were still a young man. When the House staff learned about the former lieutenant-governor's impromptu visit, they converged in the rotunda area to say hello, leaving the deputy-premier for the day, Dick Johnston, wondering who was causing the commotion.

In November 1994, the college opened its City Centre campus. The event was attended by past and present politicians, staff, students and scores of supporters. Grant MacEwan, at 91 years, had delighted the masses who came to hear him; he disappointed no one. "When I'm gone," he asserted, "the MacEwan name will live on in this institution. We had a daughter," he stated. "She had two daughters," he added. "I never had a son," he declared. "But I'm not dead yet."

The following day he gave the opening talk, "Water: A Commodity for the Future?" at J.W. Grant MacEwan Environmental Studies Institute which he helped to establish at the college. MacEwan's lecture was not only timely, it was the current issue in the ongoing North American Free Trade Agreement (NAFTA) negotiations and the topic of his next book. His stance that "Canada may have a moral responsibility to sell water to the United States" met strong resistance. After the lecture he quipped, "Things sure have changed!"

Between 1974 to 1982, it would appear MacEwan's direct and blunt comments on conservation and nonrenewable resources were out of sync with public opinion and, perhaps, the establishment, with the exception of one instance. When Alberta's Conservative government proposed the creation of the Alberta Heritage Savings Trust Fund in 1976, to "save and invest revenues from Alberta's oil and gas," Grant MacEwan wrote to the premier and applauded the idea. He supported the concept that revenues from the fund would be used to provide long-term benefits to Albertans, and ultimately Canada. Premier Lougheed was quick to request the former lieutenant-governor's permission ". . . to use your open letter as part of my remarks during the course of the debate of the Bill."

Grant MacEwan was shut out from official accolades for eight years. He continued to advocate his views about conservation, but because the resource-based economy of Western Canada was booming, his message fell on deaf ears. Media always knew that if they needed an "earthy" comment, MacEwan could encapsulate in a few words what others took hours to describe. He was very critical of the federal government's excessive spending and soaring debt. "It doesn't seem decent," he said in a 1979 Canadian Press interview. When he was asked for his opinion about Prime Minister Joe Clark, he retorted: "He's no better or worse than the leader who's let the deficit climb to where it is today."

Those years, nevertheless, were a very productive period of time for Grant MacEwan as a conservationist and writer. In January 1976, MacEwan was appointed as chairman of the joint federal-provincial committee to conduct public hearings for the 360-square-mile proposed Grasslands National Park in Saskatchewan. The hearings were, at times, heated with ranchers and environmentalists clashing openly about if and what species should be allowed to graze. In February, the federal government's Department of Indian and Northern Affairs appointed MacEwan as leader of a three-person group to evaluate native cultural-educational centres across the country. The $6 million program had been approved in 1971 on the basis that it would be assessed at the end of five years. In both cases, Grant MacEwan's reports were thorough and concluded within the given time. Like most government proposals, though, the recommendations became bogged down in bureaucratic red-tape. By the time they were tabled, there had been a change of government in Ottawa.

Between 1974 and 1993, Grant MacEwan finished writing another twenty-seven books bringing the total number to over fifty. He also began a score of other manuscripts which are "in progress" or met with rejection. Sometimes the original focus of a book changed before it was written simply because the material MacEwan unearthed during his research pointed him in another direction. His sensitivity and alertness to emerging trends was a trait that served him well as a writer.

A prolific writer of Western Canadian History. — Edmonton Journal

Grant MacEwan's ability to tailor his written voice to the topic allowed him to switch from pioneer history to conservation to humor or politics. He could write seriously or with wit, with passion or with levity. He wrote as he talked, and he talked as he wrote. His father's generation had witnessed the transformation of Western Canada into prime agricultural land: MacEwan witnessed the downfall of agriculture as a pivotal industry. His books have become a living legacy of that part of the Canadian identity.

Royalty cheques of several thousand dollars were sent to MacEwan twice a year by his publishers. Most writers of the day would have been happy to have earned half of the amount he was receiving. Few writers, however, ever become as disciplined in their technique, nor do they put forth the effort that Grant MacEwan had in his over his forty-plus years of writing.

Much of the research that formed the basis of Grant MacEwan's books was found during his regular visits to the Glenbow Library or the University of Calgary's Special Collections. The library or museum in towns and cities he visited was of prime importance for historic data. Newspapers, more than magazines, became another source.

The Glenbow Archives and Library became a favorite haunt for Grant MacEwan.
— Donna von Hauff

"Writing," MacEwan told one newspaper reporter, "has never been my master but has always been my companion." The former academic opened up files for his areas of interest and systematically clipped and collected information. When he felt he had enough to begin a book, he started to write. A pencil and some paper were the basic tools and no amount of coaxing moved him from his manual typewriter to a computer. His two-finger staccato permitted thinking between strokes.

There were as many irritations for MacEwan in writing as there were delights. He wrote as talked in his *Calgary Herald* column. Twice during his thirty-six years of writing for the paper, its internal workings challenged his patience and gave him reason to chuckle. On one occasion, the text of MacEwan's column about Spartanism appeared under Erma Bombeck's picture and authorship — his picture and byline appeared over her column about marriage breakdown. On another occasion, his material came out under Eric Nicol's name and picture which, according to MacEwan, "did no harm except that the subject of snowshoeing was not exactly his line."

"My people weren't particularly musical but we loved to sing."

It is impossible to estimate the number of forewords Grant MacEwan has authored for other writers, and for no compensation other than a copy of the book when it was published. During Canada's centennial year, hundreds of communities published their histories, and many of these books have an introduction written by Lieutenant-Governor Grant MacEwan.

When MacEwan wrote the foreword for the book *The Devil in Deerskin,* he had found, perhaps, a kindred spirit when he wrote, ". . . In many ways, Grey Owl was years ahead of his time. At his period in Canadian history, conservation was not a popular topic. Were he living today, he would find many more sympathetic listeners when he talked about the personalities and souls of the wilderness and its denizens."

In October 1982, Grant MacEwan undertook one of the most satisfying writing projects of his career knowing full well it would neither contribute to his bank roll nor to his best-seller list. It did, however, add to his pantry and his growing number of admirers. A committee of Calgary firefighters led by Bill Weisenburger had gathered up their courage, knocked on the door of MacEwan's Calgary home, and asked the busy writer, conservationist and speaker if he would be interested in writing a book. The firefighters were intent on publishing a book to commemorate the one-hundredth anniversary of the city's fire department. Although they had assembled most of the necessary research, both committing it to paper and getting it published posed a problem for them. The committee and MacEwan sat down at his kitchen table and worked out a deal.

MacEwan had two other manuscripts underway at the time, yet he completed the seventeen-chapter book, *100 Years of Smoke, Sweat and Tears* in ninety-two days. Fiona Foran, MacEwan's teenage granddaughter also contributed to the book. Fiona wrote the biographical sketch of her "Gramps" who she describes ". . . as one who is at peace with himself and the world in an age of dependence, frustration and insecurity. He lives simply, frugally and by a code he has worked through himself, and if a granddaughter may judge, he has found the secrets to good and useful living."

His payment was as requested, one jar of peanut butter. The firefighters also presented MacEwan with a pair of airline tickets for a round trip to his beloved Scotland, and they made him an honorary fire chief. The writing of this limited edition remained one of MacEwan's favorite projects.

Moreover, the friendships that he developed with the firefighters were a source of special pride. One morning, MacEwan was busy writing in his office which was located at the back of his house. Despite his poor hearing, he had heard the sounds of solid footsteps on his roof. He stuck his head out his front door and shouted, "Who's there?" Firefighter Weisenburger yelled down from above, "It's me. I'm cleaning your eavestroughs."

Grant MacEwan reciprocated the favor by inviting the firefighter and his family to one of his famous porridge parties. Over the years, Grant MacEwan had evolved his own recipe for the hot cereal. It was made from a combination of grains, raisins, nuts, and "a couple of slices of dark bread cooked thoroughly and served with a scoop of ice cream."

Weisenburger, however, not knowing what to expect in the way of food thought it wise to sternly forewarn his two preteens to "eat what's served." He need not have worried. MacEwan slopped the mixture into the boys' bowls, heaped a scoop of ice cream on top and sent them on their way. Before the adults were ready to sit down with their porridge, the boys were back for more.

By the 1980s, concern for the environment, non-renewable resources and the extinction of more species had entered classroom curriculums as far down as kindergarten. Recycling programs appeared in cities across Canada, grocery stores advertised "green" products, and governments that legislated environmental protection got elected. Society's concern for the environment had finally caught up with MacEwan's lifelong philosophy.

The shutout of awards ended in 1982 and Grant MacEwan was rediscovered. Between 1982 to 1993 Grant MacEwan was awarded the Alberta Award of Excellence; Governor General's Conservation Award; Calgary Negev Honoree; Alberta Culture's Nonfiction Award; Zeke Young Memorial Award; Sir Frederick Haultain Prize; and Emerald Award for Environmental Excellence (Lifetime Environmental Achievement Award). In addition, the University of Calgary established the Grant MacEwan Student Center, Greyhound Lines of Canada made him an honorary bus driver and he was inducted into the Manitoba Agricultural Hall of Fame.

"When I'm alone now, I sing at the top of my voice. I'm glad no one can hear me."

On November 18, 1982, the City of Calgary and numerous other sponsoring associations held a tribute dinner in honor of the former lieutenant-governor. The audience of 630 Albertans, who had paid $25-a-plate, were treated to his humorous reflections on how it felt to turn 80-years old. The former Calgary mayor and MLA told the guests that because of his age, "I can get away with kissing women, spilling soup on my necktie and walking around not properly zippered because people make allowances when you officially become an old man."

Grant MacEwan became more cherished and listened to with every additional decade. He had been well into his "golden years" by the time he officially retired, but he was far from taking up residence in a rocking chair. Moreover, he felt the contribution that seniors could make to society was being dismissed by all-too-ready youthful legislators who deemed age as the factor to determine "the capable from the incapable." The generation MacEwan was born to, farmed and performed physical work well into their seventies and eighties. They were a fit and alert lot who were not pastured out into old age homes. In 1979, he told a group of Alberta's seniors, "I've walked past too many senior citizen residences and seen older people looking eagerly out the window for an adventure — if only a mental adventure."

At seventy-five, eighty and ninety years of age, MacEwan continued to be a popular speaker within the golden-age club. He would hike himself up on a table, as he did during his university years, and talk about the subjects that were near and dear to the hearts of the audience: government spending, the need to conserve for "our grandchildren" and the days when people put in an honest day's work if they wanted to get paid. "I strongly resent the fact that our society literally cuts people off all activities at age 65," he told 150 seniors. At the time, MacEwan was eighty-years-old.

One of the more unusual tributes paid to Grant MacEwan was made by Greyhound Lines of Canada. On MacEwan's eighty-eighth birthday in 1990, the company made him an honorary bus driver and gave him and his wife, Phyllis, free lifetime bus passes. Before he could become a bus driver, however, MacEwan was obliged to become a member, also honorary, of the Amalgamated Transit Union. In January 1994, Greyhound dedicated coach 956 to John Walter Grant

MacEwan ". . . in recognition of his longstanding service and contribution to his country."

Fifty-eight years had passed since his Greyhound honeymoon trip with Phyllis. The roads, like the coaches of the time, were dusty and unreliable. With the passing of the years, both improved. MacEwan travelled by bus during the Depression because "it took the least charge on the environment." His reason was the same in the nineties.

Staying at the "Y" for most individuals signifies a cheap place to stay. For Grant MacEwan, it became his home away from home because, "The sheets are clean and the roof doesn't leak." The cost of a room was also what he was prepared to pay. More importantly, the YMCA was where "average" people stayed — individuals without power, prestige or money. The breakfast was hearty, and the conversation cheap. There was always a story to be captured in print or used in a speech. The movement also promotes much of what MacEwan believed to be important in this world: physical fitness, harmony with nature, adult education, youth activities, and humanitarian work.

The Edmonton YMCA became the overnight stopping-house for the former vice-regal when his visits to Grant MacEwan Community College required more than the usual one day. The college president's secretary would telephone and make reservations, although the Y's policy is first-come, first-served. But it's not often a hostel can brag that a western Canadian legend is their best client.

The Priddis property remained a source of enjoyment for MacEwan, particularly now that his daughter and her family lived there. Heather had made numerous improvements to the property since moving to it in the early 1970s. The muddy road was now packed and gravelled, and she had planted grass and fruit trees around the house. When Heather decided to build an addition onto her home to house her growing collection of Canadiana, she asked for her father's help. After some discussion, the two decided the only way to prevent damage to the new lawn and trees was to dig the basement for the addition — a 55-square-metre hole, 2.5 metres deep — by hand. "It was the cleanest excavation site in Alberta," recalled Heather MacEwan-Foran.

Grant MacEwan's love for horses was shared by his daughter. He had given Heather her first pony, Molasses, when

"Bagpipes were a rare article on the Frontier. I never learned to play them. I played at them. There's a sacred quality about 'Amazing Grace' on the bagpipes that I can't explain. It's always brought tears to my eyes."

Phyllis MacEwan. 1909 - 1990
— Edmonton Journal

she was seven-years old. When she moved to Priddis, it became possible for her to have her own horses. In July 1984, Grant MacEwan and Heather's husband, Max Foran, had gone up on the half-section farm to find the roaming horses. The eighty-one-year-old MacEwan, who had been working with Heather's part-Arabian mare, climbed onto the animal and was promptly bucked off. He suffered a broken pelvis and bruises in the accident. Phyllis MacEwan suggested her husband should heed his age.

Phyllis Cline MacEwan's marriage to Grant MacEwan was far from average. During their honeymoon, the groom finished writing his first book. When Phyllis went to church one Sunday, she learned that her husband — who was supposedly away on business — was in a city hospital having his haemorrhoids fixed. The couple's first pets were a pair of young skunks that Grant brought home after a walk. And her husband liked to work — all of his waking hours. It was, perchance, some of these occurrences which convinced Phyllis MacEwan that she had married a "rather unusual individual."

Grant MacEwan's constant round of teaching, community work and travel left Phyllis alone for much of their marriage. She responded by developing a life of her own. When Heather was grown, she travelled the world. Grant bought her plane ticket, and Phyllis paid for her accommodation and expenses from household money she had saved during the year. Mexico became her favorite destination, and as her arthritis worsened, the holiday was therapeutic rather than adventurous.

She scoured auction sales in Edmonton and Calgary for milk glass dishes, brass candlesticks and antique Canadiana furniture. It was one pastime which Grant was persuaded to share. Her assortment of teddy bears would rival any Steiff shop. During the course of Grant MacEwan's political career, Phyllis became known for her musical talents, her sense of humor and the wide-brimmed hats that she wore to public functions.

Phyllis's death on October 12, 1990 dealt a staggering blow to her husband of fifty-five years. She died of meningitis just as Grant's brother had in 1924. When George passed away, Grant had been a young man concerned for his parents and busy with his education. There was no time then to grieve for the brother he'd hoped to grow old with. The similarity between the death of his wife, and longest friend, and his brother triggered emotions in MacEwan that had been stored for years. He suffered an outpouring of grief that lasted for months.

His life became a lonely pattern of going to the library and writing. Heather, Max and the girls all helped, but the loss of a companion who has shared over half a century of your life is difficult if not impossible to overcome.

MacEwan's den in his house continued to be his refuge. The years of research — magazines, papers and books — lined the walls of the room from the floor to the ceiling. He had removed a portion of the window and replaced it with plywood. A small hole in it with a flap-style door allowed a squirrel he had befriended as an orphan to come and go as the animal pleased.

Early in 1992, Grant MacEwan turned over a good part of the fortune he had gathered in his lifetime to the Calgary Foundation. His donation of over $600,000 was divided into two trusts. In accordance with his wishes, the $500,000 MacEwan Family Charitable Fund annually disperses money to the Mennonite Central Committee of Alberta, the Animal Defence League of Canada, the Dr. J.W. Grant MacEwan Environmental Studies Institute, the archives and library of the Glenbow Museum, Operation Eyesight Universal, and the Sea Shepherd Conservation Society. The $101,000 Grant MacEwan Nature Protection Fund is designated to encourage conservation of wildlife and natural habitat and the $20,000 Grant MacEwan Nature Protection Auxiliary Fund provides food for wildlife. MacEwan told reporters, "I lost my ambition to make a million dollars. I thought I was making a mistake letting my money pile up."

On November 28, 1992, MacEwan slipped on a patch of ice in the back lane behind his house. The fall broke a few bones but not his spirit. Friends and family, however, convinced him that it was time to give up his house and to move into a seniors' lodge. Six months later, though, he was back living on his own in an apartment in downtown Calgary. He wasn't ready to call it quits, yet.

His body was slower to recover from the fall than his intellect. The recovery time, however, gave him an opportunity to set down for youth a catechism to guide their lives.

Phyllis MacEwan with some of her many Western Canadian artifacts.
— Edmonton Journal

J.W. Grant MacEwan (circa 1990)
— Edmonton Journal

"When funeral day comes for old man MacEwan — I hope the pipes will be there to play 'Amazing Grace.'"

1. *Thou shalt love and cherish the Great World of Nature, God's House on loan to us for a season. Conscientious tenants should aspire to nothing less than the lofty, practical and moral roles of caretakership. Good citizens should be grateful for the privilege and honor of answering to the challenge of those roles commonly known as conservation and environmental protection.*

2. *Thou shalt hate war and all forms of cruelty touching humans and other living creatures — all God's Children. Better to be a caretaker and peacemaker "in the House of my God" than to dwell in the "tents of the destroyers."*

3. *Consider well thy regard for money. In the lives of young people, exercises in making and saving money may be good but when wealth becomes a object of worship for wealth's sake or is accumulated in greedy and dishonest ways, there is not much to be said for it and there are many better shapes for a lifetime purpose.*

4. *Thou shalt hold thine own body and its myriads of working parts as things of unsurpassed wonder, deserving the best nutrition and the best care you or I can give.*

5. *Thou shalt firmly refuse entry to thy precious body of those habit-forming evils like cigarette smoke, alcoholic beverages and drugs. To yield to them is not smart and may be a forerunner of poverty and misery.*

6. *Neglect not thy personality and adorn the God-given image with smiles and laughter and clean humor.*

7. *Thou shalt despise the sins of extravagance and waste in the lives of both individuals and nations. In a world with limited resources and soaring populations, both breed hunger and misery.*

8. *Neglect not thy spiritual life; remember the words of Robert Burns that "they never sought in vain who sought the Lord aright."*

9. *Remind thyself, also, of the words of Tennyson, that "More things are wrought by prayer than this world dreams of."*

10. *And in thy search for spiritual guidelines, why not commit to memory the 6th verse of the 8th chapter of the Old Testament Book of Micah. The prophet was responding to the question: "What doth the Lord require of thee?" and answered as if the reply was for my generation: "To do justly, and love mercy, and walk humbly with thy God."*

The considerable wealth Grant MacEwan accumulated during his life was, to a large extent, an extension of his convictions. In 1950 he wrote: "Canada faces a wealth of opportunity, not the opportunity that makes millionaires, but the opportunity to serve and reap the rich satisfactions which go with service. Today the eyes of the world are on this land. It is a rich heritage. We need no imported ideologies or isms — we just need faith and loyalty and decency."

Although Grant MacEwan could be seen as a penny-pincher, his frugality was prompted by deprivation. It was the Melfort property which had saved Alex MacEwan's family from destitution. For Grant MacEwan, it was his investments and savings which, more than once, served as a safety-net for his family. He had not only learned the ditty his mother had taught him as a two-year-old, but had lived it — "Wilful waste brings woeful want, and some day you may say, oh how I wish I had the crust, that once I threw away."

Faith, loyalty and decency guided John Walter Grant MacEwan. He faced failure with self-reliance, need with resourcefulness, indulgence with caution, and the exploitation of Nature's storehouse as a protective husbandman. He lived his beliefs, and it was those same convictions that prompted him to write in 1989: "What more worthy moral cause, what more lofty human purpose than seeing to it that our grandchildren have trees, food, clean air and water, crude oil, prairie chickens and iron ore — without being shackled by heavy debts and the improvident ways of their grandparents?"

Everyone's grandfather, Grant MacEwan
— Peter von Hauff

Books by Grant MacEwan

The Science & Practice of Canadian Animal Husbandry, 1936, 1945.
General Agriculture, 1939.
Breeds of Farm Livestock in Canada, 1941.
Feeding Farm Animals, 1945.
Sodbusters, 1948.
Agriculture on Parade, 1950.
Between the Red and the Rockies, 1952, 1956, 1963, 1979.
Eye Opener Bob, 1957, 1962, 1974.
Fifty Mighty Men, 1958, 1971, 1975, 1982.
Calgary Cavalcade, 1958, 1975.
John Ware's Cow Country, 1960, 1973, 1976, 1984, 1986.
Blazing the Old Cattle Trail, 1962, 1972, 1975.
Hoofprints and Hitchingposts, 1964, 1972.
Poking into Politics, 1966.
Entrusted to My Care, 1966, 1986.
West to theSea, with M. Foran, 1968.
Harvest of Bread, 1969.
Tatanga Mani: Walking Buffalo of the Stonies, 1969.
Power for Prairie Plows, 1971.
Portraits from the Plains, 1971.
Sitting Bull: The Years in Canada, 1972, 1973.
This Is Calgary, with photographer Toby Rankin, 1973.
A Short History of Western Canada, with M. Foran, 1974.
Battle of the Bay, 1975.
And Mighty Women Too, 1976.
Memory Meadows, 1976, 1985.
Cornerstone Colony, 1977.
The Rhyming Horseman of the Qu'Appelle, 1978.
Pat Burns, Cattle King, 1979.
Grant MacEwan's Illustrated History of Western Canadian Agriculture, 1980.
Metis Makers of History, 1981.
Alberta Landscapes, in collaboration with Rusty Macdonald. 1982.
The Best of Grant MacEwan, edited by R. Macdonald, 1982.
Highlights of Shorthorn History, 1982.
Charles Noble, Guardian of the Soil, 1983.
Wildhorse Jack, The Legend of Jack Morton, 1983.
100 Years of Smoke, Sweat and Tears, 1984.
French in the West - Les Franco-Canadiens dans l'ouest, 1984
Marie Anne: The Frontier Adventures of Marie Ann Lagimodiere, 1984.
Frederick Haultain, Frontier Statesman of the Canadian Northwest, 1985.

Grant MacEwan's Journals, edited by M. Foran, 1986.
Heavy Horses: Highlights of Their History, 1986.
Paddy Nolan: He Left Them Laughing When He Said Goodbye, 1987.
Colonel James Walker: Man of the Western Frontier, 1989.
Grant MacEwan's West, 1990.
Highlights of Sheep History in the Canadian West, 1991.
Coyote Music and Other Humorous Tales of the Early West, 1993.

Books

Alberta's Parks - Our Legacy. Donna von Hauff. Recreation, Parks & Wildlife Foundation. 1992.

And Mighty Women Too. Grant MacEwan. Western Producer Prairie Books. 1976.

Between the Red and the Rockies. Grant MacEwan. Western Producer Prairie Books. 1979.

Charles Noble, Guardian of the Soil. Grant MacEwan. Western Producer Prairie Books. 1983.

Colonel James Walker: Man of the Western Frontier. Grant MacEwan. Western Producer Prairie Books. 1989.

Entrusted to My Care. Grant MacEwan. Western Producer Prairie Books. 1966, 1986.

Eye Opener Bob. Grant MacEwan. The Institute of Applied Art, Ltd. 1957.

Fifty Mighty Men. Grant MacEwan. Western Producer Prairie Books. 1958.

Frederick Haultain, Frontier Statesman of the Canadian Northwest. Western Producer Prairie Books. 1985.

Grant MacEwan's Illustrated History of Western Canadian Agriculture. Grant MacEwan. Western Producer Prairie Books. 1980.

Grant MacEwan's West. Grant MacEwan. Western Producer Prairie Books. 1990.

He Left Them Laughing When He Said Good-bye: The Life and Times of Frontier Lawyer Paddy Nolan. Grant MacEwan. Western Producer Prairie Books. 1987.

Hoofprints and Hitchingposts. Grant MacEwan. Western Producer Prairie Books. 1964.

Memory Meadows. Grant MacEwan. Western Producer Prairie Books. 1976.

Pat Burns, Cattle King. Grant MacEwan. Western Producer Prairie Books. 1979.

Sodbusters. Grant MacEwan. Thomas Nelson and Sons. 1950.

Bibliography

Tatanga Mani: Walking Buffalo of the Stonies. Grant MacEwan. Hurtig Publishers Ltd. 1969.

The Best of Grant MacEwan. Edited by R.H. Macdonald. Western Producer Prairie Books. 1982.

The Canada Year Book: 1952-53. Edmond Cloutier, C.M.G., O.A., D.S.P. Queen's Printer and Controller of Stationery. 1953.

The Collins Dictionary of Canadian History - 1867 to the Present. David J. Bercuson and J.L. Granatstein. Collins. 1988.

Cornerstone Colony. John W. Grant MacEwan. Western Producer Prairie Books. 1977.

The Holy Bible. King James Version. A.J. Holman Company. 1916.

The Oxford Dictionary of Quotations. Second Edition. Vivian Ridler. Oxford University Press. 1953.

The Lives of Eight of Canada's Most Unforgettable Mayors. Edited by Allan Levine. James Lorimer & Co. Publishers. 1989.

The Rhyming Horseman of the Qu'Appelle. Grant MacEwan. Western Producer Prairie Books. 1978.

Uneasy Patriots. David Kilgour. Lone Pine Publishing. 1988.

West To The Sea. Grant MacEwan with Maxwell Foran. McGraw-Hill Company of Canada Ltd. 1968

Wildhorse Jack. Grant MacEwan. Western Producer Prairie Books. 1983.

Papers
The Rural Society in Transition: 1900-1914. M.L. Foran. Unpublished paper. 1969.

Additional
Audiotape interviews: CBC (archives).

Correspondence and Files: University of Calgary, University of Saskatchewan, University of Manitoba, Ontario Agriculture College (University of Guelph), Royal Bank of Canada, Greyhound Lines of Canada Ltd., Government of Alberta, Government of Saskatchewan.

Grant MacEwan's Personal Journals. Unedited.

Grant MacEwan's Personal Papers.

Media Files. Varied Sources.

Videotape interviews: March - December 1993. Donna von Hauff.

Index

100 Years of Smoke, Sweat and Tears *180*
1967 Centennial March *158*
4-H Clubs of Alberta *162*

A

Abbey, Moses *21*
Abbott, Douglas *124*
Aberdeen Angus *54*
Agrarian Party, The *109*
agrarian reform movement *171*
AIDS *166*
Alberta advantage *150*
Alberta Award of Excellence *181*
Alberta Culture's Nonfiction Award *181*
Alberta Heritage Savings Trust Fund *177*
Alberta Supreme Court *147*
Alberta Treasury Branches *111*
Alberta Was My Beat *144*
Albertan *121*
Albertan, The *152, 173*
Alexander School *33*
Alladin, Dr. Ibrahim *11*
Allied forces *62*
Alpha Zeta Honors *81*
altar *27*
American Association *151*
Ames *82*
Anglican doctrine *155*
Angus *90*
Angus cattle *73*
Anik A-1 *166*
Animal Defence League of Canada *185*
Anne of Green Gables *32*
apartheid *155*
Argall, Mamie *60*
Armstrong, Ralph *168*
Arnold, Teet *50*
arrived in Priddis *128*
Assinaboine *84*
Assiniboine River *18, 26*
associate program *68*
Associated Press *96*
ATCO Industries *144*
Athens *151*
auger *46*
Auld, F. Hedley *80*
Avro *124*
Avro Arrow CF-105 *139*
Ayrshires *91*

B

baby-kissers *133*
Bachelor of Science *64*
bag lady *84*
Baldy *104*
Balkan kingdom *38*
Bank of Commerce *64*
Bankers *25*
banking day *36*
bannock *22*
Banting *63*
Baron, Flash *30*
Baron's Pride *30*

Barr, Robert *107*
Baseline Operations *114*
Bass, Tim *121*
Battle Lake *162*
Bay of Pigs *139*
Beatlemania *139*
Beau Perfection *57*
Beau Perfection 47th *85*
Belgrade *38*
Bell, H.O. *121*
Belle Plaine *84*
Bennett, R.B. *100*
Bethune *84*
Between Red and the Rockies *127*
Between the Red and the Rockies *31, 52*
Bible Bill Aberhart *133*
Birthday, Happy *162*
Biscuit *59*
Black Forest *96*
Blackwood, Professor *73*
Blakely, Alfred *37, 48*
Blandford Group in London, The *161*
Blazing the Old Cattle Trail *135*
B'Nai Brith Humanitarian Award *174*
Board of Review *108*
Bombeck, Erma *179*
Bosnia *38*
Bowen, John *147*
Bowen, John Campbell *169*
boxcar *44*
Boy Scout *33*
Bracken, John *108*
Brandon *20, 24, 30, 31, 39, 42, 121*
Brandon Fair *37, 40*
Brandon General Hospital *19*
Brandon Sun *36, 37*
Brandon-Souris by-election *125*
breadbasket *23*
Breeds of Farm Livestock in Canada *103*
Brickley, J.J. *71*
Brigham, Harriet *96*
British Columbia *16*
British North America Act *124*
British Parliament *124*
Broadcast Ernie *132*
bronco *28*
Broom, Loch *17*
Brown, Kootenai *150*
Buchlyvie *20*
Buddhism *154*
Bulgaria *38*
Burns, Robbie *80*
Burns' Society *92*
Burrell, Hon. Martin *39*
Byfield, Link *10*
Byng, Baron *77*

C

Calgary *24*
Calgary Cavalcade *135*
Calgary council *143*
Calgary Exhibition *127*
Calgary Exhibition and Stampede *127*
Calgary firefighters *180*
Calgary Foundation *185*
Calgary Herald *136, 141, 146, 179*
Calgary Negev Honoree *181*

Calgary Stampede *154*
Calvinistic *8*
Camp, Charlie Van *53*
Campbell, Douglas *121*
Campbell, F.A. *170*
Campbell, Premier *121*
Canada's aboriginals *155*
Canada's Christians and Jews *151*
Canadian Brotherhood Council Award *174*
Canadian Cattlemen, The *128*
Canadian CF-101 *139*
Canadian Club *150*
Canadian Council of Beef Producers *113*
Canadian Council of Christians
    and Jews *154*
Canadian Northern Railway *30*
Canadian Pacific Railway *16*
Canadian Society of Technical
    Agriculturists *112*
Canadian Wheat Board *111*
Canadiana furniture *184*
Cane Mola *55, 107*
Canora Fair *77*
carpentry *33*
Carrot River *74*
Carrot River Valley *30, 44*
Carson, Rachel *136*
Case steam *51*
Catholicism *155*
Cato, Marcus *166*
Caveno, Len *70*
Caver's house, Ross *116*
CBC *91, 106*
Cecil Hotel *121*
Central Office Building *120*
Central Park *144*
Chamber of Commerce *154*
Chapman *41*
Chater *22, 24, 31, 119*
Chicago International Exposition *74*
Chicago stockyards *70*
Chief Aka-tah-si, Honorary *153*
Chief Walking Buffalo *161*
Chief Walking Moose of the Sagatawas *153*
chlorofluorocarbons *165*
Churchbridge *97*
Cité Libre *124*
City Centre campus *177*
Civic Government Association *129*
Civil Rights Movement *135*
Civil Service Commission *69*
CKCK *89*
Clark, Prime Minister Joe *177*
Claxton, Brooke *124*
Cline, Patsy *90*
Cline, Phyllis *96*
Clinkskill, James *89, 97*
Clydesdale *20, 23, 51*
Clydesdales *31, 91*
Coca-Cola *55*
Code, A.E. *55*
Cody's General Store *107*
Cold War *139*
College *175*
Columbian Six *70*
Confederation *16, 124*
conservationist *27*
Constantinople *38*

Cosmopolitan Club *80*
Council of Beef Producers *130*
Council of Canadian Beef
　　Producers *127, 137*
Country Life *117*
Cowan, James *37*
CPR *18, 39*
CPR downtown relocation *142*
Crawford, F.W. *119*
Crerar, Hon. T.A. *55*
Cross, James *165*
Cruickshank, George *74*
Culoden *17*
Cumming, Martha *18*
Curtis Cattle Company *57*
cutter *48*

D

De Galliers *41*
de Gaulle, Charles *139*
Dean, Basil *136, 146*
Dean of Agriculture *116*
Dean's parties *159*
Dean's parties, the *119*
Dennis, Marvin *169*
Department of Indian and
　　Northern Affairs *178*
Depression *102, 120, 183*
Derby, Canadian *162*
Devil in Deerskin, The *180*
Diefenbaker's Conservative
　　Government *139*
Dinsdale, Conservative Walter *125*
Dinsdale, MP Walter *146*
diphtheria *25*
Dirty Thirties *88*
dole *88*
Dominion *16*
Dominion Exhibition *37*
Donald, Geo. *94*
Douglas, Tommy *139*
Downham, Howard *70*
Dr. J.W. Grant MacEwan Environmental
　　Studies Insti *185*
Drew, George *124*
Drury, Jim *60*
Drury, John Grant MacEwan *60*
Duck Lake *84*
Duke of Connaught *33*
Durnin, Jas *45*
Durnin, Miss *49*
Durnin, Olive *48*
dysentery *17*

E

East River *18, 32*
Eaton, Gladys *71, 89*
Eaton's *64*
Edmonton *24*
Edmonton College *175*
Edmonton Journal *146, 168*
Edmonton YMCA *183*
Edwards, Bob *135*
Elizabeth II, Her Majesty Queen *153*
Elrose United *95*
Emerald Award for Environmental
　　Excellence *181*
Englishmen *91*

Enoch Band *153*
Entrusted to My Care *150, 161*
entrusted to my care *38*
Environmental Studies Institute, J.W.
　　Grant MacEwa *177*
Eppard sheep drive *135*
Erickson, Eric *148*
Estevan *136*
Ethiopia *174*
Europe *95*
Evans, H.H. *119*
Evans, Muriel *92*
Ewen, Al *89, 92, 96*
Ewen, Prof. *94*
Expo 67 *139, 153*
Extension Department of the
　　University of Saskatchwan *57*
Eye Opener Bob *135*

F

F.G. Lenn Renfrew Motors *105*
Falher Hotel *133*
Family Herald *88*
Farm Boys' Camp *57*
farms, bonanza *16*
Feed Manufacturers' Association *109*
Festubert *47*
Fez *38*
Fifty Might Men *108*
Fifty Mighty Men *135*
Fillickener, Rudolf *46*
Firefighter Weisenburger *181*
Fitton, George *37*
Flood Control Headquarters *120*
flood damage *120*
FLQ *139*
foot and mouth disease *129*
Foran, Fiona *162, 180*
Foran, Max *141, 170, 184*
Foran, Maxwell *105*
Ford *61*
Ford, John *135*
Fordson *56*
Forestry Farm *97, 103*
Forks *93*
Fox, White *148*
free farmer *56*
Free Press Prairie Farmer *88*
Freedom from Hunger *158*
From the Red to the Rockies *170*
Front de libération du Québec *165*
Fry, Harold *119*
Frye, Northrop *165*

G

Galloway *90*
Gamma Sigma Delta Honors *81*
gang *23*
Gardiner, J.H. *108*
Gardiner, James *113*
Gardiner, James G. *101*
Gardiner, Jimmy *113*
Gardiner, Rt. Hon. Jimmy *122*
Garson, Premier Stuart *121*
gas-guzzling car *168*
General Agriculture *103*
Geordie *34*

George *54*
George Wambeke *105*
Germany *38*
Germany. *103*
Gillson, A.H.S. *120*
Gillson, President *122*
Givenchy *47*
Glen Urquhart *17, 91*
Glenbow Library *179*
Glenbow Museum *170, 185*
Glenbush *84*
Globe and Mail *111*
gluten *17*
Governor General's Conservation
　　Award *181*
Grade Eight Certificate *37*
Graham's Confectionery. *55*
Grain Growers *63*
Gramps *180*
grandfather *15*
Grandmother Grant *35*
Grandsire *32*
Grant, Bella *29*
Grant, Bertha *8, 19, 23*
Grant, Bertha Gray *15*
Grant, Chrissie Gray *19*
Grant ethic *53*
Grant, George Alexander *29*
Grant, James *17, 29, 58*
Grant, James Alexander *19*
Grant, John *29*
Grant, John Gray *18*
Grant, John Walter *18, 58*
Grant MacEwan Community College
　　65, 174, 183
Grant MacEwan Nature Protection
　　Auxiliary Fund *185*
Grant MacEwan Student Center *181*
Grant MacEwan: No Ordinary Man *154*
Grant, Marion *29, 111*
Grant, Uncle John *128*
Grant, uncle John *109*
Grapes of Wrath *88*
Grasslands National Park *178*
Gray, Dorothy *11, 175*
Great Britain *38*
Great Depression *94*
Great Majestic *24, 26*
Great Production Fleet, The *56*
Great World Trade Depression *17*
Greed *174*
greed *155*
greenhouse effect *165*
Greenpeace *165*
Greyhound *14, 98, 176*
Greyhound Lines of Canada
　　10, 14, 181, 182
Group of Seven *88*
grubstake *22*
Guelph *20, 74*
Gunns Limited *77*
Guthrie, Tyrone *88*

H

Halifax *18*
Halligan, Pat *170*
Halligan-Baker *158*

Halligan-Baker, Patricia *10, 157*
Hannam, Herb *74*
Harbor, Pictou *17*
Haultain, Frederick *84, 109*
Haultain, Sir Frederick *83*
Hawke, Dr. *59*
Hays, Harry W. *140*
Hays, Mayor Harry *142*
Heather *117*
Heather and Phyllis *141*
Heather, Daughter *141*
Hector *17*
Hereford *90*
His Honour *156*
Hnatyshyn, Governor General Ray *10*
Homburg, black *164*
Homestead Act of 1872 *16*
honorary LLDs *172*
Hood, Dr. Grace Gordon *118*
Hoofprints and Hitchingposts *28, 47, 135*
Hopkins, Johnny *141*
Horace Mann *61*
House of Commons *124, 126, 165*
Howe, C.D. *124*
Hudson Bay *61*
Hudson Bay Company *84*
Hudson's Bay Company *15*
Hughes, President *80*
Hughton *95*
Hunley, Lieutenant-Governor Helen *176*
Hurtig Publishers *161*

I

Icelandic *33*
Idaho *20*
idiosyncrasies *103*
IHC engines *50*
immigration *17*
income tax *51*
income tax returns *185*
Institute of Applied Art *161*
Institute of Applied Art, The *135*
International Harvester *47*
Iowa State *80, 87, 96*
Iowa State University *79*
Irish Catholics *69*
Israel *151*

J

Jacobite *17*
James, Dr. Norman *118*
Jnwaltergran *25*
Johanason, J. *33*
John Deere *53*
John Ware's Cow Country *135*
Johnston, Dick *176*
Judaism *155*
jump centre *72*

K

Kelly, Gerald *176*
Kennedy, Arnold *74*
Kennedy, Fred *144*
Kilgour, Honourable David *10*
Kindersley *14*
King, Dr. Martin Luther *154*
King George VI *124*

King, Mackenzie *88, 100*
King, Prime Minister Mackenzie *124*
King, W.L. Mackenzie *77*
Kirk, Dean *112*
Kirk, Dr. L. E. *101*
Kirk, L.E. *111*
Kiwanis Club *92*
Kiwanis International *114*
Knox, Bill *74*
Knox Church Mission Band *41*
Knox, Herb *74*
Knox Presbyterian Church *33*
Knox Sunday school *33*
Knox United Church *90*

L

Landis *84*
Laporte, Pierre *165*
Last, Best West *16*
Laurence, Margaret *88*
Laurier, Sir Wilfrid *25, 30*
Leader-Post *113*
Lévesque, René *165*
Levy *49*
Liberal administration *111*
Liberal administration, federal *121*
Liberal nomination *122*
Liberal Party, Alberta *131*
Liberals *25*
Lincoln Park *143*
Lion's Club *80*
Little Red Deer River *169*
Loch Ness *91*
London *151*
Longview *105*
Lougheed, Peter *168*
Lougheed, Premier *177*

M

MacCallum, Mrs. *99*
Macdonald, Rusty
   10, 87, 92, 115, 119, 154, 168
Macdonald, Sir John A. *16*
MacEwan, Alderman *131*
MacEwan, Alex *8, 23, 29, 42*
MacEwan, Alexander Hedley *15, 20*
MacEwan, Bertha *40, 71*
MacEwan Day *176*
MacEwan, Dean *117*
MacEwan, death of Bertha Grant *110*
MacEwan died, Alex *110*
MacEwan Family Charitable Fund *185*
MacEwan, George *20*
MacEwan, George Alexander Grant *73*
MacEwan, Grandfather *64*
MacEwan, Grant *9, 15, 23, 42, 74, 126*
MacEwan, Grant and Phyllis *148*
MacEwan, Heather born *103*
MacEwan homestead *31*
MacEwan, J.W.G. *96, 113*
MacEwan, John Walter Grant *14*
MacEwan, Lieutenant-Governor Grant *151*
MacEwan, Lt. Gov. Grant *147*
MacEwan Mayor *143*
MacEwan Medallion *176*
MacEwan, Mr. *127*
MacEwan Nature Protection Fund *185*

MacEwan, Phyllis *158, 169, 184*
MacEwan, Phyllis and Grant *119*
MacEwan women *185*
MacEwan, Young Heather *110*
MacEwan-Foran, Heather *10, 89*
MacEwanmania *118*
MacEwan's marriage, Phyllis Cline *184*
Mackay, Mayor Don *131*
MacKenzie, Reverend James *90*
MacPhaden, Laughie *46*
MacPherson, Willa *59, 64*
Madrid *151*
Manitoba *18*
Manitoba Agricultural Hall of Fame *181*
Manitoba Agriculture College *109*
Manitoba Boom *39*
Manitoba, left *127*
Manitoba, Province of *16*
Mann, James *133*
Manning, Ernest *132*
Manning, Premier Ernest *147*
Manning, Premier Ernest C. *132*
Maple Creek *84*
Maple Leaf flag *139*
Marchand, Jean *139*
Marconi, Guglielmo *25*
Margo *40, 43*
Margo farm *42*
mari usque ad mare *16*
Maritimes *17*
Marquis wheat *63*
Martin, Curtis *57*
Martin, Dr. Glenn *11*
Martin, Jack *150*
Martin Sr., Senator Paul *151*
Matador Ranch *90*
Matthews, Don *143*
Mayfair Club *160*
Mayo Clinic *80*
Mayor, MacEwan *143*
mayor of Calgary *138, 140*
McConnell, Isabell *68*
McGugan, Archie *74*
McKay, Ian *70*
McKay, Norman *119*
McLean, Chief George *154*
McLean, James *97*
McLean, Malcolm *78*
McLuhan, Marshall *166*
McNair, Hugh *105*
McPhail, Malcolm *64*
McPherson, Aimee Semple *80*
McSpadden, Maurice *79, 98*
McTavish Avenue *33*
meagre allowance *185*
Meighen, Arthur *77*
Melfort *30, 43, 84*
Melfort farm *73, 99*
Melfort Mirror *75*
meningitis *184*
Mennonite Central Committee
   of Alberta *185*
Messiah *102*
Messiah, The *80*
Mexico *184*
Michaels, John *175*
Mike's Newsstand *175*
Miles for Millions *158*

Miller, Harry *74*
Misery Pudding *156*
Mission Band *33*
Mississippi River *70*
Mitchell, W.O. *88*
Model A *70*
Molasses *183*
Monarchy *49*
Moore, Barry *174*
Moose Jaw Milk Producers' Association *105*
Moosomin *84*
Morte d'Arthur *81*
Mortlach *84*
Morton, Arthur Silver *99*
Morton, Brig. R.E.A. *120*
Morton, Dr. *111*
Mother Nature *42*
Mount Pleasant Cemetery *110*
Mount Royal College *144*
Mowat, Farley *88*
Municipal Hall *120*
Munsinger, Gerda *139*
Murray, President *87, 89, 100, 111*
Murray, Walter Charles *83*
musician *33*

N

NAFTA *177*
Nagel, Walter *145*
National Energy Policy *166*
National Research Council *90*
NATO *124*
Nature's storehouse *187*
Nevada *20*
New Democratic Party *139*
New Glasgow *18*
New World *26*
Newcomers *16*
Newfoundland *17, 124*
Nicol, Dr. *103*
Nicol, Dr. John L. *97*
Nicol, Eric *179*
Nigeria *175*
NIMBYs *130*
nomination *122*
NORAD Bomarc-B missiles *139*
Normal School *33*
Norris, Premier *31*
North Africa *38*
North America *18*
North Battleford *84*
North Vietnam *139*
North West *16*
North West Mounted Police *16*
Northrop Frye *165*
Nova Scotia *17, 32*

O

OAC *63, 85*
Of Mice and Men *88*
Officer of the Order of Canada *174*
Ohio State *98*
oil crisis *173*
Oka crisis *155*
Oklahoma City *96*
Old Polly *36, 40*

Old World *18*
Olds Agricultural College *171*
Omigosh, it's the mayor! *142*
Ontario *17*
Ontario Agriculture College *61*
Operation Eyesight Universal *185*
our grandchildren *182*
Our Natural Heritage *136*

P

Paarl Boys' High School *157*
Page, Dr. J. Percy *147*
Page, J. Percy *149*
Paine, Doc *66*
Panama Canal *39*
Park School *33*
Patterson, W.J. *109*
Peace River gas *173*
Pearson, Lester *124, 139*
Pearson's government, Mike *145*
peasant *20*
pecan pie *67*
Pelletier, Gérard *124, 139*
penny-pincher *187*
Pepita *117*
Peterson, Kevin *170*
Philip, Prince *153*
Phyllis's death *184*
Pictou County *32*
Pilling, Bertha *33*
Pleasant Valley Church *78*
Plymouth sedan *106*
pneumonia *59*
Point Barrow *98*
Poking into Politics *125, 129, 134, 144, 161*
Polish Hal *126*
Polish Hall *126*
Poole family *46*
Poole, Isaac *45*
porridge parties *181*
Port of Churchill *91*
Prairie Farm Assistance Act *108*
prairie funeral *28*
prairie grass *18*
Prairie promise *39*
Prairies *15, 62*
Premier Norris *31*
Presbyterian *20, 90*
Presbyterianism *26*
Priddis *105, 134, 170*
Priddis, arrived in *128*
Priddis, living at *170*
Priddis property *183*
promise, Prairie *17*
protective husbandman *187*
Prowse, J. Harper *132*

Q

Qu'Appelle Hall *94*
Qu'Appelle Valley *84*
Quebec *20*
Québécois, Parti *165*
Queen's cowboy *169*
Queen's representative *164*

R

racism *155*
Radville *87*
raffia work *49*
Raithby, George *74*
Rand, Sally *109*
Raymond Sewing Machine Factory *20*
Rayner, John *57, 77*
RCMP *94*
Reaves, Bill *66*
Red River *120*
Red River Valley *21*
Red River Valley Board *121*
Reed, Dr. Hugo *65*
Regina *24, 87*
Regina Exhibition *57*
Regina Farm Boys' Camp *85*
Regina Leader-Post *113*
Reid, Rod *51, 52*
Remington *105*
Renner, Bob *128*
Renner family *105*
Resource district *87*
resourcefulness *187*
reverence *27*
Richard *84*
Riel Rebellion *21*
Roaring Twenties *72*
Rochne, Knute *80*
Rogers, Will *79, 98*
Romance of Canada, The *88*
Romanticism *32*
Rome *151*
Rose, Irwin *135*
Rosetown *98*
Rosetown, Saskatchewan *14*
Rotary Club *154*
Rowe, G.R. *121*
Royal Bank of Canada *111*
Royal typewriter *162*
Royal Winter Fair *67, 74*
Royal Yacht Britannia *153*
Royalite Oil Company *131*
Royalty cheques *179*
Ruhl, Glenn *175*
Rupert's Land *15*
Russia *38*
Russian thistle *101*
Rutherford, Dean *63, 79, 83, 85, 111*
Rutherford, Ernest *63*
Rutherford, W.J. *57, 81*

S

Sabbath *28, 48*
Salonika *38*
salt pork *22*
Sampson, Inspector *94*
Saskatchewan *30*
Saskatchewan Cattle Improvement Train *77*
Saskatchewan Farmer *88*
Saskatoon *24, 30*
Saskatoon Archaeological Society *99*
Saskatoon Exhibition *92, 108, 112*
Saskatoon Little Theatre Club *109*
Saskatoon Riding Club *92*
Saskatoon Star Phoenix *96*

Saskatoon Star-Phoenix *97*
Saunders, William *63*
Scarlet Pimpernel, The *115*
School of Agriculture *101*
Schweitzer, Albert *8, 62*
Science and Practise of Canadian Animal
    Husbandry *100*
Scotland *91, 180*
Scott, Sir Walter *20*
Sea Shepherd Conservation Society *185*
Seattle *98*
self-reliance, *187*
self-imposed segregation *155*
Seventh Street campus *176*
Sevigny, Pierre *139*
shack *45*
Sharing the Continent *165*
Shaw, Dean *100*
Shaw, Malcolm *111*
Shaw, Professor *90*
Shaw, Professor A.M. *83*
Shorthorn *90*
Shorty *104*
Shutt, Frank *63*
Sifton, Clifford *20*
Silent Spring *136*
silver bullet *117*
Simmons, Dr. P.M. *95*
Simpson, George *150*
Simpson, Jim *74*
Sir Frederick Haultain Prize *181*
smallpox *17*
Smith, Art *140*
Smith, Bella *23*
Smith, Chief Justice S.B. *146*
Smith, John *151*
Smithfield *91*
Social Credit *111*
Socred administration *134*
sod-busting *16*
sod-busting *16*
Sodbusters *23, 106, 108*
Souls in Action *41*
South America *95*
South Saskatchewan River *93*
Sowbelly beans *22*
Spanish flu *58*
Sparrow *44*
Sparrow and Poole *148*
Speech from the Throne *149*
spinal meningitis *73*
Spokane *98*
Springville *18*
Spry school *48*
SS Silksworth *91*
St. Andrew's *92*
St. James Presbyterian Church *48*
St. John's School *153*
St. Laurent, Louis *115*
St. Laurent, Louis Stephen *124*
St. Paul *21*
St. Petersburg *38*
Stack, Judge Ed *174, 175*
Stampede City *129*
Standard Bred *28*
Staples, Milton *79*
Star City *61, 73*
State of Israel *150*

Steckley, Jack *74*
Steel, Commissioner John *143*
Steinhauer, Lieutenant-Governor
    Ralph *158*
Stirlingshire *20*
Stoughton *84*
stowaway *41*
strict frugality *138*
Sundre *169*
switch properties *170*

T

T1 General Tax Form *137*
tabernacle *27*
Tatanga Mani *161*
Taylor, Frank *121*
telephone *59*
Temperance Movement *62*
thalidomid *139*
This and That *102*
thistle, Russian *14*
Thomas Nelson and Sons *100*
Thompson, J.A. *105*
Thomson, J.S. *111*
thriftiness *27*
Tisdale Fair *65*
Tolton, Tubby *70*
Tool, Wade *74*
Toronto *66*
Toronto General Hospital *110*
Toynbee, Arnold Joseph *145*
Trudeau, Pierre *124, 139*
Trudeau, Pierre Elliot *140*
Trudeau, Prime Minister Pierre Elliot *160*
Trueman, Dr. A.W. *114, 119*
Trueman, President *119*
Truscott, Steven *139*
Tucker, Walter *113*
Turriff *49*
Turtleford *84*

U

Uncle James *35*
Unionists *90*
United Farmers *63*
United States *20*
University of Calgary *170, 179, 181*
University of Chicago *81*
University of Chicago Meat Packing
    Institute *81*
University of Lethbridge *160*
University of Manitoba *96, 114, 122, 137*
University of New Brunswick *120*
University of Saskatchewan *96*
urban sprawl *28*
Urquhart, Glen *17*
Utopia *26*

V

Valentine, George *90*
Vancouver *98*
Vanier, Governor General Georges *162*
VE Day *112*
vegetarian *154*
Vernon *136*
Vickers, Brenda *171*
Victor Lauriston Public School *156*

Victoria *98*
Victoriaville College *58*
Victrola, Edison *60*

W

Walker, Bob *31*
Walking Buffalo *154*
Walsh Cattle Marketing Association *151*
War Assets Corporation *143*
War Measures Act *165*
Ward, David *10, 158*
water *46*
Watrous *84*
Wawanesa Mutual Insurance Company *160*
Wayne, John *135*
Weber, Henry *155*
Weber, Wilf *64*
Weir, Austin *88*
Weir, Robert *97*
Weisenburger, Bill *10, 180*
welfare *88*
Western Producer *87, 127*
Western Producer Prairie Books *135*
Westin Hotel *65*
Wheat Board *62*
White Fox *105*
White Rock, BC *107*
Windsor uniform *149*
Winnipeg *17, 116*
Winnipeg Free Press *97, 121*
Wood, W.A. *121*
World War II veterans *116*
Wright, Esther *97*

Y

Yanks *76*
YMCA *64, 183*
York Road *20*
Yorkton Fair *84*
Youth Detention Centre *151*
Youth Development Centre *151*
Ypres *47*
Yule, H. Charles *127*

Z

Zeke Young Memorial Award *181*

The Elf of the Brook

Far within the crevice of this old brown
Where the fairies dwell in daylight, I the witch
I have a little cavern with its moss green
And most of mortal people never know I'm
I'm the elf who plans the courses of this way
I'm the voice that in its babble tells the fairies
If you believe in fairies you can always hear me
(2) you think there are no fairies you will never

I paddle in the water when there's no one near,
And I hide within the crevice when a voice I hear
And you would be astonished at the things I know
About these mortal people as they come & go.
Sometimes some happy children come & paddle in the str
How I love to watch them playing as they laugh & scream,
Sometimes a lonely poet comes & listens to the brook
I know he understands it by his quiet happy look.

Many a thirsty traveller stoops beside its cool brink
And blessing its soft music, takes a long refreshing drink
And often happy lovers sit & whisper in the shade,
(Adam told the same old story when first the world was mad
Then the brook goes "babble, babble" for fear that I will hear,
But I do not need to listen, for I hear it every year.
So I hide within the crevice as these people pass along
And I sing each little story in the brooks sweet song.
And if you believe in fairies you can always hear me sing,
(But if you think there are no fairies, you will never
Written May 24/26